BLUEPRINTS FOR THE EAGLE, STAR, AND INDEPENDENT

Revised Fifth Edition

Will Good

ISBN: 979-8-89419-452-3 (sc)
ISBN: 979-8-89419-453-0 (hc)
ISBN: 979-8-89419-454-7 (e)

Because of the dynamic nature of the Internet, any web addresses or links contained in this book may have changed since publication and may no longer be valid. The views expressed in this work are solely those of the author and do not necessarily reflect the views of the publisher, and the publisher hereby disclaims any responsibility for them.

THE EWINGS
PUBLISHING

One Galleria Blvd., Suite 1900, Metairie, LA 70001
(504) 702-6708

PREFACE TO THE FIFTH EDITION

Since the First Edition of this book was written in 2011, substantial changes and events have further shaped the political landscape of national politics. These events include the debacle over the national debt limit between the President and the Republican Party, the influence of the *Citizens United* decision of the Supreme Court on elections, and the presidential primaries and the election of Presidents Obama, Trump and Biden. Whether the latest decision on presidential immunity stands remains to be seen.

Several "blueprint recommendations" in the First Edition have proved to be prescient, especially regarding gun controls after the Newtown and Aurora shootings in Connecticut and Colorado, the cautions against the influence of violent movies, and the importance of military drone aircraft. The recent large meteorite that crashed in Russia was a dramatic wake-up call that was foreseen in the First Edition. The blueprints for investigation of the bond and securities rating agencies materialized in recent Justice Dept. indictments. The burial of electrical lines that were overhead in New Jersey and New York would have substantially decreased the property damage incurred by Hurricane Sandy. The recommendations to cease sending non-violent drug offenders to prison for possession of small amounts of narcotics or other illicit substances is presently being considered for implementation by the Justice Department.

The Second Edition contained an expanded section on the need for an Independent Party and what it should stand for, particularly in the light of the current schism in the Republican Party over its proper role and perspective on the purpose of national government, and the general reluctance of the Democratic Party to uphold its own traditions of safeguarding the interests of the general population and adherence to constitutional values.

The Fourth Edition devoted attention to the surprising election of Donald Trump as President and his defeat by former VP Biden, and analyzes the faults associated with the antiquated Electoral College system of voting for President. Changes are recommended to assure that electors will represent the intent of the voters in each state by replacement of the present "winner take-all" system of electoral vote allocation with popular votes assigned in proportion to the electors that the people actually voted for.

The Trump Administration has been a tumultuous ride for the United States. Numerous controversies regarding the influence of Russia on the election of 2016, the immigration situation on the US-Mexican border, the large number of resignations of key cabinet officials due to disputes over policy with President Trump, and the impeachment due to solicitation bribe of military aid to Ukraine in exchange for damaging political information from foreign sources. The irony is that the information sought regarding Hunter Biden, his eventual opponent's son, was rendered to little value due to a pandemic that Trump minimized in public statements. The intervention of the author to stop the government shutdown over the barrier wall on the US-Mexican border is also described in detail. The incompetent handling to limit the spread of the corona virus by the Trump Administration is also discussed, which is attributed by most commentators as to why he was defeated in the election of 2020, and his urging of extremists to overturn the vote of the electors on January 6, 2021, led to his second impeachment by the US House of Representatives.

The Fifth Edition focuses on the Biden Administration, his accomplishments in office, and his ultimate displacement due to his age, the set-aside by his own party, and the assertion of his Vice President as a surrogate candidate due to concerns that the evenly divided House and Senate would return to Republican control. The normal convention process was set aside in order to place Vice President Harris and Governor Walz on the presidential ballot for all the States to consider. Two assassination attempts are covered.

INTRODUCTION

The ballot symbol of the Republican Party is an eagle, and the ballot symbol of the Democratic Party is a five-pointed star. The election of 2008 left the Republican Party seeing stars like a disoriented fighter after sustaining too many left hooks to its jaw. Although knocked down, but not out, the GOP took the mandatory eight counts, and came back with a vengeance. The Republican Party publicly opposed every major Democratic legislative initiative, particularly the health care and the stimulus packages. Behind the scenes, many Republican objections were incorporated in the legislation as Democrats sought "bipartisanship", but these massive bills largely moved along party lines.

In the interim elections of 2010, the Republican Party, largely based on independents and some Democrats showing mild indifference to the candidates slated for the US House of Representatives, the Democratic Party lost control of their majority in the House but retained control in the Senate. The influence of the so-called "Tea Party", a group largely composed of disaffected Republicans, and received significant support from the wealthy Koch brothers, whose combined fortune is estimated at $44 billion. The "Tea Party" sought to reduce spending and reduce the size of the Federal deficit. Many of their candidates were elected for the first time to Congress. Minority Leader John Boehner of Ohio then replaced Nancy Pelosi of California as Speaker of the House.

Because of the energy exerted by this Republican sub-set was so influential in achieving the Republican majority, each position of the new Speaker was nuanced and convoluted to take their ideology into account into policy decisions and drafting legislation. Boehner on many occasions spoke like a doubly-gridlocked Speaker, locked in by a sub-set of his own party and by the Democratic opposition. Boehner traditionally believed in the House as an institution, frequently cautioning Republican members to take sufficient measure before undertaking any radical actions. Boehner ultimately resigned as Speaker and was subsequently replaced by Paul Ryan of Wisconsin. The Senate also changed hands with the Republicans holding only a thin majority, whereby Democrat Harry Reid of Nevada was replaced by Mitch McConnell of Kentucky.

In the election of 2016, after primaries were concluded, Donald Trump was chosen to represent the Republican Party and Hillary Clinton the Democratic Party. Although Mrs. Clinton received 1.3 million more votes than Mr. Trump, the Electoral College system of selection determined him to be President. The election of 2020 lead to some of the most contentious moments in American history as rioters stormed the US Capitol to assert Trump's eection.

This book traces the roots of the modern Republican and Democratic Parties, largely through the actions of their presidential and party leaders, progressing up to the elections of 2008, 2010, and 2016, the present gridlock of the two major parties continues today.

The Republican Party has several good qualities that attract voters. Republicans place heavy reliance on individual initiative, and they emphasize values and character in their candidates. Patriotism is pervasive in their messages, as they give high priority to the national security of the United States and usually give lavish support to its military forces. Other Republican characteristics include the upholding of lawful order, and their advocacy of enterprise. Ostensibly they support rigorous competition from companies and corporations operating in good faith. In recent elections, Republicans have placed great emphasis on religion as a positive force in America, and the importance of individual success and achievement. Fiscal discipline in government is another one of their ideological cornerstones, although their recent tax cuts have generated large deficits. Depending on circumstances and the time period of history involved, Republicans have often expressed reliance on the US Constitution to preserve the intentions of the Founders to have good governance, based on appropriate checks and balances, although recent developments over special counsel appointments seem to have attenuated their zeal on checks and balances. The recent Supreme Court decisions on presidential immunity and abortion now give pause to their support of liberty.

The Democratic Party also has many admirable traits, although its guiding philosophy is more diffuse and less ideological. Democrats since the days of Andrew Jackson have represented the interests of the common man, insuring that his voice is heard through voting and representation. The value of work and its relationship to family unity is held in high regard by the party, and Democrats have long stood up for the rights of workers, employment safeguards and workplace safety in many industries. Solidarity with unions has long been one of the strongest planks in their platform. Democrats have additionally placed high importance on the value of education in American life. For more than 50 years, Democrats have provided support on behalf of the civil rights of minorities, and they have been active in writing legislation to preserve the natural resources of the United States and mitigating the effects of industrial pollution on health and the general environment.

However, both parties have adopted some other traits in recent years that contradict their many good qualities and added other aspects to their core ideologies which have substantially lessened their attraction to voters in many states. Republicans of late have heavily tilted toward reliance on corporate and wealthy interests as being the guiding beacons of job creation and prosperity. Democrats, on the other hand, although ostensibly in favor of unionization and labor rights and safety, have largely acquiesced to corporate demands and watched over the decline of labor unions and organizing. They seem quite content to tax the middle class, putting lids on credit card and auto loan interest deductibility, and placing caps on deductions for medical, dental, casualty and job-related expenses. To retain homosexuals in the military and solidify an arms reduction treaty that was endorsed by many leading Republicans, Democrats traded in exchange with Republicans the extension of tax cuts for the wealthy, and further tolerated Republican rhetoric which decried the burgeoning size of the Federal deficit that such tax cuts help to incur.

This author has lost much optimism about the future of the two-party system. The often-strident views of certain members of the Republican and Democratic Party often contravene their good intentions. Approximately 40% of Americans no longer align themselves with the two major parties, and their approval of Congress is less than 20%. If present trends continue, a third major party can emerge that can provide a middle ground for the common good. Such a party would adopt the best attributes of the two major parties. The recent attractiveness of the policies proposed by Senator Bernie Sanders in the presidential primary of 2016 and other independent progressives have highlighted that independents can be elected in substantial numbers to Congress and to various State offices, although campaign funding mechanisms must be established and the opposition of the two major parties must be overcome.

EVOLUTION OF THE IDEOLOGIES
OF THE REPUBLICAN AND
DEMOCRATIC PARTIES

Party ideology solidifies itself when the President and his party prevail on major issues of the time period of history and are then adopted in succeeding years by the general public and praised by historians and legal scholars. Parties support their President to carry out their ideological agendas in law and by executive order, and are aided by legislators, party loyalists, contributors, and commentators. Even newspapers and broadcasters adopt a party slant in their editorial opinions and in the orientation of the stories they carry, either in print or by electronic media. Party ideology is also influenced by events and problems at hand, and by prior history or actions. For these reasons, the history of the United States and party ideology cannot be separated but are intimately intertwined.

The Influence of Theodore Roosevelt
Theodore Roosevelt was the first Republican that embodied many of the expansionist and modern concepts that the United States has a prominent role as an exceptional world power to act as mediator between the other great powers.

After the assassination of President William McKinley, a young Theodore Roosevelt assumed the Presidency. Roosevelt was a graduate of Harvard who excelled in the study of history. He was elected to the New York Assembly at the age of 23 and was known for his opposition to "machine" politics. After a spell ranching in the Dakota Territory, he returned to be a member of the US Civil Service Commission and later as President of the New York City Board of

Police Commissioners, where he rooted out corruption. His strong sense of volunteerism manifested itself in the formation of the First Volunteer Cavalry (the "Rough Riders"), where he valiantly led his troops against Spain near Santiago, Cuba. These exploits brought him fame, and eventually he was elected as Governor of New York. Most historians have considered him as an outstanding governor.

As president, his administration was successful in taking legal actions against major banks and railroads that were engaged in anti-trust activities. Roosevelt formed the Bureau of Corporations whose function was to examine the accounting ledgers of corporations engaged in interstate commerce. When the Coal Strike of 1902 threatened the country, even though Roosevelt understood that large unions represented a counterforce to large corporations, he recognized and affirmed that the interests of the people came first in precedence over the opposing factions. To counter the strike, he threatened to use the Army to open the mines. His work on behalf of the country by mediation and eventual settlement was a statement of the supremacy of the public interest.

He was taken aback when revelations about the adulteration of food and drugs and unwholesome practices in meat packing plants began to surface through the published works of leading journalists of the day. Roosevelt responded by offering the formation of the Food and Drug Administration, which was legislated into law, as was the passage of the Meat Inspection Act. His diplomatic skills won him the Nobel Prize for mediating peace agreements between the Russians and Japanese.

Roosevelt believed in a strong army and navy, largely due to the growing military strength of Germany and its allies. With its growing industrial power, the United States began to build its own ships and armaments, rather than relying on imported foreign weapons.

Roosevelt also employed the Sherman Act to disrupt restraints of trade or commerce by various trusts and contractual agreements and held individual officers of corporations responsible for such contracts.

Although seeming to his critics to be a progressive activist, Roosevelt considered himself as a centrist, cautiously balancing the demands of the conservatives and the progressives.

Contributions of William Howard Taft

Roosevelt's successor, William Howard Taft, was not as politically clever as Roosevelt in balancing the conservative and progressive members of the Republican Party. However, he believed in fiscal discipline, and brought about a formal annual Federal budget. Taft was rigorous in the enforcement of anti-trust laws. But his disagreements with Roosevelt led to a three-party split, whereby Woodrow Wilson was elected instead in 1912.

Photograph 1. Theodore Roosevelt was the youngest President of the United States. He oversaw the emergence of the United States as a world power but encountered many of the same problems confronting us today. Brave, fit and conspicuously honest, he disdained corruption in all its forms. He was the first environmentalist of the modern era, championing the preservation of natural parks and reservation lands free from private exploitation. Startled by the adulteration of food and abuses in the meatpacking industry, he led efforts to establish the Food and Drug Administration. His nephew Franklin would later serve four terms as President. His placement of the public interest first above special interests is a worthy model of emulation.

An Academician as President

As the Republican Party split itself over Roosevelt and Taft, a professor from the South was elected as President with 41% of the vote. Woodrow Wilson became the first modern Democratic President. Born in Virginia, his father was a minister and served as a chaplain to the Confederate Army, tending to the wounded of that fallen army. Not only did Wilson as a boy witness the suffering of the Civil War, he had a basic southern allegiance, having stood next the General Robert E. Lee during the conflict. This personal encounter left him with a lasting impression of southern leadership under extreme pressure.

Although trained as lawyer, he found greater satisfaction as a student of history, eventually earning his doctorate at Johns Hopkins University. His many papers and publications on government and his debating skills were keys to his rise to become President of Princeton University, where his organizational skills were put to work establishing academic departments and core curriculums. His resignation from Princeton was partly due to his inability to compromise with powerful political figures, a foreshadowing of the fate of his role in the formation of the League of Nations. His election as Governor of New Jersey was in large part due to his relative lack of connection to "machine" politics. To minimize the power of the party machine to "hand select" candidates, he established state primaries. Because of Wilson's dim view of Wall Street, he garnered the support of William Jennings Bryan, the most influential Democrat of the day, a man who fiercely defended the rights and interests of the common people. Wilson's southern roots curried the favor of Southern voters who helped to carry him into the White House.

One of Wilson's first acts was to create the Federal Reserve, a compromise between those who wanted a central bank vs. the financial community who wanted stability but minimal oversight. The Federal Reserve is quasi-governmental entity, where its governors are appointed by the President and confirmed by the Senate. It was broken down into regions to lessen the influence of the New York banks. However, the New York "Fed" still is the most influential bank and has the largest reserves.

Wilson's most prominent Democratic achievement was the passage of the Clayton Act, which reinforced the Sherman Act. The Clayton Act made cut-throat price cutting illegal and banned preferential arrangements to product distributors and forbid interlocking directorates of corporations. Lastly, it permitted workers to form unions, permitting strikes without violence through picketing or walkout or boycott of products. Unions were excluded from the Sherman Act as "restraints of trade". After wages and hours were subject to an orderly process by this Act, unions expanded, and they cooperated to limit disruption of war production during World War I.

Due to general opposition to involving the United States in a European war that could lead to the slaughter of Americans, Wilson adhered to neutrality, and tried to act as an intermediary. This policy lead to his re-election, but the Germans adopted a strategy of unrestricted submarine warfare, which eventually forced a declaration war on Germany by the United States. Wilson's concept of bringing democracy to countries without such ideals through military force would find its way as a basis for American interventions in Korea, Vietnam, Somalia, Iraq and Afghanistan.

Photograph 2. Two-time Presidential candidate William Jennings Bryan, shown campaigning, was the most influential Democrat and the greatest orator of the times who lent his support to Woodrow Wilson. Through his newspaper articles and Chautauqua circuit lectures, Bryan introduced populism into American politics. He advocated conversion from the gold standard to bimetallism to increase credit for farmers and working people. His efforts led to many reforms, including permitting women to vote, elimination of child labor, and prohibition. He advocated resolution of war by arbitration, a concept embodied today in the form of the United Nations.

Wilson established a "Committee on Public Information" that provided anti-German propaganda, censoring newspaper stories that were critical of the war effort. Conscription was ordered to help build up the armed forces, and much of the war was paid for by war bonds and the progressive income tax of the Revenue Act of 1913.

After the American intervention into the conflict, and the horrendous number of deaths and casualties sustained on both sides, eventually Germany felt that prolonged conflict served no great purpose, and an armistice was signed. Although the Allies punished Germany as principal belligerent through the Treaty of Versailles, the Germans felt that its terms were "severe", and this temperament began to sow the seeds for World War II.

Wilson and his advisors felt that establishment of a League of Nations could resolve many conflicts through limited force, diplomacy, and called for the "outlawry of war". Unfortunately, the League was not approved by the Senate, largely over the issue of American sovereignty over its armed forces and the power of Congress to declare war. This contentious problem persists today over the control of US forces by the United Nations.

Because of his Southern background, Wilson's race relations were dismal. Unlike his predecessors, Wilson gave no opposition to a segregated Federal workforce, setting back gains made after the Civil War that would not be regained until the administrations of Franklin Roosevelt and Harry Truman.

After the War ended, millions of returning soldiers and sailors, many of them volunteers or conscripts from rural communities, were faced with plummeting commodity prices and farm failures after the collapse of wartime prices. No real veteran's bonus pay or benefits materialized to make the transition back to civilian life. This lack of orderly transition may have been due to Wilson's failing health and his impatience to return to a peacetime world. The labor peace that had prevailed during the War deteriorated into a series of strikes in the meatpacking, coal and metalworking industries.

Incapacitation of Wilson

Due to exhaustion and overwork, Wilson suffered a debilitating stroke, although this was kept secret for an extended time from the general public. The importance of choosing a Vice President who has the confidence of the President, along with considerable experience and stature in case of death or incapacitation, was never addressed either during or after Wilson left office.

This problem would arise again when Franklin Roosevelt died. Vice President Harry Truman, who never had the confidence of President Roosevelt, had to make the awesome decision of whether to deploy top-secret atomic weapons against Japan. The problem of succession was finally covered in 1967 by the 25th Amendment, whereby transfer of the Presidency to the Vice President is by "death or resignation". It is assumed that "incapacitation" is equivalent to virtual resignation of duties.

Photograph 3. President Woodrow Wilson is shown here with his second wife Edith Galt, who acted in his stead during his illness for a short period of time. Wilson was a Southern lawyer who decided that academic life as a historian and expert on government was more suited to his talents. He rose to prominence as the President of Princeton University and then become the Governor of New Jersey. Elected with the support of two-time Presidential candidate William Jennings Bryan, Wilson presided over a neutral United States, but eventually was forced into World War I due to unrestricted submarine warfare by Germany.

The Harding Administration

After World War I, the nation craved a "return to normalcy", and elected Warren Harding to the presidency. He oversaw the passage of high tariffs and tried to limit naval expansion among the great powers of the day. Harding's Administration was a dire warning to the appointment of politically connected friends to key cabinet positions and a "laissez-faire" attitude toward their activities. The so-called "Teapot Dome" scandal was the result of the discovery of secret oil leases granted to various business associates by the Secretary of the Interior Albert B. Fall. It was a lesson that had severe consequences for a lax and passive government. Many of Harding's appointees were convicted of fraud and some committed suicide.

The Caution of Calvin Coolidge

When Warren Harding abruptly died, attributed to food poisoning, Vice President J. Calvin Coolidge rose to the presidency. Coolidge found a political situation in disarray, but cautiously guided the nation forward without fanfare. It was a time of economic prosperity. He did not believe in direct involvement in or influencing business operations as Roosevelt did. His philosophy, very similar to many conservative Republicans today, was that regulators were the assistants of industry, and that taxation should give capital investment preference over the efforts of "ordinary labor".

Unfortunately, Coolidge's general detachment and non-interference led to massive stock market speculation, due to minimal margin requirements, insider trading, and an unbridled faith in capitalism, but ignored its cyclical nature and the greed of stockholders, brokers, bankers and corporate executives.

Photograph 4. President Calvin Coolidge congratulates star pitcher Walter Johnson of the Washington Senators baseball club after winning the American League Championship in 1927. After the death of President Warren Harding, whose administration was plagued with corruption and scandal, Coolidge provided a more cautious and stable approach to government, generally advocating cooperation with business, encouraging prosperity and expansion of private enterprise.

The Paradox of Herbert Hoover

After Coolidge decided not to run, the election of 1928 brought the presidency to Herbert C. Hoover, a highly capable mining engineer who had graduated from Stanford University. Prior to his assumption of the presidency, Hoover was head of relief operations whose commission distributed massive quantities of food during and after World War I. As Secretary of Commerce, he was instrumental in establishing programs that helped develop radio broadcasting, civil aviation, a uniform code for traffic safety, and numerous waterway projects, including the massive Hoover Dam.

When the stock market crashed, and the country began to sink into depression, Hoover's approach was to largely rely on private donations and encourage personal initiative. He did not favor any direct aid to the unemployed; rather, he contended that any aid should be handled by charities and from contributions from the affected cities and towns. He constantly stated that no one was starving through the throes of the Great Depression, although many did. He vetoed a bill that would have established an agency of the Federal government to provide unemployment assistance. Likewise, he killed measures to provide direct public works spending for job creation. Hoover did provide credit for large corporations, but without demand for their products from unemployed consumers, these programs produced little change.

Even after Franklin Roosevelt was elected, Hoover continued to oppose any meaningful relief for the unemployed. It has never been understood how Hoover could have been so successful at foreign relief efforts yet turned his back on his own countrymen who had been so devastated by the Great Depression.

The Influence of Franklin Roosevelt

In 1932, Franklin Roosevelt was elected because of his optimism and promise to raise the United States out of the Great Depression through a series of programs and policies designated as the "New Deal". Upon taking office, industrial production was off by more than 50%, and about 25% of the eligible workforce was unemployed. Roosevelt appointed three Republicans to his cabinet along with other Democrats.

Photograph 5. This is an informal photograph of Herbert Hoover as Secretary of Commerce, standing with Secretary of State Charles Evans Hughes, taken during the Coolidge Administration. Hoover would later be elected President and Hughes selected as a Supreme Court Justice. Although Hoover had overseen many successful foreign relief efforts and a progressive champion for the development of new enterprises, his indifferent attitudes during the Great Depression appeared to be as if summoned from his youth in Iowa. The strong work ethic which brought him to the Presidency seemed to make it difficult for him to understand that the Depression could not be solved just through hard work. Hoover considered the Great Depression to be largely a matter of panic, not a systemic disorder.

Roosevelt's first steps were to close the banks and permit only those in sound financial condition to re-open. He persuaded the Congress to form the Federal Emergency Relief Administration which provided direct funding to the states to support their relief agencies. The Civilian Conservation Corps was designed to put men back to work on public works and conservation projects. Mortgage relief was provided to cash-strapped farmers and homeowners.

Crop prices were either diminishing or just stagnating, depending on the staple commodity involved. The purpose of the Agricultural Adjustment Administration was to raise crop prices through "supports" or subsidies on seven basic commodities. This program was slow in relieving farm problems, but eventually did raise farm income to pre-Depression levels by 1941.

Public works received special treatment in the Roosevelt Administration, focusing on projects that would eventually recoup the cost of their construction. Typical projects were stadiums, schools, college and university buildings, water projects, locks and dams, and port facilities.

To provide labor uniformity, codes of wages and hours were governed by the National Recovery Act. Because of the numerous codes proposed, enforcement was difficult. Many businessmen felt these measures were unconstitutional, whereas the unemployed and working men and their families often felt these measures were insufficient and just a starting point. Although the Supreme Court later struck down these codes, many eventually were legislated into law regarding collective bargaining rights, limits on hours and wages, and the prohibition of child labor.

In 1934, the Congress established the Securities and Exchange Commission (SEC) to curb abuses in securities trading and investment banking. The Works Progress Administration was established to find or create meaningful work for the skilled unemployed. The Social Security Administration was formed to cover disability, death of a spouse and "old-age" insurance, now termed retirement. Both the Social Security Act and the National Labor Relations Act were challenged by conservatives all the way to the Supreme Court. Roosevelt contended that they were constitutional, and the legislation was eventually affirmed so by the Court. These court decisions validated the ability of the Congress and the Executive Branch to regulate the economic activity of the United States.

Alfred Landon, the Republican governor of Kansas, opposed Franklin Roosevelt when he ran for his second term in 1936. Although Landon was a progressive, and supported many of the ideas of Theodore Roosevelt, he was soundly defeated, winning only the states of Maine and Vermont.

Photograph 6. Franklin Roosevelt was a truly remarkable president. He assumed the presidency in the midst of the Great Depression, whereby his Administration closed insolvent banks and immediately sought public works appropriations and created agencies to help stabilize businesses to create jobs for the unemployed. Although this did not immediately solve this deeply systemic problem, it provided a pathway for recovery. Roosevelt was an administrator that brought organizations and people together for a common cause. He brought these skills to fully bear in forming alliances with the British and other allies during World War II. His administration was able to coordinate war production on an extremely large scale to provide the eventual victory over Germany, Italy and Japan in support of the Allied Powers. Unfortunately, his ailing health prevented him from seeing the final victory over Japan. He passed away having been elected to the Presidency four times, more than any other President.

The Counterpoint of Wendell Willkie

In the election of 1940, Franklin Roosevelt faced Wendell Willkie, a brilliant lawyer from Indiana. Like Ronald Reagan, Willkie began his career as a Democrat, but later changed parties after he felt there was too much constraint placed on business by the Roosevelt Administration. He was a successful industrialist who had never run for public office. Although Willkie supported many of the relief agencies and programs of the "New Deal", he felt that there should be more respect on the government's part toward business. However, Willkie did support the creation of more jobs. He felt that business could benefit if it embraced some of the better ideas contained in the "New Deal" reforms.

Wendell Willkie was a tireless candidate and a leading figure for the Republican Party during World War II. He recognized that many of the relief agencies of Roosevelt's "New Deal" provided stability to a country depressed by the inability of individual enterprises to collectively bring about prosperity without government intervention, but he felt they could be more effective and efficient. His criticism was leveled at excessive rule-making, and emphasized that for business to flourish, it had to have confines, but ones not as onerous as to stifle initiative and profitability. The thrust of his message was that constructive ideas would produce balanced legislation superior to that proposed by a single party. Willkie tended to be more isolationist than Roosevelt. Willkie won 22,305,000 votes as opposed to 27,244,000 votes for Roosevelt. Although defeated, he generally supported most of Roosevelt's policies and aid to the Allies during World War II.

Photograph 7. Wendell Willkie in 1940 was a Republican Senator from Indiana. Although starting out as a Democrat, he changed parties, siding with industrial and financial interests, and sought to temper much of the governmental regulation and expansion. He maintained that he was the leader of the "loyal opposition" but supported the war effort and many of Roosevelt's policies. Many of his ideas would later be adopted and further truncated by Ronald Reagan and persist in discussions today as to the role of government and business in everyday life.

Willkie frequently used the term "loyal opposition" to describe his party and was instrumental in championing the concept of international cooperation during the War. He proposed establishing an independent peacekeeping organization after the end of the war. He did not receive a second nomination from his party in 1944 and died later that year.

During World War II, the conversion of civilian manufacturing toward the production of tanks, guns, ships, ammunition, bombs and aircraft was remarkable. In a few years, the United States would lead in the production of all key weapons used in the war compared to any of the Axis powers. The American people generously purchased war bonds, and more women took jobs in war production plants than at any time in its history. The sense of patriotism was much higher than in World War I, and the war was also a liberating time from the poverty and depression of the 1930s. This massive infusion of public debt for the war effort dwarfed the lesser magnitude expenditures of the New Deal. It created millions of new jobs, but it was also discovered that many persons with key wartime skills were working in jobs ill-suited to their professions. This was a result of the Great Depression whereby those out of work sought any job that could feed their families or support themselves.

The attitude and admiration of the American people toward its military services was certainly noticed by both parties as a means of garnering support for programs and candidates who had served their country in its time of need.

Photograph 8. An ailing President Franklin Roosevelt sits between Prime Minister Winston Churchill of Great Britain and Premier Josef Stalin of the former Soviet Union, surrounded by military leaders of the respective countries at the Yalta Conference in 1945. President Roosevelt would pass away shortly after this meeting.

The Incorruptible Thomas Dewey

Franklin Roosevelt was opposed for his fourth term in office by Thomas E. Dewey, a prosecuting attorney and popular Governor of New York. Dewey was a man of great integrity, and his reputation as a prosecutor for fighting corruption and racketeering was legendary. Eventually he would serve three terms as Governor of New York. He believed in the "pay-as-you-go" process of legislation, and in principled fiscal discipline. Dewey was an excellent administrator, well-organized, and disliked discrimination in government. Although he did not defeat the highly popular Roosevelt, most political analysts predicted victory for him in 1948 against Harry Truman. However, Dewey did not receive enough support from farmers or labor and was beset by party in-fighting between Republican conservatives and progressives, leading to an unexpected loss to Truman.

Photograph 9. Exuberant supporters display picket signs of nominee Governor Thomas Dewey of New York at the Republican National Convention in 1948. Dewey had a reputation for fiscal integrity, strength, and organization, was free of corruption and made crime fighting one of his top priorities. Although popular, he underestimated the strength of President Harry Truman and his down-home appeal in the rural and western states. In a surprising election, Harry Truman was elected to a second term as President.

The Assertive Harry Truman

Although Truman rose to the US Senate with the backing of Democratic machine politicians in Missouri, he exposed waste and fraud in government contracts and found deficiencies in war materiel during World War II. He was a last-minute Vice-Presidential choice of Roosevelt to replace the controversial Henry A. Wallace. His most important decision was the release of atomic bombs over Hiroshima and Nagasaki that lead to the immediate end of the war with Japan.

His defeat of Governor Thomas E. Dewey was due to the complacency of Dewey while Truman traversed the country complaining about the "do-nothing" Congress.

Photograph 10. President Harry Truman was Vice President during the fourth term of the Roosevelt Administration. He was chosen at the Democratic Convention as an alternative to the controversial Henry Wallace. Because Roosevelt primarily dealt with his staff, Truman was not kept informed on many official matters. When Roosevelt died, Truman was left with the responsibilities of concluding military operations in Japan, and with the rise of the post-war Soviet Union as a rival to the United States. He was elected to another term in 1948. The Truman Administration created the Dept. of Defense, oversaw the rebuilding of Europe, and dealt with the warring factions in the Korean Peninsula.

In many ways, the harsh rhetoric of Truman solidified and energized opposition against his domestic policies. However, he did receive substantial support to reduce Communist influence in Greece and Turkey, and for other anti-Communist measures in Europe.

A wide-ranging plan to reconstruct Europe devastated during World War II was put together under the leadership of Gen. George C. Marshall. During this period of time, the Central Intelligence Agency (CIA) was formed (1947), and the divided German city of Berlin received supplies via airlift after the Soviet Union blocked access to roads and check points in 1948.

In 1950, the North Korean Communists and their army invaded South Korea, leading to a long and bloody conflict, whose bitterness persists to this day. Gen. Douglas MacArthur was placed as commander of American armed forces. MacArthur pursued a course of ultimate defeat of the North Korean forces, eventually invading Manchuria. His entry into Communist China without authorization of the Joint Chiefs of Staff precipitated his dismissal. The Korean War dragged on even after the replacement of MacArthur with Gen. Matthew Ridgway.

Charges were raised by Sen. Joseph McCarthy of Wisconsin that Communists were serving in various government departments, which lead to a gradual erosion of Truman's popularity and public confidence in him as President. The issue of Communist influence and the growing military power of the Soviet Union was a significant concern of many Americans at the time, and it became one of the leading ideological issues of the Republican Party for years to come. The Korean War was another lesson that wars fought on foreign soil had to have great strategic significance for the continued involvement of American military forces. If not quickly decided within a few years after the start of first deployments, domestic disenchantment rapidly escalates as casualties mount when no visible resolution is in sight.

The Rise of Dwight Eisenhower

In 1942, Gen. Dwight D. Eisenhower was selected by Gen. Marshall to be the Supreme Commander of Allied Forces in Europe due to his military knowledge, his adeptness at strategic planning, and his diplomatic skills in dealing with other Allied commanders.

When Eisenhower returned to the United States, he was greeted as a great military hero, and was named by Pres. Truman to replace Gen. Marshall. During that time, he administered the stand-down of the armed forces, and urged a centralized command structure for the military. In 1950, he was appointed as Supreme Commander of the North Atlantic Treaty Organization (NATO), a unified confederation of Western European nations dedicated to defense against the Communist domination of Europe.

Although both major parties sought Eisenhower as a candidate, he entered the Republican primary in 1952. His principal opposition was from Sen. Robert Taft of Ohio.

Photograph 11. Supreme Commander of the Allied Armies General Dwight Eisenhower meets with Maj. Gen. Matthew Ridgway in 1944. As commander, Gen. Eisenhower was a superb planner and diplomat, holding together many generals and statesmen from allied nations in a common cause to bring an end to conflict in Europe during World War II.

Nominated on the first ballot at the Convention, he chose Sen. Richard Nixon of California for Vice President. Eisenhower easily defeated the brilliant intellectual but frequently abstruse Gov. Adlai Stevenson of Illinois in the general election.

As president, Eisenhower used a military-style staff structure, delegating tasks to his cabinet officers and advisors. Eisenhower was only involved in major decisions and felt that his role as a post-wartime president was to return the country to peaceful pursuits. Offshore oil reserves were returned to the states. He believed in reduced taxes and balanced budgets, and since the war was concluded, less government involvement in corporate and business affairs was needed.

In response to Sen. McCarthy's charges of Communist infiltration of the government, Eisenhower required "loyalty oaths" to be administered, whereby those in government service swore that they were not members of the Communist Party, nor did they advocate violent overthrow of the government.

After the death of the seemingly avuncular but evil Joseph Stalin of the Soviet Union, Eisenhower brokered a stable truce between the belligerent North Korea and South Korea in 1953. Although his Secretary of State John Foster Dulles articulated a policy of liberating nations under Communist rule, when the East Germans in 1953 and Hungarians in 1956 revolted, no direct military support for them materialized.

Photograph 12. An official portrait of President Dwight D. Eisenhower displayed at the National Portrait Gallery. Intent on returning the United States to a non-wartime footing, Eisenhower was nevertheless confronted with a post-Stalinist Soviet Union that continued the build-up of nuclear and conventional weapons. Intimately familiar with undesirability of war, he pursued policies intended to lessen world tension and tried to discourage the formation of a permanent American military-industrial complex.

Eisenhower was concerned about the potential of starting another major war with the Soviet Union that could potentially involve nuclear weapons.

In his run for a second term, Eisenhower again defeated Adlai Stevenson and his Vice-Presidential candidate Sen. Estes Kefauver of Tennessee but faced a Democratic majority in both the House and Senate.

Throughout the country, there was rioting, marches and civil disobedience in the South after the Supreme Court struck down segregation in the public schools. In 1957, Eisenhower, who had no affinity for racial segregation, sent Federal troops to integrate the public high school in Little Rock, Arkansas. Later that year, the Soviet Union launched an artificial satellite named "Sputnik" into earth orbit. The confidence of the American public was shaken as to the superiority of the Soviets in space technology.

After the death of Dulles, Eisenhower assumed the mantle of diplomacy, personally inviting Premier Nikita Khrushchev of the Soviet Union to the United States. At first, these efforts proved successful in easing tensions between the two countries. Unfortunately, a U-2 spy plane was intercepted over Soviet airspace and crashed, but the pilot, Francis Gary Powers, survived and was promptly arrested. Details came out that flights had been ongoing for four years prior to their public disclosure. After this incident, diplomacy between the Soviet Union and the United States collapsed. Subsequently, the Cuban dictator Fidel Castro aligned himself as a Soviet satellite in the Western Hemisphere, resulting in the breakage of diplomatic relations with the United States. An ongoing buildup of Soviet military aid, later including offensive missiles in Cuba, would lead to Cuban isolation for the next 48 years and counting.

In general, although Eisenhower tried to set a course for domestic tranquility and for world peace, he was blocked by Communist ideology and expansionism. Despite his long and esteemed military background, Eisenhower warned of a growing "military-industrial complex" that even he could not control, whereby military budgets became so intertwined with corporate support and money influence on legislators that military contractors became permanent adjuncts to the armed forces. Throughout those Cold War times, Eisenhower remained a president of sincerity, warmth and consistently retained substantial popularity throughout the country.

The Kennedy-Johnson Transition

The election of 1960 was a very closely contested election between the incumbent Vice President Richard Nixon and Sen. John F. Kennedy of Massachusetts. Sen. Kennedy's election to the Presidency was decided by only 118,550 votes out of a total of 68,335,462 popular votes. The election was largely decided by a series of television debates. Kennedy had served three terms as a Congressman, and two terms as a Senator, where he emphasized foreign policy and advocated full employment.

In his first year as President, he was advised by the CIA and the Joint Chiefs of Staff to invade Cuba with the support of Cuban exiles, which supposedly would lead to a "general uprising" against the regime of Fidel Castro. Upon landing on the beach, the exiles were either killed or captured. This abortive attempt at destabilizing Castro further accelerated the movement of the Castro government toward greater military involvement and overt support of the Soviet Union.

Photograph 13. Three Kennedy brothers in 1961, from left to right, Robert as Attorney General during the Kennedy Administration, Ted as campaign manager, and John as President of the United States. With their engaging personalities and personal ambition, all three would be senators and seek the Presidency. The Kennedy Administration was marked by international confrontations between the United States and the Soviet Union over the militarization of Cuba. This led to unprecedented expansion of strategic missile arsenals and defense spending for both countries, a legacy that we must deal with today and in the future.

In October 1962, reconnaissance photos showed a Soviet military buildup in Cuba, including missile launching sites and various support facilities. Missiles were being shipped from the Soviet Union to the island. When consulting with Congress, leaders of both parties recommended an invasion of Cuba. Kennedy preferred a less confrontational approach, declaring the island under "quarantine". Soviet ships carrying missiles and other armaments were blockaded, and eventually were withdrawn. In response to the withdrawal, American intermediate range ballistic missiles (IRBMs) in Turkey were subsequently removed.

During the Eisenhower and Kennedy Administrations, military assistance and a small number of military advisors were provided to the Vietnamese government located in the southern portion of the former French colony of Indo-China. Initially, this conflict seemed to be a relative minor containment effort during the Kennedy Administration, but came into sharp focus after Vice President Lyndon Johnson assumed the Presidency after the assassination of President Kennedy.

President Johnson was sworn in hastily on Air Force One at Love Field in Dallas after President Kennedy passed away. He kept most of the Kennedy appointees in his cabinet. Johnson had been a highly effective Senate Majority Leader for six years, where he thoroughly analyzed each legislator as to philosophy, interests and voting records. During this period, friction over segregation in the Deep South, as well as housing, education and employment conditions in the North, led to protests and disruptions. It became evident that the inequities had to be remedied by law. Because of his persuasiveness and persistence, a substantial number of major legislative initiatives passed, including the Civil Rights Act of 1964, which prohibited most forms of overt racial discrimination. Medicare, a Federally-subsidized health program for elderly care was also passed, along with various anti-poverty programs, voting rights, and aid to schools that primarily educated poor children.

After the civil rights leader Martin L. King was assassinated, major riots broke in many large cities. Newark and Detroit were hardest hit, suffering severe acts of arson and looting, requiring the call-up of National Guard troops to bring order to those devastated cities.

Photograph 14. President Johnson and Secretary of Defense Robert McNamara ponder over Vietnam War plans and tactics. Despite substantial achievements in civil rights legislation and the establishment of Medicare, the Vietnam Conflict would overwhelm the focus of the Johnson Administration, leading to Johnson's abandonment to seek re-election, turning that task over to Hubert Humphrey, his leading supporter in the Senate.

Johnson encountered opposition to his spending programs and the gradual escalation of the war effort in Vietnam from both the Republican and Democratic Parties. After an incident in the Gulf of Tonkin where two American destroyers were "attacked" by the North Vietnamese, the Congress gave President Johnson complete and exclusive discretion to combat the potential "domino effect" of Communist expansion in the Pacific. Casualty rates were precipitously high each month, generating widespread dissatisfaction by academia, the press, television commentators, and a growing sense among the public that the conflict had questionable strategic significance. The Republican Party was divided as to its opinion of the conflict; some desired a complete blockade of North Vietnam and wholesale bombing; others wanted a gradual reduction of conflict intensity and incremental troop withdrawals.

In 1968, with challengers Sen. Eugene McCarthy of Minnesota and Sen. Robert Kennedy of New York leading in various early primaries, President Johnson announced that he would not run for re-election. After Sen. Kennedy was assassinated after winning the California primary, the Democratic Party Convention chose Sen. Hubert Humphrey of Minnesota to face former Vice President Richard Nixon, the Republican candidate.

The Re-Emergence of Richard Nixon

In November 1968, Richard M. Nixon was elected president. He was one of the most experienced men in Federal service to assume the presidency. Although he graduated second in his law school class from Duke University, he had minimal interest in a career as a lawyer, preferring politics and public service. After the Japanese attacked Pearl Harbor in 1941, he volunteered to become a naval officer, and was awarded numerous non-combat citations, including a special letter of commendation from James Forrestal, the Secretary of the Navy.

As a Congressman, he came to prominence as a member of the House Un-American Activities Committee. As a Senator, he espoused conventional positions opposing the spread of communism, price controls, and limiting government power. These positions would change after he became President Nixon.

Photograph 15. President Richard Nixon throws out the first ball on opening day for the Washington Senators. Former batting champion and manager Ted Williams stands to the left. Nixon loved sports, especially baseball. A complex man with many insecurities, he concentrated on foreign affairs that was his expertise, but was unable to obtain the accolades and approbation from either the press, the Congress or popular opinion that he so badly desired.

Nixon greatly expanded the role of the Vice President as a political representative of the United States, visiting numerous foreign countries on behalf of President Eisenhower.

As president, Nixon portrayed his early administration as a beacon of stability in the midst of turmoil created by the Vietnam War, with its strident voices, draft evasion, mounting military casualties, and limited prospects for an honorable settlement of the conflict.

As part of a strategy to get the North Vietnamese to the peace table, Nixon ordered that the sanctuaries in Cambodia be bombed to disrupt their supply lines. He later announced that troops would enter Cambodia to complete the campaign of disruption. He encouraged the South Vietnamese to increasingly shoulder the military burdens of the war, but the transition proved ineffective. Amidst public unease and critics labeling the military campaign as a revisit to the Johnson Administration, Nixon continued the war effort. After bombing military and industrial targets in North Vietnam, gradually the warring parties settled on a peace agreement in 1973.

Nixon implemented the powers granted to him by the Congress to impose wage and price controls to temper the inflationary spiral of 1970. Wage controls limited growth to 5.5%, and price controls were set at 2.5%. Further concerned about inflation, Nixon indexed social security to the cost of living. To counteract the growing gold reserves of rival nations, Nixon desired a "floating" currency so as not to hold the United States hostage to foreign currencies. Accordingly, Nixon took the dollar off the gold standard.

Although Nixon was opposed to busing of children into neighborhood schools, he had his Secretary of Labor George Schulz establish local bi-racial committees to decrease the number of all-black schools. By the end of the Nixon Administration, the number of all-black schools had been markedly reduced from 70% to about 20%.

Nixon was a great supporter of NASA. In 1969, three astronauts landed the lunar excursion module onto the moon, providing the United States a psychological boost to counteract fears that NASA had sadly lagged behind the Soviet space program for many years. The Soviet Union had previously launched the first orbiting satellite (Sputnik), the first cosmonaut (Yuri Gagarin) and the first orbiting space station (Mir). Nixon approved funds to build the Space Shuttle, permitting American leadership in space technology for many years afterwards.

Through his support of the Pakistani government as a counterpoint to India, which had recently aligned itself with the Soviet Union, Nixon used these intermediary contacts to set up meetings with the leadership of China. His visit with the Chinese leaders was marked by frank discussions and led to the establishment of trade and cultural cooperation with China. Because of tension between China and the Soviet Union, Nixon exploited their differences to attempt to shift the balance of power toward the United States.

Uncomfortable with the newly-minted cooperation between China and the United States, Nixon was able to extract from the Soviets a relaxation of their adversarial relationship with the United States. In his meetings with Soviet President Leonid Brezhnev, he was able to reach agreement by treaty to limit the production of strategic armaments. Nixon also obtained signing of the Anti-Ballistic Missile Treaty, which halted deployment of American ICBM missile interceptors (Nike-Zeus) and their tracking stations, which could have triggered even more Soviet ICBM production to counter this defense. These two treaties effectively limited the production of additional ICBMs and construction of launching sites on both sides.

Nixon's agreements with the Soviets and the Chinese were calculated to lessen their support and interest in North Vietnam. These peace efforts may have been as equally effective as the military campaigns in Cambodia, Laos and North Vietnam in bringing the North Vietnamese to the peace table.

In both his terms, Nixon displayed the progressivity of the Republican Party in the passage of the Clean Air Act, the establishment of the Office of Management and Budget, the Occupational Safety and Health Act (OSHA), and the Environmental Protection Agency (EPA). In 1974, Nixon called for comprehensive health insurance to be provided by employers, and a federal health plan whereby any citizen not employed per se or self-employed could purchase health insurance, with premiums based on their income.

In the last years of his administration, Nixon had antagonized the Congress, and lost general support after revelations regarding his illegal pre-election activities and use of federal agencies to spy on his adversaries, leading to threats of impeachment and his resignation.

In retrospect, and despite his insular personality, Richard Nixon was an advocate of internationalism, defending the interests of the United States, acted as a peacemaker, and was sympathetic to the poor and disliking injustice. His many legislative and diplomatic achievements were carefully orchestrated, and he took a pragmatic approach to problems, balancing the interest of both right and left.

In his later years of retirement, he redeemed himself after his near-impeachment by providing advice to Presidents Reagan, Carter, Bush and Clinton, and traveled widely on behalf of the United States. His knowledge of foreign policy was always highly respected.

The Ford-Carter Malaise

After Congressional hearings, the House drew up articles of impeachment of President Richard Nixon, he resigned his office and his Vice President Gerald Ford assumed the office. Ford was a capable legislator and public official, with a solid military background and a degree in law. As a young collegian, he was a star football player at the University of Michigan, and he received his law degree from Yale University. In 1940, he worked as a campaign supporter for Sen. Wendell Willkie. When the United States was attacked by Japan, Ford joined the US Navy as an ensign. He served on the aircraft carrier USS Monterey, and was awarded numerous citations, including two bronze stars. After his military service, he served as a Congressman representing Grand Rapids, Michigan, rising to House Minority Leader. His confirmation to be Vice President under Nixon was nearly unanimous.

Photograph 16. President Gerald Ford testifies at a Congressional hearing regarding the pardon of Richard Nixon. Suspicions of a deal between former President Nixon and Ford continued to shadow the Ford Administration. Ford consistently maintained that the pardon was granted because potential legal actions against Nixon were a distraction to his administration. His bipartisan nature was a welcome change, and he clearly calmed the nation after impeachment efforts were terminated after Nixon had resigned the Presidency.

Although Ford was well liked in the Congress, the time period in which he held the Presidency was not good to him. The inflation rate was at 9-10%, and the general economy was in a downturn. His pardon of Richard Nixon was viewed suspiciously by many. When the economy went into recession, he vetoed numerous stimulus measures out of fear of renewed inflation. His only major achievement was the signing of a nuclear arms reduction treaty in Helsinki.

During the Presidential debates with contender Jimmy Carter, Ford stated that Eastern Europe was not under the domination of the Soviet Union. At first hearing, the statement was thought to be a simple "slip of the tongue", but Ford repeated it, much to the chagrin of his supporters. His opposition represented the remarks as a man out-of-touch with reality, especially for a Republican. Ford remains a transitional president who brought a solid base to a nation deeply troubled by the removal of President Nixon by impeachment. Because Ford was not hyper-partisan, he brought a governmental calm when it was sorely needed.

The President of Rectitude

The ensuing presidential election was very close, with Governor Jimmy Carter of Georgia defeating Ford by a slim margin. Carter was an ambitious legislator and governor who aspired to the highest office in the land. High-minded and a self-styled Southern reformer, he placed "human rights" at the forefront of his agenda. His choice for Vice President was not the preferred and better qualified Sen. Edmund Muskie, an intellectual New Englander; instead, he chose the more affable Sen. Walter Mondale of Minnesota. Carter was a micromanager and was involved in many policy details that normally are delegated to cabinet officers and agency heads. His relationship with the Congress was often frosty and remote, as Carter considered them as a large aggregate of special interests.

In response to oil shortages, Carter created the Dept. of Energy. His major achievement was the signing of a peace accord between Egypt and Israel, two longtime adversaries of the Middle East. However, his management of the Iranian seizure of the US Embassy resulted in a loss of American prestige.

Photograph 17. President Jimmy Carter at the Democratic National Convention with his wife Rosalynn to the left, and Vice President Walter Mondale with hands upraised. Confronted with inflation, oil shortages and poor relationships with the Congress, Carter and Mondale and their Cabinet officers struggled through a difficult four years.

In an attempt to rescue the hostages taken by Iran, Carter and his closest advisors devised a tri-service plan to rescue the hostages but did not disclose sufficient information regarding its implementation to key military commanders in the field. The tri-service task force had never previously worked together, nor had the rescue helicopters been properly prepared prior to launch. The mission was ultimately aborted after a fatal collision in the desert staging area.

Another example of Carter's odd decision-making in times of crises was his response to the Soviet invasion of Afghanistan. He decided to boycott the Olympic Games in Moscow, an ineffectual response to a military action. Having the United States provide a strong showing medal count, just as the United States had done during the Berlin Games in 1936, it would have demonstrated American solidarity and fidelity to Olympic sport even during times of tension.

Carter had long been an admirer of the Shah of Iran, overlooking his dictatorial regime and human rights violations. Again, Carter let his personal sympathy override the obvious potential for foment in Iran and admitted the Shah for cancer treatment in the United States. This action further exacerbated tensions with Iran that continue to this day.

Fortunately, after his defeat for a second term, Carter rehabilitated himself, putting his diplomatic, humanitarian and organizational skills to work on behalf of the United States. He continued to act as an international mediator and senior statesman in areas such as disease abatement in poor countries, election monitoring, and conducting semi-official negotiations with difficult foreign leaders to mollify their demands and effect compromise. Carter was awarded many awards for his humanitarian and international peace efforts, including the Nobel Peace Prize in 2002.

Photograph 18. President Carter, Vice President Mondale, Sec. of Defense Harold Brown and Sec. of State Cyrus Vance walk to Camp David to deal with the Iranian seizure of the US Embassy in 1979. This event would paralyze a substantial portion of the time that would occupy Carter during his Presidency, ultimately leading to his defeat in the election of 1980 by Ronald Reagan.

The Reagan Era

With the attitude of the nation looking for a more confident and less somber chief executive, Governor Ronald Reagan of California was elected President. Ronald Reagan grew up in rural Illinois, became a broadcaster and eventually a successful movie actor. He was a supporter of the Roosevelt Administration as a registered Democrat in his early years, and was head of the Screen Actors

Guild, a union organization. As his movie career waned, his concern over Communist influence in Hollywood transitioned him into political involvement. He never enjoyed the big tax bite taken out of his paycheck, a common lament among highly paid performers like actors and sports figures. This would later shape his thinking about tax reduction as President.

With the demand for his acting skills in decline, Reagan associated himself with the General Electric Company (GE), a highly organized and technologically innovative corporation originally founded by the great inventor Thomas Edison. Through a speaking platform provided by GE, Reagan became a polished communicator using wit, charm and clear speech to get across his political and social ideas across to a broad spectrum of people.

As Governor of California, Reagan clamped down on the unruly University of California campus at Berkeley which was riven due to anti-war activity. He was a firm supporter of the death penalty, and intensely disliked the continuation of welfare payments to many recipients who were simply evading work. His means of balancing the budget was to freeze government hiring, but Reagan did approve some tax increases. Although his first foray into presidential politics did not result in his selection, it provided the American people an introduction to his thinking regarding lower taxes, reductions in the size of government, and eliminating reverse discrimination. Since California was a leading state in production of aircraft and defense goods, Reagan felt that a strong defense industry, rather than social spending, was a more appropriate target of government spending to counteract communist or socialist adversaries that he deemed as a threat to the American way of life.

Photograph 19. Ronald Reagan and future wife Nancy Davis on the set of her movie in 1953. Reagan's marriage to his first wife Jane Wyman ended in divorce. In sharp contrast to Wyman, Nancy Davis would be a lifetime supporter and confidant of Reagan as Governor of California and as President of the United States.

As President, Reagan enunciated at his inaugural address Republican thinking that persists today: "Government is not solution to our problems; government is the problem." This simplistic political phrase literally reverted back to the days of Harding and Coolidge and was a truncation of a complex conundrum that the founders of our Constitution sought to counterbalance with the separation of powers of the branches of government. Reagan had seemed to be deprecating the common governmental purpose of Theodore Roosevelt, reaffirming the belief in corporate and industrial power advocated by Willkie, and bolstered the strong post-war defense stances of Eisenhower and Nixon. Governments, in Reagan's eyes, were to reduce taxes, relax regulations, permit the ambitious to prosper, favor the private and corporate sectors of the economy, and provide for the common defense through massive deficit spending.

In his first term, Reagan was almost assassinated by a deranged gunman, wounding him the chest. One of his advisors, James Brady, sustained a bullet wound to the brain. His recovery brought him tremendous support from people of all political stripes.

After his recovery, an air traffic controller shutdown resulted in a wide-ranging dismissal of all strikers. Although many returned to work, those who did not were blacklisted from Federal service. Many committed suicide. Reagan's tough stance against unions was the beginning of a long decline in union membership, which is now primarily concentrated in larger corporations engaged in aerospace, automotive, chemical, atomic, oil or mining work, and throughout Federal, State and local government.

Reagan was an ardent proponent of deregulation and placed great faith in corporate control of many aspects of American life. In his first term, unemployment was nearly 11%. Reagan urged cutting taxes, citing California academicians who propounded that tax

Photograph 20. This official White House photo of Ronald Reagan was taken in 1981. His movie career on the wane, Reagan honed his political speeches courtesy of General Electric, eventually becoming Governor of California. His first attempt at the Presidency was not successful, but the seeds of his popularity were sown. The dismal time period that Jimmy Carter was president was ripe for the election of a sunny leader with an optimistic disposition. His urging of the reduction of the size of government has unfortunately taken on in recent years a more militant and less merciful tone that Reagan never intended.

reductions would spur investment and result in job creation. Critics labeled "supply side" economics as nothing but "trickle down" economics. In line with his dim view of the "welfare state", Reagan cut budgets of various "Great Society" programs, such as food stamps, medical aid to the poor and environmental protection. Federal income taxes were reduced, and the economy gradually recovered over the eight years of his presidency.

In an effort to bring the Soviet Union to bear, massive defense spending led to huge budget deficits during his term of office. Due to heavy reliance on borrowing, the national debt increased from $700 billion to about $3 trillion. Reagan himself considered this heavy debt load as his "greatest disappointment".

He restarted military programs, including advanced versions of the Minuteman Intercontinental Ballistic Missile (ICBM) System, and deployed the newer shorter-range Pershing II ballistic missiles in Germany, which were targeted against the former Soviet Union. In various speeches, Reagan termed the Soviet Union as an "evil empire" that was destined to be dumped into the "ash heap of history." His ideology and those of his party broadly proclaimed freedom and democracy as the cornerstones of true political durability. When Soviet fighter jets apparently mistook a Korean airliner as a "spy plane" and shot it down, this resulted in a suspension of all flights to the Soviet Union.

Upon the advice of physicist Edward Teller and other leading defense analysts, Reagan began the Strategic Defense Initiative (SDI). SDI was a space-based defense system designed to intercept ballistic missiles either in their post-boost or guidance phase using lasers, high energy pellets or powerful penetrating X-rays. The cost of this system was staggering, and there was immediate opposition due to its complexity and unknown reliability. Many of the warhead intercept tests were clearly suspect as to their actual defensive capability in a real combat situation. There was understandable reluctance to adopt such a system that would be subject to easily implemented countermeasures. The explosion of nuclear devices in the atmosphere had literally resulted in loss of communications, disrupting the command and control of the system. Nevertheless, the Soviets were clearly agitated, since a potential deployment of such a system would require even greater numbers of offensive first- and second-strike missiles to overwhelm SDI.

Reagan supported covert aid to various factions that opposed Communist expansion in the Middle East, Afghanistan, Africa and South America. His support of the "Mujahedeen" in Afghanistan that ended in the withdrawal of the Soviet occupation forces in Afghanistan would later lead to the rise of the Taliban and its harboring alliance with Al-Queda in this remote land.

During the civil war in Lebanon, Reagan deployed troops as part of a multi-national; peacekeeping effort. The Marine Corps barracks was bombed, killing more than 200 personnel. Eventually this force was withdrawn.

A Communist takeover of Grenada was averted as US forces re-took the island, although 135 casualties were sustained. However, a new government was installed, free of Soviet and Cuban influence. Reagan also took swift action when a nightclub in Berlin that US military frequented where 63 servicemen were injured with one fatality was thought to be the work of Libyan terrorists. He ordered airstrikes against Libya, clearly shaking a bewildered Muammar Gadaffi. This type of decisive action was a hallmark of his administration.

Reagan throughout his two terms seemed to always re-affirm his anti-communist ideology, yet later he would seek compromise on arms reductions with the reformer Mikhail Gorbachev, the General Secretary of the Communist Party of the Soviet Union.

In his efforts to stifle the spread of Communism south of the border, the Reagan Administration embarked on a plan to covertly send funds to the "Contras" engaged in the overthrow of regime of Daniel Ortega in Nicaragua. Staff members apparently had diverted money obtained from arms sales to Iran to the "Contras". Although Reagan was only peripherally implicated, the scandal, the special commissions and the televised hearings all cast a pall over his executive actions that were explicitly forbidden by the Congress. This conflict over the limits of executive power of the Commander-in-Chief vs. the war-making powers of the Congress would continue into the Bush Administrations and test the limits of the Constitution. As Reagan testified, it was becoming clearer that some of his memory was beginning to fade.

The Reagan Administration used the strength of the military to challenge the authority of the Soviet Union, which was largely based on its superiority in numbers of strategic weapons. The Soviet economy, heavily dependent on oil exports whose prices were subject to OPEC oil production quotas, was depressed. The Soviets suffered a terrible loss of credibility when the Chernobyl nuclear reactor suffered a catastrophic meltdown, injuring thousands and spreading radioactive fallout over parts of Ukraine and Eastern Europe.

Reagan seized the initiative and negotiated several arms agreements regarding convention and nuclear forces in various summit meetings. His efforts at diplomacy and compromise with Gorbachev brought about a new détente, and a lessening of tension between the two great nuclear powers. Although Reagan is often credited by the Republican Party with the decline of the Soviet state, his actions only brought it to its inevitable tipping point. The Soviet pursuit of military adventures, its costly weaponry, its lax nuclear safety, the poor state of its infrastructure, and its continuing attempts to spread of spheres of influence beyond its extensive borders, could not be indefinitely sustained. Its people had sacrificed enough during World War II, its ideology of dictatorship of the proletariat had become outworn, and its over-planned economy based on rationing of social goods with preferences to military and political action were no longer workable. The Soviet Union just eventually collapsed due to its own internal exhaustion.

Reagan, along with his wife Nancy, felt that drug usage could be curbed by strong law enforcement and stiff sentences. This change in Dept. of Justice policy and its enactment into various laws brought about sharp increases in the prison population. This war on drugs bore a substantial cost, resulting in commingling non-violent offenders with murderers, rapists, robbers and other criminals. In some cases, the prison sentences of drug users were often more severe that those of truly violent criminals.

In his judicial lifetime appointments to the Supreme Court, Reagan secured seats for Antonin Scalia, a very staunch conservative, had elevated William Rehnquist to Chief Justice, and nominated moderate Anthony Kennedy after the controversial Robert Bork was rejected by the Senate. He had appointed the most judges of any president in US history.

The First Bush Presidency

George H. W. Bush came from a wealthy family with a history government service. Bush was a graduate of Yale University, and his own long record of government service brought visions of promise for those who had voted for him. He had an enviable military record as a young Navy fighter pilot during World War II and was awarded the Distinguished Flying Cross and other medals. In addition to his tenure as Vice President, he was Ambassador to the United Nations and served as a director of the CIA. Bush was a very successful oil executive, particularly as president of Zapata Offshore Company, an oil exploration firm that drilled wells in the Gulf of Mexico. The election for the Presidency in 1989 pitted the Governor of Massachusetts Michael Dukakis, a patrician bureaucrat and Sen. Lloyd Bentsen of Texas, his Vice-Presidential choice, against George H. W. Bush, the incumbent Vice President and his selection for Vice President, the callow Sen. Dan Quayle of Indiana. With Bush's emphasis on the suppression of crime and "no new taxes", he received 56% of the popular vote, and a much larger majority of the electoral votes.

Left with a growing deficit incurred during the Reagan Administration, his campaign pledge of "no new taxes" eventual

Photograph 21. President George H. W. Bush has a long history of government service. He began his career as a young fighter pilot during World War II, became a Congressman, a successful oil executive, and served as Director of the Central Intelligence Agency before being chosen as Ronald Reagan's Vice President.

came to haunt him as his Republican colleagues failed to support his call for spending reductions and tax increases. Forced into a box, he eventually signed a tax bill that increased taxes, as advocated by the Democratic Party, which he would later regret.

During his term in office, legislation was enacted to decrease the emissions of sulfur from coal-fired plants and diesel engines, and to provide better access to buildings and governmental services for disabled persons. Bush considered himself to be the "education president", although only minimal educational accomplishments materialized during his administration.

From 1989 to 1990, after extended talks with Soviet Premier Mikhail Gorbachev, the two countries agreed to the Strategic Arms Reduction Treaty (START I), whereby long and intermediate range ballistic missile counts would be reduced by about 35% to 50%, depending on the class of missile. This treaty was the beginning of a long-range reduction of tension between the United States and the Soviet Union, which later split apart, dissolving the Soviet federations which became independent nations. These negotiations would later lead to a tenuous partnership of these former adversaries on various global problems in the future.

The principal achievement of the Bush Administration was its decision to repel the Iraqi armed forces that had invaded and occupied Kuwait in violation of international law. Using his diplomatic skills to secure a wide array of support from allied nations, American and coalition forces easily turned back and defeated the Iraqi armed forces.

However, Bush and his advisors at the time were reluctant to pursue the complete entry and occupation of Iraq to remove the regime of Saddam Hussein. Bush and his advisors worried over subsequent insurrections, insurgent guerilla war, and the number of military personnel and their attending drain on the US budget that is inherent in any long- term occupation. Instead, Bush chose a covert means to topple the Hussein regime by supporting the indigenous opposition. That support ultimately proved to be weak, and the opposition resistance was crushed by the surviving Hussein dictatorship, resulting in cruel suppression and elimination of internal resistance for years to come.

Bush and his supporters were strong advocates of free trade. Working with the leaders of Canada and Mexico, Bush advocated the North American Free Trade Agreement (NAFTA) which virtually eliminated tariffs between the three countries and lifted restrictions on foreign investments. The proposed treaty met immediate opposition from labor and environmentalists, since it contained no labor standards, nor did it include any stringent environmental requirements, which were especially needed in Mexico.

Although many jobs have been created since NAFTA was passed in the Clinton Administration, there has been a steady decline and outflow of manufacturing jobs and production to Mexico, although to a lesser extent to Canada. Major manufacturers have commenced a steady stream of the shipment of production machinery and the construction of assembly plants in Mexico, hollowing out domestic work in the United States in the automotive, appliance and electronics industries. Trade deficits with Mexico and Canada started to substantially enlarge.

As one his last acts as President, Bush decided to intervene in Somalia, where lawless warlords ruled sections of a country virtually with any government. It would not only influence the next President's outlook on presidential power but would also act as one of several breeding rounds of an even more sinister threat to the safety of the United States.

Faced with growing corporate layoffs due to "restructuring", unemployment gradually increased during the latter part of the Bush Administration. Bush chafed at the notion that the US was in recession; his reluctance to face the problem seemed to be almost "Hoover-like" at times. In the coming election of 1993, Bush's remote approach to economic problems and his preference for foreign affairs would prove his undoing.

The Clinton Era

The election of 1992 pitted the incumbent President George Bush against Bill Clinton, Governor of Arkansas and his Vice-Presidential choice Sen. Albert Gore, and the independent H. Ross Perot, a billionaire executive from Texas. As the votes did not appear to provide victory for Perot as the campaign proceeded, he withdrew from the race. Upon the strong urging of his supporters, Perot re-entered the race, receiving 19% of the popular vote, a substantial amount for an independent. Clinton received 43% of the popular vote, and Bush 37%.

Clinton was an accomplished young president, graduating from Georgetown University, with a degree in Foreign Service. He received a Rhodes scholarship to study at Oxford University, and then attended Yale University where he received his law degree. He was twice elected as Governor of Arkansas. Much of his work as governor involved the improvement of schools and providing a better economic climate for the state, including the elimination of the sales tax on medicine. Much of this work was jointly accomplished with the help of his wife, Hillary Rodham Clinton.

Photograph 22. Bill Clinton swears in his wife Hillary Rodham Clinton as Senator for New York State, accompanied by their daughter Chelsea and Vice President Albert Gore. Bill Clinton was a moderate Democrat who oversaw the expansion of internet commerce and increased trade between the United States, Canada and Mexico. During his administration, the seeds of global terrorism began to sprout with problems in Somalia, embassy bombings, continuing attacks on aircraft in Iraq, and ethnic cleansing in Bosnia and Kosovo. The attack on the USS Cole signaled that many Middle Eastern countries could not be trusted, despite their governmental assurances of benign intent toward American interests.

In his first term, Clinton embarked on several highly controversial changes involving the armed forces and free trade. Acting upon campaign promises, Clinton proposed that homosexuals be permitted to serve openly in the armed forces without facing discharge. Eventually, after much opposition and discussion, a compromise policy emerged, whereby there would be no disclosure of identity by the service member, and no overt inquiry by the military would be made into their private life. The shorthand for this policy became "don't ask; don't tell". Notwithstanding this policy, service members were discharged when direct or indirect disclosure was apparent. Although recently reversed, the controversy over this policy remains with the House Armed Services Committee and some senior military officers.

The North American Free Trade Agreement (NAFTA), originally proposed during the Bush Administration, received support from Clinton. The agreement established tariff-free zones, allowing the movement of agricultural products and industrial goods between the United States, Canada and Mexico. There was both support and opposition in both the Democratic and Republican Parties for NAFTA. Many unions saw this agreement as a mechanism to eliminate jobs in the United States and transfer them to low-wage Mexico. Advocates touted the agreement as providing new export and markets for American products. However, in the end, the agreement provided both Canada and Mexico advantages, as US plants closed and manufacturing jobs in the United States disappeared by the hundreds of thousands.

Mrs. Clinton was appointed the head of a commission to establish a universal health care system for the United States. Due to staunch resistance from the insurance industry, the Republican Congress, and the American Medical Association, the Clinton health care initiative stalled and eventually was abandoned.

In 1993, Clinton signed legislation which provided tax cuts for small businesses, but increased taxes on the wealthy, and called for balanced budgets. During this period of time, economic prosperity occurred, accompanied by budget surpluses, and the massive expansion of the Internet as a force for information sharing and commercial activity.

In his first act as Commander-in-Chief, Clinton continued American involvement in trying to establish order in Somalia, a "quasi-nation" torn asunder by contesting warlords and unorganized militia factions. A disastrous insertion of American infantry and Blackhawk helicopter forces to quell disturbances led to the killing of 18 US soldiers and 73 wounded, although more than 1,000 Somali rebels were killed. The Congress did not support Clinton's concept of "nation-building", and troops were withdrawn. Somalia today remains a sanctuary for pirates and extremists and continues to be virtually ungovernable.

This early setback in Somalia and lack of Congressional support lead to a sense of executive hesitance for Clinton and his advisors on military matters, and a reluctance to commit troops where casualties would mount. The conflicts in Kosovo region of the former Yugoslavia, punctuated by the ethnic cleansing of Albanians by ethnic Serbs, eventually led Clinton to commit aircraft for the bombing of Serbia and release of American troops for peacekeeping. Led by Gen. Wesley Clark, an Army officer with political links to Clinton, the operation sustained only two accidental deaths and no combat casualties. It is evident that Clinton did not want a repeat of the humiliation of Somalia.

Similarly, he launched cruise missiles against Iraq when the dictator Saddam Hussein blocked UN inspectors from entering key areas where weapons production or storage were suspected. Fighter interceptors eliminated Iraqi air defense sites which interfered with allied aircraft enforcing the "no-fly zones" established after the Gulf War. Although Clinton wanted Hussein removed from power, he never authorized the use of American forces on Iraqi soil, even after the attack on the USS Cole.

Low points during the Clinton Administration included the rise and eventual demise of the Special Prosecutor, a prosecuting attorney given full resources to pursue charges of corruption. In general, most of the cases involved millions of dollars in legal investigations, but found no major transgressions, and were a waste of public resources due to the political nature of the charges.

In an effort to diminish the Clinton Presidency, the Republican-controlled House voted articles of impeachment alleging Clinton committed perjury in court testimony involving his sexual relationship with a White House intern. Although the Senate overturned the impeachment, it led to climate where there were constant demands that public officials be sexually and morally pure, causing the resignations of both Republican and Democratic legislators in subsequent years. Notably, it partially contributed to the election of George W. Bush over Vice President Al Gore, who was never involved in any improprieties, but the opposition trumpeted in their campaign "restoration of honor to the Presidency". This rectitude led to resignations of several leading Republicans in later years due to similar sexual conduct while in office.

An overlooked achievement of the Clinton Administration was his signing of the bill for a line item veto, a powerful tool to eliminate unnecessary riders or undesirable parts of legislation. This tool is widely used in many state legislatures. Unfortunately, this legislation was declared unconstitutional by the Supreme Court.

Despite his impeachment, Clinton has remained quite popular, and consistently had a favorability rating above 50% from mid-1995 to the end of his term in 2000 and continues to the present day.

The Bush II Presidency

The general election of 2000 was one of most bitter Presidential contests in American history, rivaling the disputed election of Tilden and Hayes. The actual outcome was decided by the Supreme Court in *Bush vs. Gore.* The Democrats nominated the incumbent Vice President Albert Gore for President and Sen. Joseph Lieberman for Vice President. George W. Bush, son of George H. W. Bush, was the Republican Presidential nominee for the Party and Richard Cheney was the Vice-Presidential choice, with a long record of public service.

George W. Bush was a graduate of Yale University, and received a master's degree in Business Administration (MBA) from Harvard University. He had an early introduction to politics, campaigning for Winton Blount for the US Senate for Arkansas in 1973, and in his father's presidential campaign. His service in the Texas Air National Guard was nominal at best. Although a fighter pilot, he saw no service in the Vietnam Conflict.

Photograph 23. A young George W. Bush as a fighter pilot trainee in the Texas National Guard. Bush would use some of this drill time for political campaigning for Winton Blount. He would later become Governor of Texas and his brother Jeb would be elected Governor of Florida. His tenure as President concentrated on responding to the attacks on New York City and the Pentagon by deploying hundreds of thousands of troops to Afghanistan and Iraq. The costs of these conflicts have been estimated at about 50,000 wounded and dead and a fiscal drain of at least $800 billion up to 1.5 trillion on the US Treasury.

Bush had extensive experience in the oil exploration business and was one of the owners of the Texas Rangers baseball club. His close ties to the oil industry had a significant influence on many of his decisions during his administration. Bush served two terms as Governor of Texas, where he governed in a spirit of bi-partisanship.

The general election revealed deep flaws in the method by which Americans choose their President. It demonstrated that the popular vote, which is used to determine virtually every elected office in the United States was invalidated by the "Electoral College", a non-existent physical entity in which voters select "electors" to cast their vote for President and Vice President. Because of close vote tallies in many states, Florida in particular, the actual winner of the election was indeterminate. After lawsuits were filed by the major parties, the Florida and US Supreme Courts ruled on ballot counting. The actual election is still disputed by various ballot counts and newspaper investigations as to who truly prevailed in Florida. After much litigation, the US Supreme Court halted the counting of all ballots in the State of Florida as ordered by the Florida Supreme Court, at which time Bush was leading by 500-600 votes out of about 6,000,000 ballots cast.

After assuming the Presidency and sustaining a rather slow start proposing tax cuts for the wealthy and expanding grants to faith-based charities, the World Trade Center in New York City and the Pentagon in Washington, DC were impacted by hijacked airliners. The terrorist "pilots" were primarily Saudi Arabian nationals on visa who trained at various flying schools in preparation for their attacks. Due to the Bush family's close ties to Saudi oil interests,

Saudi nationals and military pilots had long been enrolled in flight schools. Reports of their suspicious activities were discounted by higher level FBI supervisors.

The attack revealed the utter vulnerability of the airline industry, and the foggy response of the US Air Force to intercept these hijacked airliners brought little inspiration as to the effectiveness of our defenses. Presidential commissions were established to investigate, and the administration placed the country on a partial war footing. The event led to a relaxation in the constitutionally designated role of the Congress to declare war. Instead, the Congress rapidly approved defensive and anti-terror legislation in rapid fashion. Bush, augmented by the hawkish Cheney, initiated combat operations in Afghanistan, and later in Iraq after declaring the Iraqi regime as partners in the "axis of evil" that included Iran and North Korea.

Although the ostensible leader of the terrorist group Al-Queda Osama Bin Laden escaped into Pakistan, its close ally, the Taliban, was largely defeated, and its remnant stragglers sought refuge in Pakistan. In the winter of 2002, Bush and his Secretary of Defense Donald Rumsfeld and Secretary of State Colin Powell requested that the United Nations provide troops for an invasion of Iraq, based on intelligence reports now known to be either selective or specious that the Iraqi regime possessed active weapons of mass destruction. This assertion was contradicted by the UN weapons inspectors as exaggerative and misleading, stating that most of the weapons in question were largely destroyed after the Gulf War. Nevertheless, the Bush Administration convinced the Cong5ress and its key allies, especially Great Britain, that their course of action was proper.

After a short invasion and ensuing occupation, a long and protracted insurgency against the Allied occupation began, continuing until the end of the Bush Administration. During this period of time, Bush asserted the authority to ignore or overrule Congressional legislation regarding surveillance, unauthorized "wiretaps", and detention without trial of "enemy combatants" that were not subject to the Geneva Conventions of war since he was Commander-in-Chief in time of war, although "war" per se had never been declared by the Congress. Bush and Cheney considered their actions to be commensurate with many similar measures taken during the Civil War under President Lincoln.

On the domestic side, Bush enlarged the Medicare drug benefit for senior citizens. He was persistent in calling for the privatization of Social Security, although instability of the stock market led many to believe that was an uncertain and risky means to assure stability during retirement. Bush supported a revision of the immigration laws, permitting "guest workers", primarily intended for Mexican nationals who routinely crossed borders into the United States. The reformation also included a point system by which an immigrant could obtain provisional status of citizenship (the "green card"), and restricting wholesale migration of relatives based on single or family citizenship. Due to opposition by conservatives and unions, the immigration packaged withered on the vine.

Although early in his administration Bush considered global warming to be controversial and unproven, he later revised his position, proposing initiatives to increase oil production and investment in hybrid vehicles, batteries and fuel cells. His commitment of $2 billion for research in these areas was minimal at best.

Albeit heavily criticized for the Bush Administration's response to devastation to the Gulf coast by Hurricane Katrina, much of the blame lies with state and local authorities for their inadequate preparation and evacuation efforts.

In Bush's second term, events in the financial markets led to worst recession in American history. During the Clinton Administration, as a sop to Republican and commensurate with his image as a "New Centrist Democrat", a major revision of the Glass-Steagall Act was signed by Clinton. The Gramm-Bliley-Rudman Act eliminated the previous barriers erected between commercial banks and investment banks, citing the "self-regulating nature" of the American financial system. Commercial banks whose reserves that were primarily deposit-based now could be used for a myriad of other riskier security instruments.

At this same time, the concept of derivatives and other debt instruments began to enter the banking system. These instruments could be created based on various indexes and portfolios. These derivatives were protected from general disclosure by Clinton's Secretary of the Treasury Robert Rubin and his assistant Larry Summers, along with staunch support from the Chairman of the Federal Reserve Alan Greenspan. This attitude of non-regulation and non-disclosure toward these derivatives and other instruments resulted in the virtual creation of a "black market".

Bush and his many allies in Congress supported the concept of an "ownership society", whereby all segments would share in the fruits and enjoyment of home ownership. Democrats too saw this as a "win-win" solution to providing better housing for low-income and minorities, and the quasi-public mortgage giants FNMAE and FDMAC certainly obliged. The real estate industry seized the opportunity, creating new mortgage "products" to either accommodate or ignore those with credit, health or income problems. Many real estate holders purchased marginal properties, made minor repairs and cosmetic upgrades, then re-sold the properties in a process called "flipping".

All the while the banking industry floated millions of new credit cards and encouraged homeowners to pay off their consumer credit splurges by absorbing the debt as a home equity loan on properties already mortgaged. Many of the derivative portfolios were based on supposed "secure" mortgages. A home mortgage was thought to be one of the safest pieces of collateral, although the veil of vulnerability was pulled back as foreclosures started to increase. Concurrently, the price of oil and gasoline prices started to rise, squeezing consumer spending.

The old restrictions of Glass-Steagall were gone, and the interlocked nature of the banking system started to unravel, even affecting the largest investment and commercial banks. It was a repeat of the problem of excessive "speculation" that occurred during the late 1920's and early 1930's, except now it was derivatives, collaterized debt obligations and credit default swaps. It was the perfect "financial storm".

After bailing out the investment Bank of Bear Stearns, Secretary of the Treasury Henry Paulson could not secure guarantees from other large banks to bail out the investment firm of Lehman Bros. The interconnectivity and exposure of the banks led Paulson to force the major banks to adhere to the terms of the hastily drafted legislation called the Troubled Asset Relief Program (TARP), whereby treasury assets would extend loans at substantial interest in exchange for preferred stock.

Although many Republicans objected to the outright "seizure" of the banking industry, it was evident that action was urgently needed as stockholder and fund holders sold of their assets in a complete loss of confidence. The stock market had plunged approximately 40% in a matter of weeks. It was a repeat of the stock market crash of 1929, but on a lesser scale. Similarly, banks sharply curtailed lending to cover their perceived losses in the various risky securities they held.

The auto industry, so heavily dependent on credit, started to rapidly contract, and the Bush Administration was forced to offer loans to GM, Chrysler and Ford. Although Ford eventually declined, GM and Chrysler went "hat in hand" to secure bridge loans to stave off bankruptcy. The infusion of cash only forestalled the problem for GM and Chrysler.

The Bush Administration limped into the inauguration, leaving a legacy of war debt, unresolved military conflicts, sustaining excessive tax cuts during a period described as "wartime", the banking and auto industry in complete disarray, and a simmering problem of immigration as millions of Americans were placed on the unemployment rolls. Bush was stoic about this state of affairs, stating that "history" would judge whether his actions were achievements or just gross misjudgments.

THE ELECTION OF 2008

The media's preliminary assessment of the election of 2008 would be a contest between Sen. Hillary Clinton of New York, the wife of former President Bill Clinton, and a prominent Republican like Rudy Giuliani, the former mayor of New York City. The various candidates in the Republican primary were certainly fit to be president. The field consisted of many stars of the Republican Party.

First there was Mitt Romney, son of George Romney, the former governor of Michigan, president of American Motors, and a presidential candidate. Mitt Romney was the pragmatic former governor of Massachusetts who had guided a comprehensive reform of health care in his state and was instrumental in making the Salt Lake City Olympic Games a complete success. His policy positions at times seemed to shift a bit more in comparison to the other candidates as a function of the constituency he was addressing at the moment.

Photographs 24 (a) & (b). Upper photo *(a)* of then Governor George Romney of Michigan points out details to young son Mitt at the 1960 World's Fair. George Romney was the former President of American Motors and sought the Presidency. Lower photo *(b)* shows Mitt Romney exhibiting the Olympic Medals where he guided the planning and execution of the Olympic Games held in Salt Lake City. As Governor of Massachusetts, he signed into law a comprehensive health insurance plan for that state. Romney was one of a few Republicans to vote to convict former President Trump in his two impeachment trials.

There was Rudy Giuliani, the former US Attorney and prosecutor that brought the junk bond king Michael Milken and greedster Ivan Boesky to justice and led rescue and reconstruction efforts after the Islamic terrorist attack on the World Trade Center as mayor of New York City.

There was Sen. John McCain, a semi-independent legislator from Arizona who began his career as a naval liaison to the Senate, co-authored campaign finance reform, and was a strong foe of earmarks and "pork". McCain has a war record envied by many in the party who praise the military but have never served their country in a military role.

Photograph 25. Senator John McCain of Arizona, the Republican Party's nominee for President in 2008. McCain was a young naval aviator who was imprisoned in Vietnam for four years and comes from a distinguished military family. Although fiscally conservative, McCain has a history of collaborating with Democrats and Independents on major legislation on campaign finances, military spending, weapon system procurement and foreign affairs.

There was Sen. Fred Thompson, the baritone-throated actor with a folksy style who hails from the State of Tennessee. He had served as counsel during the Watergate investigations and played in prominent roles in various big-time moves such as *Cape Fear* and as a district attorney in the long-running television series *Law and Order*.

There was Mike Huckabee, the former governor of Arkansas, who began his career as a preacher, which honed his people skills and brought him populist appeal. He was noted for his prominent weight-loss program to improve the health status of his Southern constituents and political base.

There was Rep. Duncan Hunter, the defense-oriented legislator from California, who extolled the military and its culture, seeking to attract one of the core constituencies of the Republican Party.

And there was Rep. Ron Paul, the quirky intellectual from Texas, who brought libertarian isolationism to the panel. He excited many partisans who saw some logic in Dr. Paul's description of the foreign policy of the Bush Administration as semi-imperialistic.

Early prognostications from the first series of debates seemed to indicate interest among the Republican electorate around Giuliani, but he never materialized as the party's choice due to his perceived "liberalism" and Eastern roots. Romney, Huckabee and McCain all eventually vied for the top slot, with Fred Thompson showing limited enthusiasm for the office. Eventually McCain surged ahead, capturing most of the primaries and caucuses and eventually the nomination. As presidential candidate, McCain principally relied on his moderation, but did recognize that his "maverick" status in the party did not sit well with many of the party's more conservative elements. He touted fiscal conservatism, yet still felt that the United States needed to embrace policies that would increase its domestic production of oil, and to engage in support of new technologies such as wind and solar energy. Due to his naval background, he was a strong proponent of nuclear energy. Since gasoline prices at the beginning of the summer travel season of 2008 were about $4.00 per gallon, he proposed gas tax holidays.

To placate many evangelicals in his party, he chose a relative unknown, Gov. Sarah Palin of Alaska for Vice President, an ambitious and very attractive woman who is a strong supporter of gun ownership and opposed to abortion. Palin was clearly the dominant parent of her wholesome family. She was the surprise choice over Romney, the clear favorite in Republican polls at the time.

The Democrats offered a variety of choice to their base, ranging from liberals as former Sen. Mike Gravel of Alaska and Rep. Dennis Kucinich of Ohio to moderates Sen. Joe Biden of Delaware and Sen. Chris Dodd of Connecticut.

The early primaries principally focused on three candidates, Sen. Hillary Clinton, the media-perceived front-runner; Sen. John Edwards of North Carolina, and a relatively unknown senator from Illinois, Barack Obama.

Sen. Clinton represented the State of New York, where she sat on the Senate Armed Services Committee, ostensibly to prepare her for her future role as Commander-in-Chief. She came into the race with credentials as a world traveler accompanying her husband former President Bill Clinton during his 8 years in office.

Sen. John Edwards, a successful trial lawyer, was the previous Vice-Presidential candidate in the 2004 election. An excellent speaker, with a quick mind and able to respond to questions in an understandable manner, he was an advocate of health care reform and curbing the growth of corporate power and its influence over American life. But his married life was fraught with conflict and infidelity, making his candidacy flawed from the outset.

Sen. Barack Obama had limited political experience, first in the Illinois Senate and leaving no significant legislative legacy, and then only serving 4 years in the US Senate. However, Obama was a persuasive speaker, placing emphasis on changing the political climate in Washington DC, health care reform, and general cultural unity. Because he was of mixed race, the media considered him as an appealing change from the usual collection of politicians that seek office. However, their bias in his favor became most evident as the Democratic primary proceeded from state to state.

Once Sen. Obama had won the Iowa caucus over Sen. Edwards and Sen. Clinton, the media subsequently adopted him as part of a "two-horse" Democratic contest of a man of mixed race vs. a white woman, whereby Edwards became a marginal commodity.

While Clinton focused on the larger populous states holding primaries, Obama focused on a 50-state strategy to win both caucuses and primaries. In the final tally of combined primary and caucus votes, Clinton received the plurality of votes.

Photographs 26 (a) & (b). Upper photo (a), Vice Presidential candidate John Edwards, his wife Elizabeth and children Jack and Emma as they campaign for the Kerry-Edwards ticket for President in 2004. Lower photo (b) shows Edwards seeking the Presidency campaigning before crowds in South Carolina in 2008.

But the Democratic Party, in a most "undemocratic" way, saw more minority votes going to Obama than Clinton in the general election. This margin of minority votes was perceived by many Democratic Party officials to be the determining factor in the general election.

After each state primary where there was a significantly higher population of minority votes, Obama carried a high percentage of this voting bloc, based on exit interviews.

Obama was chosen at the Democratic convention to be their candidate for President. His choice for Vice President was not Sen. Clinton, but instead it was Sen. Joe Biden, showing Obama's inexperience, and his trepidation to have former President Bill Clinton overshadowing or upstaging his authority as President if Sen. Clinton was chosen as Vice President.

THE INTERVENING ECONOMIC CLIMATE

Although the three debates between the Republican and Democratic candidates largely resulted in a tie, a Wall Street and banking debacle caused by the problem of mortgage foreclosures tied to leveraged financial instruments intervened, prompting McCain to suspend his campaign and rush to the Senate to assist in drafting legislation to stem the free-fall in stocks and bank failures.

The problem had surfaced earlier in the campaign when Lehman Bros. had sought government assistance, stemming from losses due to derivatives which bound various mortgages as collateral for loans and other leveraged credit instruments. The leverage ratios of debt-to-assets often were in the range of 30 to 1. The credibility of the rating agencies like Moody's and Standard and Poor was brought into question. The massive number of sub-prime mortgages offered to persons with high debt-to-income ratios was attributed to the efforts of the quasi-governmental entities known as "Fannie Mae" and "Freddie Mac". Other investments, which were tied to commercial banks, also started to fail. The previous legislative restrictions of the old Glass-Steagall Act put in place after the Great Depression had been repealed, permitting the intermingling of the operations of commercial and investment banks. The "insurance" on these derivatives, which protected them in case of default, were re-designated as "credit default swaps", failed to secure these derivatives because of their massive size and extent. Hedge funds, sensing bank instability, saw unprecedented panic redemptions, leading to wholesale selling, which further fueled even more dumping of stock in favor of bonds and Treasury bills. This panic mode led to a literal drop in stock market value of many key stocks of up to 40% in just a few weeks.

Senators and Representatives rushed to Washington to provide legislation for the Treasury to alleviate the credit liquidity crisis. Initially it was thought, and specifically advocated by Sen. McCain, that mortgages should be handled first, since they were the root cause of the problem. Because of the difficulty of gauging the indeterminate cost of the mortgages after the housing bubble had burst, banks were reluctant to accept "mark-to-market", although the banks and lenders certainly were in support of the concept when the housing market was rising.

The Chairman of the Federal Reserve Ben Bernanke and Secretary of the Treasury Henry Paulson vainly sought to bring the problem in hand. Bernanke lowered the prime rate of interest, the interloan banking rate, and opened the money supply. Paulson requested from Congress an emergency piece of legislation, which the Congress named the Troubled Asset Relief Program (TARP) to the tune of $700 billion, of which Paulson was granted the ability to distribute 50% of that amount at his discretion.

Secretary Paulson decided instead to inject approximately $300 billion of funds into various banks to keep them solvent. Instead of purchasing the troubled mortgage assets, he purchased preferred shares of various banks in exchange for future return to the Treasury after these banks had stabilized. Although the Treasury significantly owned major shares of these trouble banks, Paulson provided virtually no oversight, nor did he require any governmental officials to become members of the boards of directors of each corporation when he acquired their shares. This would have permitted direct knowledge of the actual financial condition of the weakened banks. To date, many of the shares purchased by the Treasury have not been fully distributed in accordance with their purchase prices.

The electorate was stunned as to the turn of events. Not only had stocks fallen so abruptly, the virtual passivity of the Bush Administration and his appointees to the Securities and Exchange Commission toward government regulation of commercial and investment banks was so evident. There was a palpable laxity in which buyers and lenders causally transacted mortgages without meaningful supervision of debt-to-income ratio of buyers, often with no down payment, and banks then repackaged those same risky mortgages, despite many warnings from financial experts.

Pensions, IRAs, 401Ks and other retirement vehicles often lost 30-40% of their value.

The financial institutions that were heavily allied to the Republican Party and the anti-government rhetoric so frequently used by its many leading politicians seemed to indicate to the general electorate that the party of Gingrich and Reagan had misled them with a false sense of security and misplaced faith in a world of phony paper assets and lofty talk. The so-called "Reagan Revolution" had ended with a bang, and there was much whimpering about where to go from here. The Obama mantra of "change" sounded attractive; any change was better than the mess that was at hand.

THE OBAMA ADMINISTRATION, 2008-2012

Although Sen. Obama received 53% of the popular vote, he was cognizant that he didn't exactly have a "landslide mandate" that politicians always crave when they set their campaign promises into motion. He set about to try to put in place a cabinet that contained both Democrats and Republicans, although it was obvious that Republicans would be in the minority. He asked Secretary Robert Gates of Texas A&M University to remain at his Dept. of Defense post. He tapped Rep. Ray LaHood of Illinois to be his Secretary of Transportation.

As expected, the print and electronic media played up his uniqueness as the first President of mixed race. His personality appeared to be even-tempered and relatively conciliatory, but he chose persons of merit and experience substantially greater than his own. overall, he was surprisingly moderate in his approaches, but generally chose

Democratic Party positions but considered Republican ideas, but with no guarantee of adoption.

Photograph 27. Chief Justice John Roberts administers the oath of office in 2008 to President Barack Obama with his wife Michelle smiling in approval. Standing to the left of Obama is John Boehner, the House Minority Leader at the time. Two years later, he becomes Speaker of the House. Obama's limited governmental experience left him with little alternative but to shepherd on with the legacy of the Bush Administration's Troubled Asset Relief Program (TARP) and the fiscal stimulus package put together by the House and Senate Democrats for implementation as the American economy was crumbling.

However, his first budget submission contained controversial initiatives that seemed to be over-reaching and too expansive, considering the rocky state of the economy. It seemed more of a campaign package than a focused, serious budget that went to the heart of America's urgent banking and job creation problems. His selection of choosing Cabinet officials was fairly thorough, but many of his appointees had back-tax problems which were corrected before their nomination to the Senate. Particularly notable was former Sen. Tom Daschle of South Dakota, a longtime supporter who was picked to be Secretary of Health and Human Services, who withdrew his nomination due to a hefty level of back taxes. Pres. Obama's selection of former Deputy Attorney General Eric Holder seemed to be largely along racial lines. Holder proved to be a controversial Attorney General, starting from past actions on questionable pardons made during the Clinton Administration, to a subsequent contempt of Congress in his later years.

The immediate reactions from prominent Republicans after the November 2008 elections reflected their inability to grasp the fact that their limited unobtrusive government ideology was in tatters and becoming obsolete in view of the deep recession which had developed since the banking debacle which began in the summer of 2008, and the subsequent severe job losses in 2009.

Rep. John Boehner, the US House Minority Leader, intoned on behalf of the Republican Congressional Committee that the "... inauguration also marks a new beginning for the Republican Party." But unfortunately, Boehner went back to the "old playbook" and declared that "...the best way to help our economy would be to tax less and spend less." His positive goals were to "...to promote freedom, security and a smaller, accountable government." A sentence later he lapsed into standard GOP ideology to "protect secret ballots for workers, keep talk radio free of regulation, and unlock more American energy to reduce our dependence on foreign dictators."

This supposedly "forward-looking agenda" hardly addressed the fact that the banking system in the United States was in shambles, the number of unemployed was increasing by over 1,000,000 in just over 3 months, and major corporations and small businesses were laying off employees by the thousands. The auto industry, due to the credit squeeze, was at a virtual standstill, begging Congress to keep them on life support. The average American found little comfort in saving talk radio, or whether there are secret ballots in union elections that represent only 15% of the general American workforce. Since gasoline and diesel fuel to a lesser extent had dropped more than 50%, there were limited short term worries about fuel costs.

However, Rep. Boehner's recognition of the long-term energy problems of the United States was his only positive sign of reality. It has been frequently published in many articles that domestic oil reserves are limited. OPEC and many oil companies have stated that exploration costs are rising due to the growing scarcity of proven and easily exploited oil fields. The Saudi government has admitted their reserves are being depleted and not as extensive as previously stated.

During the transition, the plight of the American automotive industry surfaced, primarily due to its high dependency on credit availability in terms of short-term financing for dealers and customers, commercial paper, supplier payments and cash for development of new products. General Motors, with its many brands, including Saab, Hummer, Chevrolet, Pontiac, Buck, Cadillac, Saturn and GMC, was the largest corporation of the Big Three, and needed the most infusion of cash to sustain its operations. Chrysler, the smallest and 80% owned by a private equity firm Cerberus Management, also needed cash support to survive. Ford Motor Co., which had previously mortgaged most of its assets, requested no direct funds transfer, but indicated it may require a future line of credit if conditions worsen.

During Congressional hearings where the auto companies brought their case to tap additional funds from the TARP, two Senators, Bob Corker and Richard Shelby, continually emphasized that bankruptcy was the better alternative. They praised the "transplants" (read: foreign manufacturers) as models of efficiency and profitability. It was no secret that Toyota, Nissan and Daimler had assembly plants in their states. Still, as Senators from those states, they had responsibility to represent all the interests of their constituents, including dealerships, repair shops and suppliers to the Big Three located in Tennessee and Alabama. Saturn had an assembly plant in Spring Hill, TN. The anti-union bias was palpable in their commentary that "transplant" wages were less than United Auto Worker (UAW) wages. This statement discounts the fact that foreign manufacturers have no "legacy" costs, and that UAW and "transplant" wages were quite comparable. After Sen. Corker effusively praised Toyota for its automotive acumen, his credibility was virtually destroyed after Toyota posted a loss just days after his pronouncements. Further investigations found that Toyota in 2009 had disguised defects in its vehicles that accelerated without warning, leading to several deaths. These vehicles were ultimately recalled by the National Highway Transportation Safety Administration (NHTSA).

Sen. Tom Coburn of Oklahoma, a physician, offered his prescription that the banks should just collapse in response to "market forces". He felt that the economy would eventually correct itself, although he didn't seem to understand deflation or what occurred during the Great Depression of the 1930s. Republican thinking on the stimulus package was, to say the least, "stimulating".

Then there was Sen. James Inhofe, also of Oklahoma, apparently a former member of the Flat Earth Society, who stated the $700 billion Wall Street bailout was the "most outrageous vote in American history." Inhofe was the same Senator who declared that global health and climate change due to the increased production of CO_2, methane (CH4), nitrous oxides (NO_x), sulfur oxides (SO_x) and other gases from the industrialized nations of the world was the "greatest hoax perpetrated on the American people." He decried that Secretary Henry Paulson, was an "unelected bureaucrat" (he was a wealthy Republican investment banker from Goldman Sachs, and a Bush appointee) that was given authority "with no strings attached" (the TARP legislation had many conditions attached to it). Paulson had given a substantial portion of the $350 billion allocation to major banks foundering due to the unraveling of their convoluted, leveraged derivative credit instruments. Although the purchase of "bad" mortgages was originally envisaged, it was evident to Paulson and the ten major bank executives that their equity shares in exchange for government cash were needed to keep them afloat. Paulson's major error was that he did not place federal regulators on corporate boards, in addition to obtaining preferred shares of the major banks.

Paulson initially resisted efforts to reign in bonuses and establish pay restrictions to employees of the commercial and investment banks and the insurer American Insurance Group (AIG) that accepted federal bailout funds. Upon pressure from the public and lawmakers, Paulson eventually relented, but failed to call for restructuring of pay and incentive contracts prior to disbursement of federal funds. It was a mistake that would come back to haunt him and the Treasury appointments of the Obama Administration. Ironically, the Congress was equally at fault, since contract renegotiation was required for the autoworkers, salaried employees and auto executives for their bailout, but none was required for the banks.

Sen. Inhofe also offered his opinions on the closure of the Guantanamo Naval Prison for combatants from the Iraqi and Afghanistan conflicts, and actually stated that prisoners had better living conditions than our own troops. Contrary to Sen. Inhofe, our own troops do not live in cages, nor are they shackled and grossly humiliated under questioning. The question for Oklahomans is, "don't you deserve better representation in the Senate?"

Sen. John McCain, usually noted for his measured moderation, labeled the stimulus package as larded with "pork". To a limited degree, McCain's opposition was justified, since the original bill was a conglomeration of true stimulus measures and old-fashioned special interest spending legislation. Pres.-Elect Obama made a serious error in permitting the surfacing of a wide-ranging legislation to emerge without the serious cutting of "pet" Democratic initiatives that had no bearing on the matter at hand. These included funding for birth control, money for the prevention of sexually transmitted diseases, smoking abatement, and funds for the National Endowment of the Arts.

Much of the stimulus contained longer term investment measures including research & development on improving the electrical grid, developing energy from wind, solar, coal gasification and CO_2 sequestration. These initiatives were not immediate solutions to the massive unemployment that was yet to come.

However, there were many initiatives and inclusions in the package that were clearly stimulative in creating jobs over a one to three-year period. Many created infrastructure or other improvements that will have durability, increase productivity, and lessen our demand on energy derived from fossil fuels. The following efforts, besides the income tax cut for the "middle class" (albeit quite small on a per-person basis), were stimulative and had multiplier effects on the economy:

(a) $53 billion for scientific facilities, high speed internet, and other energy projects.

(b) $13 billion for weatherizing buildings, which employs many persons with light construction skills, and decreases energy costs.

(c) $20 billion for accelerated depreciation allowances for industrial equipment, which stimulated small businesses to deduct such purchases from their taxes over a shorter period of time.

(d) $20 billion for expansion of the food stamp program, which aided unemployed families and was immediately expensed.

(e) $87 billion to the States, who were suffering from their own adverse effects from the severe recession.

(f) $32 billion for improvements to the national electrical grid, which improved the distribution network, increased reliability, and created jobs for electrical workers and suppliers.

(g) $0.6 billion for new cars for the Federal government, which saved on fuel and aided the ailing auto industry.

(h) $0.65 billion to aid in the transition from analog to digital, which increased purchases of new televisions to aid the retail industry. Unfortunately, the "Buy American" provision did not apply, as most of these television sets are of foreign origin.

These initiatives totaled only $226.3 billion and did not include the tax cuts supported by many Republicans and Democrats. However, in the end, only three Republican Senators, Arlen Spector of Pennsylvania, Susan Collins and Olympia Snowe of Maine, collaborated with Sen. Ben Nelson of Nebraska, to remove portions of the bill that were clearly spending items that would create little or no stimulus multiplication. Unfortunately, they were pilloried by several Republicans as "traitors".

It was not a good start to find common ground, nor was it in the spirit "... to be a respectful, loyal opposition" as put forth by Sen. Mitch McConnell of Kentucky, the Minority Leader. John Boehner, the House Minority Leader, proposed a test for any legislation or action: "...is it in the interests of the American people?" Although these words seemed to be a good start in reforming the restricted ideology of the Republican Party that has often sacrificed the interests of the American people on the altar of free trade and corporate supremacy, they were just words, because the party embarked on a course of rigid opposition.

The Republican Party reverted back to a position of obstreperous obstruction, feigning bipartisanship, and asking for changes to legislation. When the bill actually came up for a vote, knowing that Democrats had sufficient votes for passage, its members then uniformly voted "nay". After the funds arrived in their districts, they often claimed responsibility for the funding that they voted against.

The Democratic Party, with their majority in both the House and Senate after the election of 2008, along with the assent of the newly-formed Administration, embarked on two journeys, one of success, and the other characterized by fits and starts and stumbles.

The most successful recovery program legislated by the Democrats was the so-called "Cash for Clunkers" program, which provided direct credit payments to car dealerships for the sale of new cars in exchange for vehicles with low miles per gallon ratings that had been developed years ago. Both the mainstream and the automotive press immediately attacked the program, stating that the return would be minimal, with sales of only 250,000 cars. Even though the legislation did not include either age or high mileage as a qualifier to be a "clunker", the one billion dollars allocated was quickly consumed, and a reauthorization was needed within a month. All told, approximately 1,000,000 cars were exchanged in two months, helping to revitalize the struggling domestic auto industry.

Democrats in both the House and Senate confidently felt that their stimulus package would cure the fallout from the financial collapse and marked contraction of borrowing and credit extension from the "mega-banks". Harkening back to the Presidential Campaign of 2008, the Democrats saw that health care reform was significant contributor to the election of Obama and Biden. What they underestimated was the vocal minority opposition and the fickle penchant of the media to report the dissonance against "universal" health care in such aching detail.

All major industrialized countries that have "universal" health care require that their citizens must be included and pay for treatment on a nominal basis. Without inclusion of the entire population, insurance companies in the United States can operate as the principal providers of compensation to physicians, hospitals and clinics, and can select the healthiest to minimize their risk and maximize their profitability. The chronically ill, those with prior incidences of cancer, heart problems, emphysema or other health conditions, or those without an employer, would be either excluded or pay exorbitant premiums.

Originally the Obama Administration proposed a "public option", whereby the Federal government would provide a competing plan vs. private or employer health insurance. Although the health care industry saw the need for reform, having a government insurance plan run by government employees whose maximum pay would be limited by strict classification and would not be for profit presented a grave threat to their viability. Moreover, when employers would eventually see the government alternative as less expensive and more stable than private insurers, where premiums can continually escalate, this would result in a gradual shift away from private health insurance as the government agency grew and became better organized. Much of the difference in expenses of domestic employees vs. foreign workers is due to rising health care costs, so this was also a job preservation issue for the United States.

To preserve their status quo, insurance industry representatives obtained agreement from the Obama Administration that all new entrants would be considered as eligible, pre-existing conditions included, and that a government sponsored plan be eliminated from the legislation in exchange for their cooperation to the reform legislation.

In numerous town hall meetings, both conservatives and Republican activists voiced their vehement disapproval of mandatory inclusion of everyone and increased taxes on capital gains and dividends. Also raised was the issue whether there was a sufficient constitutional basis to mandate these "universal" inclusions into health care by penalties on income, even though Medicare and Social Security taxes had long been deemed as constitutional based on the 16th Amendment, which grants to Congress the power to tax incomes.

Seeing the traction gained by this opposition, wavering Republicans withdrew their support and the bipartisan aspect of the legislation disappeared. In the end, a budget resolution was needed for passage, but the benefit of the "public option" to employers and Americans in general never came to be. The public option was a sacrificial entity offered in the spirit of compromise with the insurance industry and the Republicans, and never materialized, but was replaced by "insurance exchanges".

Financial reform legislation suffered a similar fate. Many experts felt that the Federal Reserve and the Securities and Exchange Commission (SEC) and other Federal agencies contributed to and mishandled the financial collapse by advocating derivative trading without monitoring its expansion and abuses, questionable hedge fund activities, permitting large bank consolidations and mergers, and ignored securities fraud even when reported to the SEC several times in the most direct of terms. Considering these financial and ethical lapses, the Senate, led by the retiring Sen. Christopher Dodd of Connecticut, who had received substantial support from the financial, insurance and banking interests, compromised and permitted these same two agencies to oversee circumstances if banks became too large or if they had insufficient reserves. The legislation created a board to facilitate bankruptcy of financial institutions in jeopardy and placed a consumer protection agency to monitor and foster uniformity of loans, mortgages and credit back into the Federal Reserve. However, the legislation failed to protect stockholders by requiring a majority vote of stockholders to approve executive pay and compensation. Instead, the legislation deemed such votes as "advisory", which could be easily overruled by the board of directors, who are typically friendly appointees nominated by a carefully controlled proxy vote by the corporation to facilitate its interests. Stockholder proposals, even when beneficial, are routinely derided by corporate boards, where direct statements are specifically placed on the proxy ballots to vote against the proposals.

The legislation was grandiose in its size, but accomplished little in terms of real reform, since it did not address the root causes of the collapse that could have prevented the debacle, such as placing size limits on banks, setting actual reserve limits based on bank size, requiring complete transparency on derivatives and other debt instruments, and curbing excessive bonuses, stock options and executive pay that encourage risk taking.

Then there was the Administration and the Democratic Congress push to terminate the so-called "don't ask, don't tell" policy which could result in the discharge of homosexuals from the military services. Disclosure of sexual orientation had in the past resulted in outright discharge in accordance with the Uniform Code of Military Justice (UCMJ). Even though many of the Joint Chiefs and other leading military experts were opposed to such a change or advocated additional study, the issue was still pressed. Considering the evident weariness of the country regarding the two major conflicts in Iraq and Afghanistan, it was no time to introduce an additional stressful moral challenge onto a fatigued army. Ultimately, the measure to permit homosexuals to serve in the armed services was passed by the Senate in exchange for the extension of tax cuts for upper income households after the election of 2010 where the Republicans had gained the majority in the House of Representatives.

The Administration had even dredged up the tired issue of gender pay equality at a time when males were being laid off in droves, and 60% of college entrants are women and the pay gap was at its lowest level in history.

The Democratic Congress, led by Sen. John Kerry, persisted in trying to force "cap & trade" legislation which establishes environmental emissions credits. This legislation would lead to arbitrary assignment of "carbon dioxide" costs for each plant operating under an overall emissions limits "umbrella". Those plants not achieving a specific goal in CO_2 emissions would pay for "credits" to those who had achieved their carbon goal. Such a bureaucratic system could lead to more profitable polluters delaying emissions controls due to their size and deeper pockets. Secondly, this system is domestically pointless since China and other developing countries have no restrictions on their emissions output. Although the legislation seems to be environmentally friendly, it is economically punitive and could become an unworkable bureaucracy at its worst.

In the Spring of 2010, a massive crude oil leak in a well head on an oil lease controlled by British Petroleum (BP) in the Gulf of Mexico created one of the worst man-made environmental disasters that planet Earth had experienced in recent history. It also highlighted why government regulation, oversight and preparedness are needed to protect American and international interests.

The Macondo Well was located off the continental shelf and was 5000 ft down below the surface of the Gulf of Mexico. The well was drilled from a platform owned by Transocean, and the well was serviced by Halliburton Corp. BP had placed a priority on completing the drilling of the well to minimize its costs and had skimped on use of "equalizers" which insure that the well could be properly sealed after drilling to prevent leakage. A blowout preventer of questionable safety was used, and many of its key functions were often ignored or disenabled to foster increased drilling rates and minimize interruptions. As the well continually provided warning signals of increasing pressure, measures were taken in hopes of control its erratic behavior but always with cost as the bottom line, not safety first. Pressure built up, throwing methane gas, oil and drilling mud, resulting in a massive fire, 11 fatalities, and the eventual sinking of the Deepwater Horizon drilling platform.

Subsequent investigations determined that the blowout preventer shear cut-off was unable to sever the drill pipe which was displaced off-center due to the explosion of natural gas from the well head.

BP apparently had no real backup plan to contain the massive leak, and purposely underestimated flow rates to avoid penalties. BP undertook various well head "kill" procedures, taking several months to seal the well. A large plume of oil was dispersed throughout a portion of the Gulf, along with chemical dispersants to break up the crude oil. The US Coast Guard, nor the US Navy, had any actual means of assistance to cope with sealing the well. Most of the government effort focused on assessing damage, cleanup and establishment of a claims fund of $20 billion. Congressman Joe Barton of Texas egregiously called this a "shakedown" of BP. After considerable pressure was applied, Barton later apologized for his inanity.

It was revealed later that officials from the Dept. of the Interior had been co-opted by BP. Interior official had made their primary role to be approving oil leases, rather than monitoring the safety of oil fields. Bonuses were awarded based on how many leases could be approved. It showed that "limited, cooperative" government, as advocated by many conservatives, could be disastrous under certain circumstances when public safety and welfare are at risk.

All this legislation, phased in over several years, created uncertainty, and did not address the problem of unemployment. At long last, the Administration realized that consumer demand could be better achieved by shorter term projects, tax cuts, incentives for business to hire and produce goods and to put pressure on banks to provide loans and credits.

THE INTERIM ELECTIONS OF 2012

As the interim elections approached, the Obama Administration and the Democratic Congress, led by Speaker Nancy Pelosi, finally grasped that their "landmark" health care legislation was not immediately beneficial to the unemployed. Frustration and discontent brought the Administration's popularity poll numbers down to 40%, and as low as 15% for the Congress in general.

As interim elections go in between presidential elections, typically the party in power loses a considerable number of seats in both the House and Senate. With their constant carping and pointing to lack of progress on job creation and reiterating the same mantra of deficit reduction used on the Roosevelt Administration during the Great Depression, the Republicans decried the massive deficit generated by the bailouts they created and the stimulus debt of the Obama-Pelosi-Reid alliance. Much of their harangue came from the so-called "Tea Party", a group of conservatives whose aim was to reduce the size of government and its debt, and to preserve the tax breaks they received during the Bush Administration.

True to form, the House of Representatives, under the leadership of John Boehner of Ohio, a pliable Speaker who acquiesced to demands of his more vocal members, introduced legislation to defund the health care initiative, decrease the power of the Environmental Protection Agency, further restrict abortions, and preserve the tax cuts previously awarded under the both the Bush and Obama Administration.

The House of Representatives proceeded to dominate the general debate by raising deficit concerns, even as the economy slowly recovered. It was as if Republicans were returning to the same rhetoric pitched against the Roosevelt Administration during the Great Depression where deficit spending was decried by the Republicans.

In a decisive achievement, the Obama Administration, through coordinated activity between the Departments of Defense and the Central Intelligence Agency, was able to locate the headquarters of the Al-Qaida terrorist Osama Bin-Laden. In a daring raid, specialty forces, including interrogators in case Bin-Laden was taken alive, were dispatched to a remote location in Pakistan without informing the unreliable Pakistanis. Bin Laden was killed in the raid, but a large cache of data files was obtained.

Photograph 28. John Boehner of Ohio was elected Speaker of the House by the Republicans after their electoral victory in 2010. Caught between mainstream moderates and conservatives and the radical "Tea Party" elements of his caucus, Boehner's policies and rhetoric were typically multi-lateral in tone and objectives. Faced with a Democratic Senate to block any proposal deemed too revisionist, Boehner was caught in a web of legislative and ideological entanglements, and commanded limited leadership. He had minimal respect from many House members, who refused to support many of his initiatives. His inability to work across the aisle and his partisan behavior had diminished the Speakership, whereby Boehner became "Speaker of the Republican Party", not the entire House of Representatives. Eventually Rep. Boehner was replaced by Rep. Paul Ryan of Wisconsin, Vice Presidential running mate of Mitt Romney. Unfortunately, the level of bipartisanship has not increased under the leadership of either Speaker Ryan or Senate majority leader McConnell.

Although praised by the public and most governmental officials, there were still claims that the locations were obtained through interrogation techniques which used torture prohibited by the Geneva Convention. Although Sen. John McCain decried the use of "water boarding" (a technique that simulates drowning) and the CIA noted that the leads were only obtained from standard conventional intelligence methods, many former Bush Administration officials vigorously defended their endorsement of "water boarding" and other similar physical and deprivation techniques to obtain information.

Gridlock, as predicted by most political analysts, had set in without any time to waste. The Republicans settled on the issue of deficits and the public debt as a point of political leverage. As a means to emphasize the importance of deficit reduction and curbing spending by the Congress, the Republicans in 2011 threatened to withhold authority to raise the debt ceiling of the United States. This raised hackles throughout the financial community. Standard & Poor's downgraded the US credit rating to AA+, whereas Moody's and Fitch maintained their AAA ratings but warned that spending reductions and new revenues were in order.

To address the problem, the Congress created an unprecedented Select Committee on Deficit Reduction, dubbed the "Super Committee" by the media. Composed of six Democrats and six Republican committee members and was jointly chaired by Sen. Patty Murray of Washington State and Congressman Jeb Hensarling of Texas. Other committee luminaries included Senators Max Baucus of Montana, John Kerry of Massachusetts, Jon Kyl of

Arizona and Rob Portman of Ohio, and Congressmen Chris Van Hollen of Maryland and Dave Camp of Michigan.

Although the Budget Control Act increased the debt ceiling by $400 billion in 2011, it required an additional $917 billion in budget cuts over a 10-year period. Because of the inability of the Democrats and Republicans to agree on program reductions and new revenues, a "sequester provision" was inserted that would force across-the-board cuts, half from defense, half from non-defense. Because no overall deficit plan was developed due to internal bickering and partisan disagreement, the sequestration took effect, even though it was supposed to be the onerous political equivalent of a "poison pill". This was a manifestation of the true inability of the two major parties to separate themselves from their ideologies. The Congressional Budget Office estimated in February 2013 that sequestration was estimated to impact the creation of at least 750,000 jobs, which certainly would help to sustain the sluggish recovery.

This same tactic was used again in mid-2013 after the election of 2012 where the Republican opposed the Affordable Health Care Act (ACA). If the ACA was not rejected, the federal budget would be withheld by the House, which led to a government shutdown of many key agency functions for several weeks. These included inspection of fruits and vegetables, closure of national parks, and the furloughing of federal workers.

THE PRESIDENTIAL ELECTION OF 2012

The election campaign of 2012 featured an unopposed President Obama and several prominent Republicans, some qualified, and others clearly unqualified for presidential office. An early frontrunner for the Republicans was Congresswoman Michelle Bachmann of Minnesota, a Tea Party favorite with a penchant for overstatement and frequent twisting of facts that suited her own purposes.

Another political fish out of water was Herman Cain, a wealthy businessman associated with Godfather's Pizza and the National Restaurant Association. He dropped out of the race due to disclosure of his womanizing past and extra-marital affairs.

Newt Gingrich, former Speaker of the House of Representatives, intoned various pieces of political wisdom on occasion during the various debates, and was spirited through the primary process with the financial assistance of casino mogul Sheldon Adelson. Speaker Gingrich did not help himself during the debates by championing the colonization of the moon, while 8% of the country was unemployed.

Senator Rick Santorum of Pennsylvania continued a staunch defense of his anti-abortion philosophy and other fundamentalist themes throughout his campaign, toting himself as a populist and "blue collar" candidate. However, the Republicans eventually realized that each of the previous candidates were fundamentally flawed for a general election, and gradually drew themselves to a sometime moderate-turned-conservative Gov. Mitt Romney, who seemed to be the most level-headed and electable.

Romney had made a substantial fortune as head of Bain Capital, a private investment firm that acquired both ailing and successful companies to make even greater profits by cost-cutting, labor renegotiations and leveraging. When the companies went into bankruptcy, Bain collected "consulting fees", often stripping the employees of pension rights, reorganizing the same company, and then offering the same jobs to former employees at reduced pay. Although this negativism was played up by the Democrats, Romney launched two torpedoes against his own battleship that ultimately lead to the sinking of his campaign.

Romney was very reluctant to reveal his real net worth. Such a disclosure would expose his ferreting away vast sums in Swiss banks, the Cayman Islands, Lichtenstein and several other locations that largely exist by profiting from their expertise on tax avoidance. During the campaign, much was discussed as to equalizing the tax differences between the upper 2% and the remainder of the working population, whether they are professionals, skilled trades or service workers. The tax avoidance schemes employed by Romney and his lawyers and tax advisors are not generally available to the average person, even those earning up to $200,000 per year, because salary income is taxed at more than double the rate of Romney's income, which consisted of dividends and capital gains taxed at only 15%.

Romney's biggest error occurred at a fundraiser of wealthy contributors, where he excoriated persons receiving any government assistance as "victims". The speech was recorded by a bartender of no political affiliation, who made a copy available to *Mother Jones* magazine. A sampling of his remarks is as follows: "There are 47% of the people who will vote for the president no matter what. All right, there are 47% who are with him, who are dependent upon government, who believe they are victims, who believe the government has a responsibility to care for them..."

In the same speech, Romney went on to describe a factory in China that Bain Capital owned, where the plant manager informed him that the barbed wire surrounding the factory was to prevent outsiders from coming in to take factory jobs. His description of captive labor working at less than poverty wages was spun into a fairy tale that the sweat factory was a worker's paradise. It was a frightening concept that American workers could look to more depressed wages, loss of jobs to poorly paid Chinese laborers, all with the approval of their future president.

The 47% remark was classic Romney, who also went into his home state of Michigan extolling how the auto bailout was a disaster (it was a resounding success) and literally published his opinions in a newspaper article supposedly justifying his new conservatism. His behavior was a sort of politicized Mormonism, where only ambitious and hardworking voters would support him, whereas the 47% remainder were just folks with a lesser or missing work ethic that needed constant government assistance for them to carry on with their lives. Romney's calculation was that he only needed his Republican base, which consists of 30% of all voters, plus some additional 23% more of the voting population that were ambitious Democrats or independents. For Romney, 47% of the remaining voters were a lost cause; he would only represent 53% that fit into his vision of the Mormon beehive of economic activity. The 47% remainder was just a drag on the vitality of his new vision for America.

Although Romney later claimed that he would represent "all the people", his own recorded hypocrisy resulted in the end of Romney's quest to be the first Mormon president of the United States when all the votes were tallied.

In January of 2013, President Obama was again sworn in as President for his second term but saw more obstruction in terms of opposition to the Affordable Car Act, various Cabinet positions and judgeships, and a shutdown of the government for two weeks.

THE INTERIM ELECTIONS OF 2014

The two years between the inauguration of 2012 and the elections of 2014 proved to be a gradual decline of the President and his party. The decline had both domestic and foreign origins, and the influx of campaign money due to *Citizens United* and *McCutcheon* decisions of the Supreme Court helped bolster the Republicans in their quest for control of the Senate and expansion of the House majority.

The enrollment process for medical insurance of the Affordable Care Act was plagued by a user-unfriendly web site that was subject to long delays and overload. The Secretary of Health and Human Services eventually resigned over the matter. The US Secret Service badly botched the unauthorized entry of a man into the White House, although he was eventually apprehended.

The biggest problem was the deterioration of the situation in Iraq where Sunni militants from Syria and former commanders from the army of former dictator Saddam Hussein overran large swaths of western Iraq. They claimed an establishment of an "Islamic State", whose aim was to purge any minorities who would not pledge fealty to their "ideology", slaughtering thousands of civilians and causing the Sunnis in Iraqi army to disband. Obama was unable to convince Iraqi Prime Minister Nouri Al-Maliki, a Bush favorite appointed in 2006 and serving to mid-2014 (now Vice President), to a status of forces agreement to permit American forces to remain. Al-Maliki had dismissed Sunni army officers and had replaced them with Shiite political appointees. When the Iraqi army was confronted by the radical Sunni terrorist forces, Sunni soldiers abandoned their weapons and uniforms out of distrust of their appointed Shiite officers and fear of the Sunni militants.

The Obama Administration subsequently used airstrikes to limit the expansion of the "Islamic State" and began to train and arm the Kurds and train several moderate militias in Syria who were battling the Assad regime. The situation appears to have effectively partitioned Iraq into a western Sunni region, a northern Kurdish area, and a southern Shiite Iraq. The most ironic condition of this nightmare is that the Islamic militants used captured weapons that were originally supplied to the Iraqi Army by the United States.

The election of 2014 resulted in control of the Senate by the Republicans, with Sen. Mitch McConnell of Kentucky as Majority Leader. This political realignment portended conflicts over more symbolic votes on revisions or overturning the Affordable Care Act.

THE PRESIDENTIAL ELECTION OF 2016

The election of 2016 was one of the most convoluted in the history of the United States. For both major parties, there was a large array of primary candidates and unusual undercurrents of negative activity.

The Democratic candidates included Mrs. Hillary Clinton, the Secretary of State in the Obama Administration, Senator Bernie Sanders of Vermont, an Independent running as a Democrat, and Governor Martin O'Malley of Maryland. The principal contention that Sen. Sanders leveled at Mrs. Clinton was her close alliances with Wall Street financial interests and the pharmaceutical industry. Sanders continuously railed against income inequality and the overbearing influence of wealthy individuals and families and political action committees (PACs) on the American political system. He also advocated a single payer system for health care, eliminating the patchwork network of insurance companies and exchanges set by the Affordable Care Act. O'Malley was largely sidelined, although he largely espoused standard Democratic positions on a variety of issues. Eventually Mrs. Clinton, through the overt assistance of the Democratic National Committee, eventually prevailed and was the Democratic standard bearer.

In contrast, the Republican primary almost exuded a circus-like atmosphere due to several outspoken candidates in the competition. The novelty candidate was Donald Trump, the real estate magnate from New York City who declared his independence by stating that he was not under any obligation to support the Republican nominee. The other Republican primary candidates were various prominent luminaries, including Jeb Bush, Governor of Florida; Governor

Chris Christie of New Jersey; Senator Rand Paul of Kentucky, son of former candidate Ron Paul of Texas; Governor John Kasich of Ohio; Senator Marco Rubio of Florida; Senator Ted Cruz of Texas and Carly Fiorina, former Chief Executive Officer of Hewlett Packard (HP Inc.).

Trump emerged as the dominant candidate, employing the use of deprecatory monikers such as "low energy Jeb", "little Marco" and "lying Ted". He referred to Ms. Fiorina as having unattractive features ("what a face" was his remark). Another tactic employed by Trump was his continuous emphasis on his personal wealth, stating that he had held sway and influence over politicians through his campaign contributions. He noted that he had given contributions to many of the candidates he was debating. It was a confirmation of that large political campaign contributions are legalized bribery.

The televised debates between Mrs. Clinton and Mr. Trump principally revolved around Clinton's use of a private email server containing classified information and her acceptance of contributions to the Clinton foundation run by her husband, former President Bill Clinton. Trump's negative nickname for her was "Crooked Hillary". Clinton countered that Trump was inexperienced and unfit for office due to his penchant for immediate, harsh and immature responses to criticism on his Twitter account. These descriptions of his behavior were a foreshadowing of his actual conduct as President.

The campaigns of the candidates were remarkably different. The Clinton campaign concentrated on unity and emphasis on her wide experience. Trump, on the other hand, ironically emphasized both Democratic and Republican issues. His campaign emphasis on job losses to overseas companies, one-sided trade agreements, increasing domestic employment in depressed industries such as in the coal and steel industries, which directly appealed to many blue-collar voters and their families, especially in the states of Michigan, Wisconsin and West Virginia. His deprecation of the Affordable Care Act, always dubbing it as "Obamacare", appealed to many southern voters where many Republican governors had limited the number of insurance exchanges. To many Republican voters, his criticism of "political correctness", his ability to speak on their level to "tell like it is", and his supposed business success, all seemed to affirm that Trump possessed the characteristics that would satisfy their needs in a President.

There were other Republicans who cautioned that these were just "selling points" for a Trump presidency, and that his promises would unlikely come to fruition if he was actually elected. During the campaign, Trump dismissed the warnings of his opponents and detractors as "sour grapes".

In the final tally of votes, due to the inherent unfairness of the Electoral College and the many state requirements of "majority winner take-all of electoral votes", Trump was elected president, even though he had 1,322,095 fewer votes than Mrs. Clinton. [The distortions of the Electoral College with regard to determining who shall be president are discussed in a subsequent chapter.] This was the second occurrence in recent history when Governor George W. Bush was elected with fewer votes instead of Vice President Al Gore. Even in that election, without the intervention of the Supreme Court, it was determined by newspaper counts of ballots in Florida, that Gore would have been elected President by the current system of counting "winner-take-all" electoral votes.

After the inauguration of Trump, serious signs of dysfunction in his administration began to appear. He claimed his inauguration had greater attendance than Obama, which was easily disproved. His administration was populated at cabinet level by many financial advisors from Goldman Sachs, which he had previously called out such alliances during the campaign as "crooked". Although he had appealed to the blue-collar vote and promised a "populist" cabinet, his administration was headed by individuals with great wealth. His Treasury Secretary is Steven Mnuchin, a Goldman Sachs executive, as is Gary Cohn. Betsy DeVos, his Secretary of Education, was a wealthy Amway executive; Linda McMahon of the World Wrestling Enterprise headed the Small Business Administration. Rex Tillerson, former chief executive officer of Exxon Mobil, was appointed as Secretary of State. Other appointments included Rep. Tom Price of Georgia, who opposed the Affordable Care Act, and Tom Pruitt of Oklahoma, a fierce opponent of the Environmental Protection Agency, who subsequently began to dismantle many of its regulations and programs, especially those related to climate change.

During the campaign and subsequently during the transition, Trump surrounded himself with officials with strong financial and political ties to Russia. Trump previously had agreements with Russian oligarchs with loyalty to President Vladimir Putin. American intelligence agencies had established that Russian internet hackers and propaganda teams had intended to secure a Trump victory over Mrs. Clinton. Emails of both the Democratic and Republican National Committees were hacked and the DNC emails of John Podesta were made public, particularly after it was revealed that Trump had made very unflattering comments during an interview where he bragged about placing unwanted kisses and his hands on the genitalia of women, ostensibly claimed by him to be permissible because he is "famous".

Photograph 29. President Trump meets with Russian Ambassador Kislyak and Foreign Minister Lavrov in the Oval Office after his election. No American press representatives were invited to the meeting. This photograph was made public afterwards by Tass, the Russian news agency. It reveals the close ties and cooperation Trump had with his Russian counterparts, including meetings with President Putin after his election.

The campaign and some of his cabinet officers have ties with Russian interests. Rex Tillerson has long been involved with Exxon-Rosneft joint ventures for oil exploration in Russia and has personally met with President on several occasions. He was awarded the Russian Order of Friendship from Putin himself in 2013. Paul Manafort, campaign manager for Trump, had intimate relationships with Russian interests in Ukraine and was well compensated for his efforts. Lt. Gen. Michael Flynn also had Russian ties, along with being a foreign agent on behalf of the Turkish government. Meetings of Sen. Jeff Sessions, appointed as Attorney General, with Russian Ambassador Kislyak, led Sessions to recuse himself from any investigations involving Russian influence, much to the consternation of Trump who apparently wanted such investigations to be quashed.

Faced with the possibility of the investigation of Lt. Gen. Flynn's activities, Trump then fired James Comey, the Director of the Federal Bureau of Investigation (FBI). Because of the possible involvement of Trump's sons and son-in-law also in coordination with the Russian government after the dismissal of Comey, Robert Mueller, former head of the FBI, was appointed as special prosecutor. Immediately Mr. Mueller obtained a search warrant, convened a grand jury, and subsequently arrested Paul Manafort. It is obvious that Trump desired "better relations with Russia" in order to secure his interests in future hotels and casinos in Russia; to bolster his standing with oligarchs where his debts are involved, and maintain a positive aura to surround the Trump brand around the world.

Most distressing is the manner in which Trump conducts himself and his presidency. He apparently has difficulty understanding his role as a constitutional officer but considers himself as a "businessman" or as if he is the CEO of the United States. He is frequently in conflict with both the Democratic and Republican Parties, particularly when his initiatives are not met or are placed in legislative abeyance. He was particularly perturbed when the Affordable Care Act was not repealed, faulting Speaker Paul Ryan and Sen. McConnell for "lack of leadership". Sens. McCain and Flake of Arizona were thorns in his side, as was Sen. Corker of Tennessee. After Sen. McCain emerged from his hospital stay due to brain cancer, he reminded his Senate colleagues that they "are not subordinates of the President but are his equals."

Trump's insistence on abrogating agreements with Iran, his pullout from the Paris climate accords, and criticism of NATO allies not meeting their fiscal quotas, gives pause to nations whether his agreements or "deals" can be kept as promised. Prone to exaggerations, his pronouncements often reflect a limited knowledge of governmental nuance. Trump has a woeful inability to maintain good relationships with the Congress on both sides of the aisle.

Trump governs by executive order, which have limited effect, because they are not federal law per se, and have been overturned on several occasions by federal judges. He has designated the press and the media as "enemies of the people", even though their function is guaranteed and protected by the Constitution. His two appointments to the Supreme Court were clearly judges most willing to support corporate interests. He has disputes with his own cabinet officers, particularly with Jeff Sessions and Rex Tillerson, who have already left the administration, an obvious indication of dysfunction and potential governmental disruption.

In January 2018, a new low was sustained for the administration. In a bipartisan meeting attended by senators and representatives,

Trump expressed his opposition to allowing immigrants into the United States from Haiti "because they have AIDs" and from African nations because they are "shithole countries". Sitting next to Trump was Senator Richard Durbin of Illinois. The deprecatory comment was further authenticated by Senator Lindsay Graham of South Carolina, although other Republicans evaded whether the remark was spoken because they "couldn't recall it" or "didn't hear it". Nevertheless, the comment had serious foreign policy implications. There are many who already seek Trump's impeachment, principally from Democrats and independents, but also from a few Republicans.

His agreement with the President of Turkey to recall American military personnel who were cooperating with the Kurds to quarantine ISIS fighters in Syria led to Turkish attacks on Kurdish targets leading to mass chaos because Trump desired to put a stop to "endless wars". His intent was to leave the chaotic state-of-affairs to Turkey, Syria, Iraq and Russia to settle it among themselves. This action put American forces at risk since many were remaining in Syria when the Turks started their invasion.

Facing re-election and interested in obtaining negative information on his potential presidential rival former Vice President Joe Biden, Trump withheld approximately $350,000,000 in aid to Ukraine and sent various emissaries, official and non-official, including former Mayor of New York City Rudy Guiliani to solidify the arrangement. Due to several whisleblowers and officials who knew such activity was contrary to various Federal statutes, they reported the activities to their Inspector Generals.

Because the House majority was controlled by the Democrats, Articles of Impeachment were filed against Trump. The principal charges were abuse of power and refusal to comply with congressional subpoenas. A separate annex termed "Grounds for Impeachment" in this book was created to describe this circumstance in greater detail. An additional section, called "Shutdown Intervention", describes an intervention by the author to help end the government shutdown, caused by President Trump's insistence to build a 2,500-mile-long wall on the US-Mexican border, starting at the Gulf of Mexico, terminating at the Pacific coast. Wall construction was a centerpiece of his campaign to halt the flow of supposedly "illegal immigrants".

Although there was a possibility that Trump could have adjusted his behavior in office because the House is now controlled by the Democrats after the election of 2018, his attitude of defiance and non-cooperation continued. Although immigration policy was altered that merit and experience would govern entry, most policy changes have been negative. Trump administration advisor Stephen Miller has implemented draconian measures limiting entry of asylum seekers, often in contravention of court orders and UN guidelines for refugees. Most of the entrants sought asylum due to active gangs, drug-related violence and threats against family members in their countries of origin. Instead of providing aid to curb such conditions, Trump took the opposite stance and cut off aid, thinking this would stop the flow of refugees.

One of the most distressing incidents occurred when the Chiefs of Staff of the armed forces tried to present a briefing to Trump describing why bases are needed throughout the world. Based on information obtained from persons who attended the meeting, Trump derided the generals and their staff present that they were "dopes and weak" for not seizing the oil fields in the Middle East. He further stated that "he wouldn't want to go to war with them", according to those present. Secretary of State Tillerson, who came from a military family, stood up for the generals, stating that they were not mercenaries or pirates to loot countries, but were there to defend our allies and interests. Afterwards, several officers thanked Tillerson for standing up for them. The incident is most problematic because the President is "Commander-in-Chief" per the Constitution. Such derisive behavior by a commander toward his generals is truly unprecedented in American history and despicable by any measure.

Due to the opinionated ego of President Trump, his years in office have been characterized by turbulence and uncertainty. His impeachment and complete mishandling of the corona virus pandemic led to his defeat in 2020. Even then, he refused to concede the election, hoping that recounts in GA, PA and AZ will shift the electoral vote in his favor, even though his own administration called it the safest election in US history. He opposed a peaceful transition to the Biden Administration, even though Biden received 78,781,289 votes vs. 73,140,146 for Trump (based in November 16, 2020 results). He apparently desires to continue to promote division and disunity for revenge purposes, as shown by his repeated claims that he won the election, that the results were "fraudulent", and contested the results up to the Supreme Court after numerous State courts affirmed the accuracy of their counts. Greater detail is described in a subsequent section on the Electoral College.

At best, the future political climate for the United States appears visibly stormy between the two major political parties and justifies the need for a major independent party.

PARTY IDEOLOGIES AND THE CASE
FOR AN INDEPENDENT THIRD PART Y

In this chapter, the history and evolution of the two major political party ideologies are chronicled to their present state.

"We the People of the United States, in Order to form a more perfect Union, establish Justice, insure domestic Tranquility, provide for the common defense, promote the general Welfare, and secure the blessing of Liberty to ourselves and our Posterity, do ordain and establish this Constitution of the United States of America."

From this preamble to the Constitution, it seems that the two major parties have drawn out only certain portions of the general preamble to suit their respective ideologies which have evolved over time. The Republican Party appears to favor defense and justice and law and order, whereas the Democratic Party promotes the general welfare and prefers domestic tranquility.

How the two parties have been drawn to separate the overarching purposes of the preamble of the Constitution follows pathways that began in the presidency of Theodore Roosevelt. President Roosevelt faced a Republican Party divided in loyalty to industrial interests vs. populism. Roosevelt saw that the dominance of corporate power could change the democratic nature of the United States through the formation of trusts, corruption, monopoly power and the subjugation of labor. He witnessed it during the Great Steel Strike where steel barons virtually treated him as a pawn to further their interests. The Democratic Party was divided by its Southern interests and its advocacy of agrarian populism, personified by the great orations of William Jennings Bryan.

When the United States was finally drawn into World War I, there was a general unity of purpose, but its aftermath saw a yearning for normalcy of business as usual, with the expansion of wealth, enjoyment and prosperity. Even during the days after the 18th Amendment was passed in 1919 where liquor was prohibited, people found it easy to evade the law, and the general population turned toward business and its success through consumption and investments. Republicans saw this as a natural alliance where successful businesses, unfettered by restrictive and undesirable laws like prohibition, meant prosperity and reward, and their faith in this ideology began to gel.

Democrats equally shared in this belief but concentrated their political efforts in the larger urban areas like New York, Boston and Chicago. Their alliances with labor began to be more coherent as the US economy became less and less dependent on agriculture.

When the Great Depression came about, Republicans primarily kept their allegiance with business and the moneyed classes, whereas the Democrats realized that there must be governmental creation of jobs because demand had fallen to its lowest depths, and there was no grand business alliance to rescue the country from its state of economic and mental depression. As the Roosevelt Administration struggled to find means, methods and programs to provide work through various governmental agencies like the Civilian Conservation Corps, the Works Progress Administration and the Tennessee Valley Authority, its critics scolded such efforts as "make work", although many public works, parks stadiums, ports and highways were built that served the country for decades to come.

After the United States was attacked by the Empire of Japan in 1941, massive government expenditures were appropriated to provide war goods in the form of airplanes, ships, tanks, guns, ammunition, and foodstuffs. Although many conservative historians discount the pre-war programs as halting the Great Depression, the massive government expenditures of World War II lifted the United States out of its economic misery.

Both parties marveled at the dedication of the citizenry toward the war effort, with the Republican Party emerging as the most ardent supporter in the post-war era of the "common defense". The Democratic Party concentrated its political efforts around urban affairs, but still recognized the importance of the support of business and labor. Always looking for new votes, the Democrats gradually started to embrace the civil rights movement, whereby its Southern support of both politicians and voters started to fall away and slowly gravitated toward the Republicans.

During and after the disastrous Vietnam War, the Democratic Party lost much credibility within its own ranks, whereby Republicans gradually gained traction as an alternative party that seemed to provide peace through military strength and would advance our commercial interests throughout the world.

The election of Ronald Reagan over the ineffective Jimmy Carter caused a major shift in Republican thinking where the government was made the scapegoat for the country's ills. The concept of "good government", as personified by Thomas Dewey, began to fade away. A gradual conservatism began to seep its way into political thinking, focusing especially on how taxation was paralyzing initiative, creativity and hard work. It was a harbinger of the severe inequality of incomes that would manifest itself in the 21st Century.

At the same time, the United States touted its leadership, emphasizing "free trade" as if that theoretical concept were a reality, but began to face the foreign competition that it had vanquished in World War II. The Democratic Party gradually adapted their general philosophy to accommodate "free trade", asking for "fair trade", but still allied the party with labor and sought the voting support of minorities and the poor.

The attack on the World Trade Center in New York and the Pentagon in Washington, DC by the terrorist group Al-Queda was a terrible re-visitation to the days of Pearl Harbor. As the Army and Air Force counterattacked hostile military training bases in Afghanistan, misguided decisions based on faulty intelligence were made to invade Iraq by the Bush Administration. Plunged into two wars costing in the range of $1 trillion dollars or more total, and then later witnessing the collapse of banking due to insecure housing assets, excessive leverage and fiscal fraud and mismanagement, the United States faced one of its biggest crises in recent history.

The Democratic Party largely adopted the philosophy of massive government spending to remedy the Great Recession, similar to the steps taken in the Great Depression, whereas the Republicans reverted to decrying government spending and relying on tax cuts for the private sector and bailouts for the banking and insurance giants who were exposed to these potential losses by holding "bad paper". The Republican strategy of reliance on the private sector did not work during the Great Depression due to lack of work and severely reduced demand for products and services.

During the Great Recession, government spending was insufficient and off-target in many areas. Businesses continued to lay off employees in the millions, but executives still increased their pay by 27%, and the unemployment rate persisted at 8-9%. This is a simple concept to grasp, because businesses act in their own common interest, and they react to the financial climate of their specific sectors of the economy, and they not linked by law to provide for the common welfare as does the government.

The United States is faced with a choice between Republicans intending to provide further tax relief to the moneyed class, reducing the benefits of the middle class and insuring a limited opposition by either attacking or decertifying unions, or the Democratic Party, which has a seeming lack of will to generally support the middle class that would rather place its concentration on supporting minorities, immigration, diversity, and long range projects of selected interest.

Ideology of the Republican Party

When Theodore Roosevelt assumed the presidency, the Republican Party was in ascendency as a progressive force in American life. It supported successful industries and their leaders but understood exploitation of labor and trade had its limits. Laws to restrict monopoly, hazardous and poisonous products, child labor and fair competition and trade were necessary ingredients to stimulate the economy and promote societal harmony in a heavily capitalist society. These progressive ideas carried over into the Taft Administration. Progressivity, however, had its limits, as long as it did not inhibit prosperity and the wide discretion sought by private enterprise. Natural resources, the free exchange and transfer of capital and an abundant labor force that was paid tolerable wages provide the needed fuels for the engine of growth.

President Coolidge and Hoover both felt that government was the steward for industrial expansion and success. Limited government meant limited regulation, and its hallmarks should be frugality, limited spending and the abhorrence of government debt. Debt by leverage and speculation in the private sector were a different matter; those were decisions made by industrialists, bankers and investment houses. Capitalism was to be largely left unfettered in these matters.

Unfortunately, when the bubble of prosperity collapsed during the Great Depression, individual corporations and businesses had to contract in order to stay afloat. Republicans, believing that capitalism alone would save itself, led substantial opposition against government relief, public works programs, and wage controls. But without the general demand due to lack of work and no income, government was the only last resort, because no corporation, bank or enterprise could be held responsible for the entire population, the establishment of general prosperity, and work security. The general welfare of the people was a matter for the government, and it was specifically stated so in the preamble of the Constitution.

Most Republicans of the time, whether publicly or privately, understood that capitalism alone could not have dug the United States out of the Great Depression without government intervention. They grudgingly cooperated in many instances with the Roosevelt Administration. Yet their faith in capitalism and private enterprise as the purveyor of market-based prosperity was only partially diminished. Their policies of limited government had permitted the free reign of the financial industry, which had wrought an economic depression that affected 25% of the working population, and slashed deep scars into the optimism of the American people.

As the clouds of war began to gather and then began to rain hell on the people of Poland, France and the low countries of Europe, Republicans received a reprieve as they joined with their Democratic counterparts in securing the transfer from the production of civilian consumer goods to war materiel and weapons. Instead of cars and refrigerators, tanks and armored vehicles were produced. Shipyards, aircraft and ammunition plants were activated and many more were built. Government debt soared, but it was for the war effort, and could not be realistically opposed.

Republicans saw how patriotism, industry and loyalty to the United States could work in their political favor. Their candidates after World War II deeply opposed communism, and the popular solidarity with the military demonstrated that people in general had fidelity to the concept of peace through strength. Military appropriations were routinely attached to legislation, especially with the rise of Communist adversaries in the Soviet Union, China and Eastern Europe. The support of military and intelligence operations easily garnered votes in a fearful "cold war world" as Republicans vigorously pledged to protect the United States from hostile states and ideologies.

Their support of defense was especially strong during the Eisenhower and Nixon Administrations. Not to be outdone, the Democratic Administrations of Kennedy and Johnson also opposed Communist expansion and influence. Their incursion into Vietnam, however, proved to be disastrous for the United States. After billions of dollars of aid, bombing missions, prolonged coastal and inland combat, and the widespread use of toxic herbicides and defoliants, these actions did not dislodge the North Vietnamese from South Vietnam. The Vietnam Conflict ended with the withdrawal of a sustained military presence in the hundreds of thousands of Army, Navy, Marines and Air Force personnel, many of whom returned embittered, especially after receiving limited homeland support from a substantial portion of the American people.

President Nixon secretly continued the Vietnam Conflict, with clandestine incursions into Cambodia and Laos. Although the conflict was eventually settled, the continuance of this war sapped the morale of the armed forces. It forced a reassessment of whether the United States needed further interventions into these ideologically driven military conflicts. With their dedication to the military and free trade among all nations, Republicans hesitated to declare whether the American role of carrying the "beacon of freedom" should ever be sharply curtailed or its light be dimmed.

Republicans were not disappointed when Ronald Reagan assumed the Presidency. He agreed with the Coolidge doctrine of limited government and questioned the role of many government programs to lessen the effects of discrimination and poverty. Reagan felt that prosperity was granted by market forces that were best left alone by government to enable the economy to flourish. His skills as a movie actor, his humor and personality gave him an aura unlike other politicians of the day that masked his actual political philosophy that originated in the 1920s.

Inserted as a campaign document during the 1994 Congressional elections, led by Congressman Newt Gingrich, a former history professor from the University of West Georgia, the Contract with America outlined supposed core principles that Republicans cited as their continuation of the "Reagan Revolution", which abruptly ended after the economic collapse of 2007-2008. Gingrich eventually became Speaker of the House, serving from 1994 until his resignation in 1998.

Gingrich rose to power in the House of Representatives as Speaker based on a document termed the "Contract with America", which started out as a campaign plan, but morphed into an agenda for the reformation of Congress. It contained many good ideas for improvement of government, but also reflected Republican penchants for budget restrictions and the denial of funding for programs they did not favor or support.

There were eight recommendations to supposedly restore Congressional integrity, although some were unrealistic. Favorable requirements included that all laws that apply to the people must also apply to legislators. This concept was partly adopted many years later when Congress banned insularity from insider trading to members. Limiting the terms of committee chairs made sense, where some chairman could rule for years on end. Banning proxy votes also was beneficial, and opening meetings to public scrutiny gave some degree of transparency. However, the requirement for a 3/5 majority for tax increases was onerous and unrealistic, as was zero-based budgeting, which could cause undesirable single-year funding cycles. Many other governments use longer-term plans of five years or more to provide continuity for large or enduring programs.

Bills were also introduced in the Contract for America, calling for many old-line Republican ideas such as a "balanced budget"; many anti-crime and prison sentencing guidelines removing the discretion of judges; denying welfare to mothers out-of-wedlock and cutting benefits to discourage fatherless families and teen pregnancy; improving or securing child support from fathers, and cracking down on pornography. Marriage was also encouraged, and the child tax credit was increased, which was well received. The United Nations was singled out to not command American troops. Unfunded mandates were condemned, and special treatment for capital gains and small business tax relief were proposed. To limit litigation, the concept of the losing plaintiff paying for legal costs seemed tilted in favor of business to supposedly curb "frivolous" lawsuits. Congressional votes on term limits were also proposed.

Some of these measures came to pass or continued to be part of Republican ideology, but many of the favorable initiatives seem to have been forgotten since their initial introduction in 1994.

In the transition from Reagan to acolytes Gingrich, Mitch McConnell and John McCain, there has been a gradual tilt toward general conservatism that sought out certain voting groups in American society that more naturally would tend to support Republican concepts of self-determination, faith in private enterprise, strong military and fundamental values of family life.

Republicans set about conveying their message to the more fundamentalist religious denominations, including Baptists, Lutherans, Roman Catholics and Mormons. Those in the military, and states that had large military populations or were home to large defense contractors, were targeted for votes to elect senators and representatives. Republican support of gun manufacturers and gun owners has always been rock-solid. To garner the support of the wealthy and corporations, Republicans vigorously supported tax cuts, reduction of taxation rates on capital gains, restricting Social Security and Medicare taxes to cut off at certain income levels, and allowing deductions for home mortgages and large charitable contributions. To further solidify their religious support, they vigorously opposed abortion and whined about the "secularization of America".

They induced fear into the general population during recent recessions that taxes would devastate those with very high 1% of the upper incomes, terming them the "job creators". They heavily practiced the political maneuver known as "gerrymandering", whereby state legislators split voting districts based on past voting history to their favor. Sensing that this may not be enough to secure election for their candidates, they have turned to forcing voters to produce picture identification cards or birth certificates issued by each state. All this opposition because they were convinced that lower income voters would come out in droves to defeat them.

Legislative obstructionism is another tactic employed, including and re-voting against the Affordable Car Act even though its validity and mandate as a tax measure was affirmed by the Supreme Court. Republicans have ideologically opposed all three segments of the supposedly "unholy socialist trinity" of Social Security, Medicare and Universal Health Care as a slide toward establishing a permanent bond between government and the common population. Numerous infrastructure bills have been stalled by the Republican by overuse of the Senate filibuster requirement of 60 votes to invoke cloture to permit the bill to reach the floor for final passage. Disgust with this procedure led to the Democratic-controlled Senate overturning the 60-vote filibuster rule in 2013. This change unfortunately came to bite back when conservative judges were nominated in droves after the Republicans subsequently controlled the Senate.

The future uncertainty of the strength of the Republican Party stems from its monolithic reliance on support from the wealthy 1% without providing for the 99% remainder. Continuing faith in "trickle-down economics" can only work when the 99% receive fair compensation for their work that actually is supporting the 1%. By continuously advocating and encouraging an egregious tax disparity where 15% applies to the 1%, compared to 28% for the 99% remainder, the sharp distinctions between the rich and middle class will only further magnify and ultimately turn away even the politically inept or inert portions of the electorate from the Republicans at the ballot box.

The ideology of the Republican party appears to favor a 21st Century "overlord class", whereby the wealthy keep their favored legislators in power by negativism against even good policy, write legislation through their lobbyists, support their favored legislators with campaign support as permitted by the egregious *Citizens United* decision of the Supreme Court, and continue to urge their supporters to reject any comity with the government. Instead, voter and employee loyalty would belong to the corporations, who would dictate their wages, force them to increase their productivity and break any of their associations, alliances or unions that supposedly would limit corporate control over their employees. To some extent, the exportation of jobs to foreign shores has accomplished this, and the off-shoring of wealth into tax havens has kept the monetary power of corporations and their officers intact, all with the cooperation of the Republican Party.

The Republican Party claims to be a constitutional party, although nowhere in the Constitution does it mention or grants any rights to corporations. The 16th Amendment simply states that "Congress shall have the power to lay and collect taxes on incomes from whatever sources derived, without apportionment among the several states and without regard to the census or enumeration." It does not set aside separate classes of persons for taxation, but the general trend has been tracking in the opposite direction, whereby the rate of taxation of income for one class of persons is not the same as the taxation rate of income for another class of persons.

Currently there is a supposed rift in the Republican Party over the tactics advocated by "Tea Party" members that feel government must be shrunk, and the supposed "moderates" who are generally in line with corporate interests have been largely compliant or silent. Although the Democratic opposition claims a split in the party, it is still noted that these anti-government and corporate ideologies are actually concomitant, and not really at odds, because the shrinking of government means less regulation, less taxation, and greater latitude for corporate activity without government interference. The decisions to withdraw budgetary funding resulting in government shutdown meant losses were sustained through the United States, affecting ordinary citizens, trade, tourism, travel and loss of product inspections. Threats not to raise the debt ceiling harm rattled practically everyone and seemed to be irrational political futility.

The Republican Party is at a crossroads of whether it chooses to be the constructive loyal opposition for the common good, or continue to be virtually shills for wealthy individuals, corporations and radical anti-government fringe elements. By continuing down this pathway, the Republican Party will further widen income disparity, generate more fear of the future, and increase disaffection among the American people.

The Ideology of the Democratic Party

At the turn of the 19th Century, the concentration of economic power rested in the hands of Carnegie, Rockefeller, Morgan and Gould and several other men of great wealth who literally controlled many legislators and were able to amass large fortunes in the absence of labor laws, lack of restrictions on monopoly power, kickbacks, employment of strike breakers, intimidation, child labor, and the unrestricted exploitation of the natural resources of the United States.

Many citizens of the time turned to Democratic populism to curb these barons of industry, choosing William Jennings Bryan as their leader and advocate for the people. The cities of the East saw a huge influx of immigrants that provided a vast labor pool permitting large corporations to decrease wages and depress working conditions. Bryan was defeated by William McKinley, a staunch supporter of capitalism, who eagerly backed the monopolists of the day. After McKinley was killed by an assassin in Buffalo, his Vice President Theodore Roosevelt assumed the mantle of progressive reform. Both Roosevelt and William Howard Taft demonstrated that legislation could be passed to counter workforce oppression and exploitation. During the Wilson Administration, anti-trust legislation and protection of the working class finally came to pass after much strife and violence. To pay for the Great War, the income tax amendment was ratified, firmly requiring that the Constitution would mandate that both the wealthy and the commoner must support an army and navy to protect and permit their commercial interests and enterprises to flourish.

Although the Democratic Party continued to support American economic success after the end of World War I, they generally took a back seat to the Republican ideology of small government that did not interfere with business and finance. The rumblings of corruption during the Harding Administration were a prelude to the speculation bubble that were abated during Coolidge's term, but would later burst during the Hoover Administration.

Many Democrats waited their turn until the stock market collapsed. During the ensuing Great Depression, Democrats came to power with their ideology that government must be the source of re-ignition of economic fire when private enterprise could act collectively because of individual corporate and stockholder interests. The concept of government programs providing work for private enterprise and the unemployed on a grand scale had only been accomplished during wartime.

Democrats during the New Deal set out to control working conditions, set minimal and fair wages, and provided for old age and disability. These programs often clashed with employer prerogatives of the past, the spending programs accumulated public debt, and were vigorously opposed by many Republicans and their business supporters.

The attack on naval forces at Pearl Harbor by the Empire of Japan changed the opposition to accept Democratic programs and ideas of governmental control at least for the duration of the war. Both parties praised and supported the military, industrial participation was overwhelmingly patriotic, and weapons production was highly prolific. The war effort was a shining example of American cohesion, both politically and socially, against tyranny, injustice, dictatorship and the need for cooperation with our allies against the Axis Powers.

This cooperative spirit with the greater Allied powers was embodied in the belief by Democrats in the merits of the United Nations (UN), a concept that saw defeat prior to World War II in the form of the League of Nations. Republicans and some Democrats to this day still have reservations over sovereignty and control over American forces by foreign UN commanders, just for the same reason the League of Nations was opposed and defeated by the US Senate.

As the United States returned to a peacetime economy, the Democratic Party was at a crossroads between the Southern wing of its party and its Northern and Midwestern wings over integration. With the election of John Kennedy and Lyndon Johnson, the party gradually moved toward an expansion of civil rights voting and educational improvements for colored people, principally of the South, but also on the West Coast and Southwestern portions of the US. Because of much targeted opposition from Southern leaders trying to sustain prior restrictions on personal liberties and livelihoods placed largely in state statutes since the conclusion of the Civil War in 1865, Democrats gradually embraced and affirmed the constitutional rights of African and Caribbean Americans and others of similar racial heritage through legal means and affirmative action. It was the beginning of a solid voting block for Democrats that continues to this day.

During that same time period, President Johnson markedly expanded the military conflict in Vietnam. He and his advisors were concerned over a "domino effect" on nations of the South Pacific, resulting in an expansion of communist ideology, intimidation and influence. The communist takeover of China equally disturbed Democratic leaders and their Republican counterparts, especially as China aligned itself with the Soviet Union for advice and military weapons. Concerned about United States prestige as a great power, not wanting another debacle like the defeat of France at Dien Bien Phu, the American military plunged ahead and firmly supported the weak and corrupt government of South Vietnam.

The Vietnam Conflict proved to be a disaster for the Democratic Party and its leadership, and tilted many Democrats against the military, especially those eligible for draft conscription. The opposition was further magnified by the adverse effects on the families of those who volunteered or were drafted. The disillusionment towards the military continues to this day, with many Democrats reluctant to enter into foreign conflicts with tenuous rationales for authorization. The lingering effects of defeat or stalemate and the long-term costs of caring for wounded veterans continue to make any rational Democrat waver before making a strong commitment to war or conflict. This skepticism has been even more reinforced after the questionable invasion of Iraq and Afghanistan after the attacks on the World Trade Center and the Pentagon.

The rise of feminism during this period and the concomitant problem of abortion and sexuality led to Democrats tilting their orientation toward "equal pay for equal work" and a pro-abortion policy that was asserted by the Supreme Court in its decision to allow abortions up to six months of a typical nine-month gestation to birth. While this policy brought support to Democrats from many women, it alienated others whose religious beliefs decried the performance of some or all medical abortions.

Although labor had long been a staunch supporter of the Democratic Party since the Great Depression, the party witnessed how labor membership had dwindled, since many corporations and businesses started offering many of the same benefits conferred by union membership. They saw, but did not overtly oppose, the passage of the so-called "right-to-work" laws in many states whereby union membership could not be made compulsory. Democrats saw contributions from large donors, lawyers, individuals and contributions from industry groups as sufficient, and gradually began to adopt an "observer" status when it came to strikes, arbitration and other labor disputes. In some cases, some unions started to endorse Republican candidates when it suited their union interests.

In current times, Democrats have finally seen the light that their interests cannot be supported alone by business or corporate interests due to their belief in regulation, taxation of the wealthy, and the continuation of many governmental programs that support the poor that started in the Johnson Administration. Only recently have they come to adopt the mantra of the former Speaker of the House Richard Gephardt of Missouri that the middle class provides the productivity, stability and solidarity of America. Most Democrats believe that science and education must be supported to provide upward mobility for lower- and middle-class citizens that are willing to sacrifice their time and effort to make a commitment to a better life.

To garner further support for their party, Democrats have turned to key voting blocs and emphasized how their programs can help these blocs. This political strategy tries to unite the middle class, minorities of blacks, Asians, liberal women and the poor into a grand coalition of voting "diversity". The greatest virtue of Democrats has been to reveal the marked contrast of income inequality, although the voting patterns of many Democratic legislators indicates a strong reluctance to alienate wealthy interests and contributors, even though they project strong rhetoric against the sharp divides of the poor, middle class and the wealthy. The clear majority of elected Democrats, like their Republican counterparts, are financially well off and are comfortable with delay of needed legislation if passage could jeopardize their re-election or their standing and reputation with key supporters.

This remoteness among many Democrats has been most evident in their hesitance to curb ownership of assault weapons by ordinary civilians, supporting stockholder rights, restrictions on banking and environmental regulation, and curbing the continuing production of weapons systems of limited military value.

Even when consensus among the American people is very strong on some issues, many Democrats are hesitant to act. The public support for required background checks in order purchase guns and weapons is estimated at 90%, yet many key legislators failed to act due to their fear of the National Rifle Association. To some extent, the Democratic Party has elements of unpredictability within itself, and does not always act in concert even when it controls the majority due to its open attitude toward disagreement and its continual fear that it will be in the minority in the future if it makes the wrong step. Although the Democratic Party deems itself as "progressive", it embraces a half-hearted form of progressivity.

The general ideology of the Democratic Party is that government is a necessary and integral part of the life of America and its citizens. They believe in the continuance of programs that have been successful in the past. They are much more willing to compromise than Republicans, but often cannot convince their own members to agree on a general consensus on the ownership of guns, abortion and other controversial issues. They often mistake their ideology as acceptable to everyone and their members, promising a great future for all, yet often end up missing the mark, especially when it comes to financial matters. Blocked by gerrymandered districts and relying on certain voting blocs, Democrats frequently fall short of their goals. It is their great emphasis on certain minority interests and set-asides that give pause to their ostensibly good intentions of common cause that ends up appearing as another vote grab for special interests.

The Democratic Party often claims itself to be the "party of the people", but in recent years it also tacitly accepted and cooperated with Republicans to withdraw its support of the poor and the middle class and provided nominal lip service as union membership gradually declined. They saw a need to raise revenue for expansion of government, partially secured by establishing deductible limitations on medical expenses, casualty losses, employee business expenses, and only allowing deductions for either state taxes or property taxes, but not both.

The support of many Democrats for the North American Free Trade Agreement, led by the "new Democrat" Bill Clinton, resulted in substantial job losses as many corporations transferred production to Mexico. Many Democrats voted for the Iraq War, literally deferring their constitutional oath to determine if war should be declared by Congress. Instead, they allowed the executive branch to make that decision. They seem to have neglected the male wage earner and his well-being as a head of a household, instead encouraging his replacement by women and minorities in exchange for their votes and loyalty.

It is only in the last few years that Democrats have finally recognized that the upper 2% of the population have absorbed 60% of the wealth of this country, whereas the remaining 98% have gained little ground. This disparity has become a political tool for the wealthy to funnel vast sums of money into political action committees to oppose the fair taxation of incomes. Whether the disastrous decision of the Supreme Court in the *Citizens United* case can be overturned by a constitutional amendment remains to be seen.

In the absence of an independent party, the only alternative to the Democratic Party for most voters is the Republican Party, a party that seems to have forgotten the legitimate way to win elections, which is by proposing an attractive, positive agenda that embraces the concept of common sense for the common good, and a vibrant economy that benefits all economic classes, not just the upper 2%.

The Basic Platform of an Independent Party

Any party that presumes to represent the American people must follow both the spirit and letter of its Constitution. Its preamble begins with "We the People, in Order to form a more perfect Union..." does not state "We the Corporations" or "We the Special Interests" or "We the Special Classes of People". The Constitution and its many amendments over many years of service have emphasized uniformity and equality. The Civil War demonstrated that "states' rights" have limits, and that suppression of rights and liberties is a prescription for suffering, deprivation and enduring animosity, and the subordination of the concept of equal protection of the laws.

The focus of any meaningful political party must be promotion of comity between its diverse peoples, insuring the safety and defense of the country, and the passage of laws that are intended to provide for the general welfare of the nation.

Although the Federal Constitution grants the majority of powers of governance through the Congressional legislatures, it has become increasingly evident that the executive branch has become the dominant force in modern times due to the fractured nature of the House and Senate, and the larger number of personnel and resources that the executive branch has at its disposal. An independent party must become the mediator and arbiter of the discord between the branches of government through moderation and intellect, and absolve itself of bitterness, cults of personality and the partisan bickering and behavior of its predecessors. Its focus must be on the common good for the people in general and reflected so in its policies and proposed legislation. The Constitution actually spells out pathways for this purpose, and it seems that the other two parties cannot find their way due to their fixation on self-preservation, the influx and dependency on the campaign dole from special interest contributors, and a general duplicity of their words vs. actual legislative or executive deeds.

The Constitution grants the clear majority of governmental powers to the Congress. The President, through the various departments he supervises, must carry out the statutes passed by the Congress, generally without question after becoming law. The recent introduction of "signing statements" by many presidents in recent times is contrary to the Constitution. It is truly necessary that the US government, by the passage of a constitutional amendment, use either an amendatory or line item veto to eliminate "riders" that are not pertinent or germane to the bulk of the legislation, or contain onerous or unconstitutional provisions. The veto would be overridden by the current 2/3 majorities of the Senate and the House.

Taxation must have a certain uniformity that is commensurate with a legitimate governmental purpose, not one which favors one set of interests over another, unless there are truly overriding circumstances to justify such disparity. A very good example of taxation unfairness is the favorable treatment of executive pay in the form of stock options as capital gains vs. the taxation of "ordinary income", which literally discriminates against professional, technical or skilled labor that directly generate the profits that flow into executive compensation.

The defense and the general welfare of the United States were extremely important to the founders of this Republic. No political party can downplay these most important aspects of governance. The defense of the United States often comes at a high price, both in the sacrifice of its people who sustain deaths, casualties, wounds and a reduced quality of life, and to its treasury where war debt is not easily extinguished in a few years.

In recent years, the decisions to enter conflicts have been tenuous at best, often decided based on piecemeal information, upholding the national stature or its perceived standing among the many nations, and augmented by the emotional zeal of the proponents of war. The Congress has often left the actual decisions to the executive branch, even though declaration is specifically stated and placed upon the shoulders of the Congress by the Constitution. The Congress must extend not only oversight, but its own investigations of whether the conditions and situations warrant a declaration or war or extended conflict involving any or several of our military services.

The proper constitutional role of the President was recently tested in 2013 tested during the build-up of naval forces carrying Tomahawk cruise missiles that would be targeted against Syrian military sites due to the use of chemical weapons in that civil war. Initially President Obama asserted that it was his prerogative as Commander-in-Chief that he possessed the authority to use military force because he felt that international law had been breached by military forces under the control of the Assad Regime. Wisely, President Obama deferred the decision to use military force to the Congress because there was no imminent threat to the United States under the War Powers Act, a statute propounded during the Vietnam War. Fortunately, a proposal by the Russians to dispose of the Syrian chemical weapons under international supervision saved the day, which placed the US military in a delay mode until the matter could be concluded by diplomacy, inspection, supervision and ultimate destruction of Syrian chemical stockpiles and production facilities.

Nevertheless, an Independent Party must staunchly support the Army and the Air Force, provide and maintain a Navy, and insure that the rules and regulations that services must adhere to are both uniform and fair. The concept of different sets of discipline and punishment in each service breeds contempt and disrespect for military service; disparity is not a badge of honor.

The National Guard has been called into service numerous times, requiring the services of specific units in Iraq and Afghanistan. Many of these units have been overtaxed, and many businesses have failed to keep positions open for guard members while on combat duty or other civil relief operations. In a time where military service is no longer mandatory, service in any State Militia must be held in high esteem and respect. Position retention for guard members on military deployment working for corporations or private companies must be fully supported by national and state law.

Although the militia and the armed forces and our closest allies require continuing support, the United States must not continue to be the world's greatest exporter of arms, along with Russia and China. It must be committed to the reduction of the distribution of armaments, and against the spread and production of nuclear and biological weapons. Although we often hear articulation of this principle from leading politicians, we see limited set-asides of funds for these purposes. Moreover, the United States needs to apply its money, influence and leverage with the United Nations to act in a more responsive and direct manner to settle conflicts, and to provide more rapid relief for refugees in conflict zones. It must assert that American troops and equipment commanded by American officers under UN auspices is a means to carry out these goals to suppress further conflict. The appointment of assertive, knowledgeable and confident diplomats has proven to be an effective means to carry out workable solutions to complex political problems.

The phrase in the Constitution "...to promote the General Welfare..." is not a difficult concept to grasp. It entails promotion of job creation, aid during natural disasters and unemployment, preventing the spread of disease, health programs, ensuring a safe food supply and clean drinking water, and safe working conditions for all employees, whether employed in public, private or military, and an efficient transportation network to carry goods and the general population. No political party can downplay these important aspects of governance, as they are the lifeblood of a vibrant economy.

The founders recognized that borrowing and payment of public debt was vital to the growth and expansion of the United States. Trade with other nations was especially important as the early republic gradually established itself, and the encouragement of fair trade continues to be of great significance, especially as competitor nations try to circumvent or dump their products and simultaneously discriminate against American goods and commodities. An independent party must be ever vigilant against trade predation and theft and piracy of intellectual property.

The issue of immigration is of particular importance in recent years, whereby talented, skilled and educated immigrants must be welcomed and assimilated into American culture and understand adherence to our laws. Immigrants who enter the United States to use its services and gain employment, but have no real intention of becoming citizens, can only be allowed to remain on limited and trackable visas or limited work permits, to prevent the loss of jobs to American citizens. When refugees ask for asylum, they should not be summarily turned except for reasonable cause. The American military is more than capable of setting up temporary and permanent shelters for refugees, so they can eventually become productive citizens over a reasonable amount of assimilation time.

The building, repair and refurbishment of infrastructure must have priority of an independent party. Operable and well-maintained highways, bridges, ports, electrical distribution networks and water and waste facilities are the basis of any great industrial power. The means to support these elements of infrastructure can take the form of a separate utility fund, similar to Social Security, and would not be used for other unrelated projects.

The support of industrial, academic and governmental research is vital to maintaining the technological and economic superiority of the United States vs. its many other competing nations. Support can be provided in the form of grants, tax credits, and assistance to inventors, expediting the patent process, and at the same time, aiding patent holders against foreign infringement.

Several amendments to the Constitution have established the United States as a nation that truly respects liberty. Unfortunately, we have seen that the two major parties seem to pick and choose which amendments suit their purposes. An independent party adopts them in totality.

The first amendment is the most sweeping of all, and its interpretation and implementation has not been entirely uniform by any means. "Congress shall make no law respecting an establishment of religion, or prohibiting the free exercise thereof..." does not seem to be sufficiently clear for religious zealots or atheists. Some wish to establish Christianity as the Federal religion; others wish to remove "In God We Trust" from coins and currency and eliminate Christmas trees. Religion has always been contentious, and it is best for any party to adhere to a moral code personified in all religions that others must be treated as one would treat themselves.

Americans have always been able to express their views publicly, whether friendly or unfriendly. However, in recent days, speech in the form of mass advertising, funded by certain wealthy citizens or special interest groups, have begun to dominate much of our political speech in manner intended to influence elections. There are elements contained in much of this "free speech" that is either libelous or slanderous or patently inaccurate. This is a distortion of free speech, generating undesirable consequences, and limits must be placed on forms and intent of speech.

The right of the people to "peaceably assemble" is not only confined to demonstrations, but also to form unions, and petition the government for fair wages and working conditions. The United States has been one of the leading nations to provide for safe work environments, encouraging the granting of employee benefits and promoting high productivity for both union and non-union employees. The decision to form a union is a constitutional right and should not be interfered with unless the union uses violence or intimidation to achieve its purposes. During the turn of the 19th Century, working conditions were so dreadful that employees resorted to violence, often in response to equally violent strike-breaking tactics of their employers. Such conditions are rare today, and most employers now use a more constructive approach to employee relations. Nevertheless, as the cost of living increases, and wages have been nearly stagnant since the recession of 2008, unionism appears on the rise for many occupations on the lower ends of the pay scale. As in any employer-employee dispute, fairness on the part of the government and its truly independent leaders, is the only tried-and- true approach to labor and management relations.

The second amendment is one of the most controversial additions to the Constitution and is frequently misinterpreted. Its actual intent by the founders was to provide for a well-regulated militia, now known as the National Guard, so that citizen-soldiers were able to "keep and bear arms" when called to duty in case of riot, floods, suppression of rebellion, or other emergencies. At the time the Constitution was ratified, there were no state or local police forces. Citizen-soldiers, not ordinary citizens, were to carry military rifles, pistols and other arms. Automatic rifles and pistols did not exist at the time of ratification of the Constitution. Many modern-day proponents of arming anyone ignore the preface of the amendment, stating that "the right of the people to keep and bear arms shall not be infringed". Even the Supreme Court did not allow in the *Heller* decision that all persons shall have the right to bear arms, restricting those who have mental disability or felony records to have guns. Some states basically have unfettered gun rights due to lack of enforcement, whereas others place sharp restrictions on ownership. An independent party needs to establish uniformity of what type of guns can be held and by whom, what are the protocols of sale and registration, and the penalties for violations of sale and illegal transfer. Automatic and semi-automatic rifles, with the ability to carry ammunition in the form of clip magazines, are clearly military weapons and not intended for ownership by the general population, but only by "militia", which now means State guardsman, police and special agents of federal and state agencies.

The fourth amendment is a guarantee of privacy from unreasonable searches and confiscation of persons and property. In the light of recent disclosures of unfettered and widespread monitoring of telephone and cellular phone traffic by the National Security Agency without warrants, this amendment needs close adherence to prevent innocent persons from being accused of wrongdoing. An intelligence court where both prosecutors and defenders appear before a Federal judge can at least be a first step in preventing excessive breaches of privacy which are ostensibly made in the name of national security. This very fundamental freedom must be upheld to prevent any government or police department from acting on unwarranted authority and must be one of the cornerstones of an independent party.

The fifth and sixth amendments are also bulwarks of freedom and provide protections for the people. Considering the often-slow process of justice, "the right to speedy and public trial" remains a safeguard against long internment before trial whether by judge or jury. In many countries, persons can be detained without being "informed of the nature and cause of the accusation", and there is an inability to cross-examine witnesses and the evidence against persons accused of crimes. The right of silence is a presumption of innocence, although many police seem to take that constitutional right with a big lump of salt. Although "due process" seems a vague term, it prevents a court or legal authority to imprison, execute or seize property. The right to have counsel by an attorney is a constitutional right, permitting the accused to present his own witnesses and evidence to exonerate him. These rights of the people must be one of the strongest cornerstones in the belief system of an independent party.

Because governments can seize property by eminent domain, it is vital that such seizures provide just compensation to the property owner. There must be valid reasoning applied before any seizure occurs, such as building of a vital transportation artery, cleaning up land to clear it of toxic waste, or the designation of a flood plain. The appropriation of land and property for development to benefit land speculators or developers that contribute to legislative campaigns can result in a permanent scar on the reputation of an independent party.

Several amendments to the Constitution reserve undesignated rights and powers to the states and to the people. Independents should emphasize and foster good relations and cooperation with the states to benefit the people in all regions of the country, but always recognizing that the party represents the United States, not a rough conglomerate of disparate elements that are not really politically or culturally connected. This has been the approaches of the two major parties that have divided the country up into favorable and unfavorable regions, and further exacerbating this partisanship by dividing up states by gerrymandering. An independent party acts on the interests of the whole country and must refuse to gerrymander it.

The 16th Amendment was originally passed to raise revenues to support the military in World War I during the Wilson Administration. This amendment establishes the power to levy and collect taxes on incomes. An Independent Party needs to recognize the growing income equality among the people of the United States, and attempt to unify its taxation of income, whether it is derived from hourly wages, salaries, capital gains, dividends, rents or other sources of income. By assigning sharp distinctions to income "from whatever source derived" is formula for division of work and rewarding certain types of income as superior to another. It is the intent of the 16th Amendment that "income is income" and should be taxed on a relatively uniform basis.

Over the years, the 16th Amendment has been altered so a relative few can benefit from the tax code. These benefits take the form of special exemptions, allowances, different classes of income and different tax rates, depreciations and deductions. As a result, the tax guides, forms and documents produced by the Internal Revenue Service cannot even be relied on as absolute; taxpayers must reference Tax Court decisions for definite rulings and be represented by counsel.

Since the late 1970s to the present, the income equality between the average American and the wealthiest 2% has grown to great disparity. The average American family in 2017 earned $61,372 per year. In contrast, the average CEO of medium to large corporations earns about $5,000,000 per year, and is often compensated with stock options of $2,000,000 or more, depending on how much appreciation of stock value occurred between the time period of 2008-2013. The difference of $7,000,000 ÷ $61,372 is a factor of 114. In addition, the ability of corporations of corporations, their executives, attorneys and accountants to divert their assets to tax havens such as Switzerland, the Cayman Islands, Maldives, the Isle of Man, Cyprus and many other countries has deprived the United States of the ability to tax an estimated $10-20 trillion dollars, causing a deficit between expenditures and revenues. This loss of revenue deprives many programs which benefit common causes, strains our defense budget, and extends the retirement of public debt.

The United States itself allows foreign and shell companies to similarly park tax avoidance assets in the States of Delaware, Nevada and New Jersey. If the United States is truly willing to halt the flow of legal and illegal off-shoring of income assets, its needs to order transparency of its own house and restrict the ease by which foreign capital and assets can be deposited without proper scrutiny of their legality and the sources of the transfers.

The Byzantine American tax system also permits inherent tax avoidance by permitting wealthy taxpayers who can afford tax counsel the best guidance to minimize their tax burden, whereas ordinary taxpayers are generally advised by low-level commercial tax servicers. The tax forms, terms, language and nomenclatures used by the Internal Revenue Service are not taxpayer-friendly and are not intended to be generally understandable. As a result, the tax code is uniformly disliked by most Americans, except for accountants and other occupations that derive their income from its complexity. An independent party would make tax policy understandable, uniform and eliminate the inherent class distinctions of the American tax code.

There have been many amendments to the Constitution as to how the President and Vice President of the United States shall be determined. Although every other political office is determined by direct vote of the people, whereas only the President and Vice President are chosen by the antiquated "Electoral College", which really doesn't exist, disappears every four years, doesn't grant degrees, and even does not have students or members. It is apparent that presidential elections must be determined by a majority of popular votes or by plurality if there is more than one candidate. Presidential selection should be determined by assigning the number of electoral votes of each state in direct proportion to the popular vote. It should not be determined by majority of votes in a legislative district, because those districts are or can be gerrymandered. Recent polls have indicated that Americans are profoundly tired of partisanship, and desire that their legislative districts be determined by independent commissions, not by the predominant party in control of the legislature.

With 40% of the electorate considering themselves as independent of the major parties, there is great potential for success of common ideals and electability of moderate, intelligent and considerate candidates. Although there is uncertainty of how parties and their campaigns will be funded in the future, the independent base is hungry for a change in direction of this nation to support candidates who consider the interests of all American, not a select few or a special voting bloc.

The number of independents in the United States constitutes about 40% of eligible voters. An Independent Party can be founded on the simple motto of "common sense for the common good". This was the general intent of the founders in the preamble to the Constitution. This document was not only for defense, nor just for corporate profit, but was intended to provide for the general welfare of the people living in a tranquil Republic where there is prosperity that permits the "pursuit of happiness".

Happiness was not to be just conferred to the upper 5%, because the founders were trying to provide a general environment where "domestic tranquility" would be obtained so that inequality was limited. This is evident because the founders relied on the theory of checks and balances and the consent of the governed as proposed by concurrent political philosophers John Locke in *Two Treatises of Government* and Charles de Montesquieu in *The Spirit of Laws*. Although elitist founders like James Madison and Noah Webster found the initial proposition of the Bill of Rights to be offensive, eventually the more thoughtful Madison gradually came to understand that many of those rights became the real spirit of the United States that separated it from other countries. The framework of American government has been copied by other countries, but it is the belief and support of the Bill of Rights that makes the United States a nation to be envied.

The United States has steadily moved toward a two-tiered society, one of wealth, and the other a mere worker status that serves executives as technical, professional and social servants. Prior to the American Revolution, resentment of the English aristocracy lording over the colonists led to the founding of the Republic. During the expansion of the United States, moneyed interests and corporations, especially in the western portion of the United States in the late 1800s, controlled livelihoods, legislatures, housing and incomes. Much of that corporate control had been halted since the late 1930s, but it is reappearing again as American nationals are not seen as individuals who can band together for common purpose through associations and unions, but as mere inheritors of uncertainty except for a select few.

The founding of a vibrant Independent Party is not a simple effort. First there must be prominent political, philanthropic and wide social interest in starting a viable party. The leaders of the party must be independent thinkers and advocates for changing how we elect our representatives, choose our leaders, how to tax people fairly and spend their revenue wisely, and are willing to broker compromise with the Republican right and the Democratic left. Proposed legislation should be based on issues and benefiting the common good, not just for lobbyists, select industries, well-connected corporations or special interests.

Who would be the leaders of such a party? There are several leading independents that could be heads of the party. Examples of political figures include former Senators Evan Bayh, James Jeffords, Judd Gregg, Joseph Lieberman, Kent Conrad, and Russ Feingold. Former Sec. Ray La Hood and Gov. Jon Huntsman are also prominent independents, along with Senators Angus King and Bernie Sanders presently serving in the US Senate. Philanthropic contributors could include Warren Buffet, Bill Gates and the Hewlett Family. Independent military leaders, such as Sec. Robert Gates, Gen. Wesley Clark, Sen. William Cohen and Adm. Michael Mullen could be prominent advisors. There are large organizations who call for "common sense for the common good" as their desire for American advancement, including Common Cause, Public Citizen, founded by Ralph Nader, and many other progressive non-profit political organizations. Moreover, there are millions of independent voters willing to donate by the internet and by mail if a "common good" party platform is adopted.

As the Independent Party grew in strength, disaffected members of both the Democratic and Republican Parties would join. In a sense, these competing major parties would serve as breeding grounds for future independents because of the stifling ideologies and habits of the two major parties.

The blueprints for an Independent Party, or the two major parties if they wish to adopt such measures, are found in the next sections of this book. They are common sense solutions for many common problems that confront us today.

Photograph 30. Senator Evan Bayh is the son of former Senator Birch Bayh, both of Indiana. Bayh was the Governor of Indiana, where he was successful and well-regarded. His service as a senator was with distinction, and he was considered by many neutral commentators and journalists to be one of the most thoughtful and well-balanced men in the Senate. He resigned from the Senate as he felt his moderation often seemed to be out-of-place in these highly partisan times.

Photograph 31a. Rep. Adam Kinzinger of Illinois (left photo) is one of the few conservative Republicans to vote for impeachment of Donald Trump. A military veteran with an abiding loyalty to his oath to defend the Constitution, Kinzinger is a leading voice in opposition to radicalism and believes in long term alliances to preserve American interests.

Photograph 31b. Sen. Ben Sasse of Nebraska (right photo) has been a critic of Trump and also voted to convict him of incitement of insurrection. Sasse was heavily criticized by the Republican Party of Nebraska for his vote, but he has an abiding loyalty to the Constitution. Sasse is literally a student of the Constitution, receiving a masters and doctorate in American history from Yale University.

These two independent Republicans could advocate center-right interests that would be an integral part of an independent party for all Americans.

Photograph 32. Senator Kent Conrad of North Dakota has always considered himself to be a fiscal "hawk", but with a friendly demeanor and compromising approach to problems. Conrad was an innovative and thoughtful legislator, frequently positioning himself as an intermediary and contributor to federal fiscal policy and legislation forged together by Democrats and Republicans.

Photograph 33. General David Petraeus was an intellectual officer, but commanded respect from his staff and subordinate troops as an Army Ranger, leader and diplomat. As principal author of the Army manual on counterinsurgency, he witnessed and helped to counteract asymmetrical warfare as commander of both American and NATO forces in the Middle East. He was subsequently appointed by President Obama to head the Central Intelligence Agency (CIA). However, his stature was seriously diminished after being forced to admit to an extramarital affair with his biographer, causing him to resign from the CIA. Nevertheless, his diplomatic, military and organizational skills would certainly still be a great asset to any independent party.

Photograph 34. Photograph of a young Ralph Nader taken circa 1962. Nader's road to independent status began with publication of *Unsafe At Any Speed*, an indictment of automotive safety. Subjected to surveillance by General Motors, he won a lawsuit and used the seed money to start several public interest groups and helped co-author many safety and environmental laws. He ran for President several times. Although possessing marked intelligence and a lawyer's penchant for advocacy, his hard-edged and unrelenting criticism of special interests and political parties sidelined him, where he garnered no more than 2% of popular vote.

Photograph 35. General Wesley Clark is a gifted military officer who commanded US and NATO forces stemming the ethnic cleansing of the Balkans. General Clark is a dynamic leader whose motivational and organizational skill are well known, and he has consistently had an interest in politics and foreign affairs for many years.

Photograph 36. Senator Angus King of Maine is a true independent, serving as Governor of Maine from 1998 to 2003. A graduate of Bowdoin College and possessing a law degree from the University of Virginia, King is a thoughtful legislator who caucuses with Democrats. An advocate of progressive education and sound environmental and energy policies, he is well respected on both sides of the aisle.

Photograph 37. Senator Bernie Sanders of Vermont is also an independent legislator who is an ardent spokesman for decent health care, regulation of financial transactions, banks and investment firms, expansion of job programs, increased investment in infrastructure, and a staunch supporter of other progressive programs. In this photo, he shares the podium with Senator Sherrod Brown discussing veteran's health care. Senator Sanders also caucuses with Democrats on almost all legislative issues.

Photograph 38. Jon Huntsman was the former Governor of Utah. Scion of the Huntsman family that runs a large industrial chemical company of the same name, Huntsman is a Republican with progressive ideas and is without the usual ideological taint that seems to be synonymous with many Republicans of today. Fluent in Chinese, he was Ambassador to China. Although unsuccessful as a candidate for President, Huntsman articulates a vision that is more centrist and independent of the anti-government rhetoric that permeates the Tea Party wing of the Republican Party.

BLUEPRINTS FOR THE COMMON GOOD

Common sense solutions can be adopted by Republican eagles, Democratic stars or by a new Independent Party of the Republic. They are divided into the following categories: (a) national defense; (b) taxes and financial reform; (c) manufacturing; (d) national identification and immigration; (e) education; (f) the courts; and (g) energy policy.

National Defense

The Department of Defense (DOD) is the largest Federal employer. Both military and civilians work in this complex department, numbering at least 1.5 million military personnel among the Army, Navy, Air Force, Marines and Coast Guard, and approximately 1 million civilian employees, depending on funding and the state of involvement of the United States in global affairs. The head of this large department is the Secretary of Defense. Robert Gates replaced Donald Rumsfeld during the Bush Administration and continued for two more years in the Obama Administration. President Obama appointed Leon Panetta of the CIA to replace Dr. Gates, who was then succeeded by Sen. Chuck Hagel. The military services are commanded through the Joint Chiefs of Staff, which was created in 1948 to better coordinate their activities through centralized control. The level of expenditures for the DOD fluctuates, with spending depending on involvement in various wars and conflicts, the needs for increased pay, benefits, and housing, along with weapons and armaments procurement and maintenance of the existing inventory of ships, aircraft, tanks, trucks and other materiel. For many years this level of spending ranged from approximately $450-500 billion per year but has substantially increased due to conflicts in Afghanistan and Iraq. Moreover, conflicts of the past obscured the magnitude of spending by making them "supplemental", and not being part of the normal budgeting process. Based on published data, the approximately spending for defense of the United States is about $700 billion per years, which has begun to diminish as the phase-out of troop deployments to Iraq and Afghanistan progresses.

Because of the massive size of the DOD, the sophistication of its weaponry, its remarkable command structures, and its large budget, there is a great tendency for other nations to ask the United States to enter into too many conflicts around the world.

Decisions to Enter into Conflicts
The lessons of both Vietnam and Iraq are that conflicts should be entered only when several key conditions are met. First and foremost is whether the United States has been directly threatened by either an overt attack on American soil or one of its bases, either by foreign or domestic enemies, and what is the extent of casualties and damage incurred. The second requirement is whether military action would nullify this threat, and if nullification is achievable within a reasonable amount of time. A third requirement is the extent of the threat. A fourth, how does it affect the spheres of influence in the general region. A fifth requirement, would pursuit of the conflict involve additional aid from allied nations, including the slow and generally amorphous United Nations.

This process is even more clouded when the doctrine of "first strike" or "preventative war" is introduced into the equation. The amount of intelligence and its accuracy are absolutely key to taking action in a proper format. The use of foreign intelligence sources, who may be reliable or unreliable, poses a difficult question as to whether those sources are acting principally in their own interest or that of the United States. The antiquated notion that the "enemy of my enemy" will provide truthful intelligence needs extremely close inspection before any American blood is spilled and our Treasury depleted.

Fortunately, the American military is presently commanded by post-Vietnam outstanding general officers who are thoughtful, intelligent and have risen through the ranks of all-volunteer force and have great respect of the armed forces in contrast to the days of the Vietnam War. It is now patently understood that with an all-volunteer force, personnel are precious resources, and the days of massive casualties sustained due to poor strategic thinking, continually fed by a large contingent of conscripts, is long gone. They understand that constant rounds of re-deployment and place a great strain on both men and equipment when in a state of "perpetual war", and that soldiers, airman and sailors and valuable weapons and materiel are not to be wasted in battles, such as those of the Civil War and many other conflicts this country has been engaged in. A volunteer military requires the sacrifice of a select few, while the remainder of the country goes about its ordinary business. The notion of Woodrow Wilson that countries under dictatorial rule need liberation must be tempered with the realization that a subjugated population must crave the ideals of liberty and are willing to equally sacrifice toward a common aim along with American military personnel who are committing their lives and resources to the same goal.

The Role of the Secretary of Defense

The founders recognized that civilians must have control over the military; otherwise the newly created Republic could have devolved into states controlled by military governors. In the tradition of the Roman Republic, militias were limited, relying on volunteers when conflicts arose upon the State or the Union.

During the Vietnam Era, one of the most controversial but influential Secretaries of Defense was Robert S. McNamara. A former executive from Ford Motor Co. with prior military experience, McNamara was concerned about the constant inter-service rivalry and duplication of similar weapons and equipment. Military procurement involves massive expenditures for aircraft, communications and supposedly "service-compatible" arms. Probably the most radical and controversial proposal put forward by McNamara was the acquisition of a joint service fighter-bomber, which had a variable wing geometry that could turn the aircraft from a fighter to a bomber. This concept eventually materialized as the FB-111 fighter-bomber. Although intensely disliked by high-ranking military of the day, it was a nimble aircraft and highly prized by the Europeans who considered it as a major strategic asset to their defense. The lesson of this acquisition is that well-designed weapons are compatible to any service, whether it is a truck, clothing, helmets, communications equipment, or small arms.

The M-16 was originally designed as a rifle on a linear platform using lightweight aluminum and plastic intended for infantry troops in Vietnam. Due to field inoperability at key moments, the DOD eventually had to change the ammunition which was jamming the receiver, and its barrel was chrome-plated to reduce its susceptibility to corrosion. By gradual evolution, the M-16 became the rifle of choice of all the armed services because of its universal appeal. Before any weapon or piece of equipment of commonality is developed, it needs to be examined not only by one service, but by each service to truly determine if modifications to a common platform can accommodate any service-special capabilities by using the concept of modular construction.

Photograph 39. Secretary Robert McNamara briefs the press regarding war actions taken in Vietnam. Although many of his Vietnam initiatives proved faulty, McNamara brought the concept of "jointness" to the Armed Forces by insisting on cost-saving measures, eliminating duplication, combining and coordinating forces, and improving weapon systems and their acquisition.

The opposite of this logic is found in the Marine Corps insistence on the V-22 Osprey, a vertical takeoff and landing aircraft that was unstable, killed many test pilots, and was subject to numerous cost overruns. Even after several modifications, the V-22 proved to be an unreliable weapon system desired only by a single service whose function could have been provided by numerous other similar aircraft that already had proven reliability.

Another method to foster commonality is to de-emphasize highly restrictive military specifications for commonly-used items and rely instead on standardized commodities and components governed by the American Society for Testing and Materials (ASTM), the Society of Automotive Engineers (SAE), American National Standards Institute (ANSI) and many other accepted standards-making bodies.

Robert Gates was one of the best civilians to ever guide the DOD through some of its most difficult moments. Called upon from his previous post as President of Texas A&M University, Gates rapidly made the transition to Secretary of Defense, and was willing to make difficult decisions regarding re-deployment of additional troops during the so-called "surge" to tramp down the intransigence and reaffirm American commitments to partner with the fledgling Iraqi government to provide continuity to that war-torn region.

His recognition of the severe physical and mental harm caused by improvised explosive devices (IEDs) in Iraq and Afghanistan led to his abiding support for the rapid production of mine-resistant ambush-protected (MRAP) vehicles, earmarking $1.1 billion for their high-priority acquisition. MRAP vehicles can dissipate the explosive energy of an IED using V-shaped hull, rather than continuing the use of more vulnerable flat-bottomed, four-wheel drive high mobility multipurpose vehicles (Humvees).

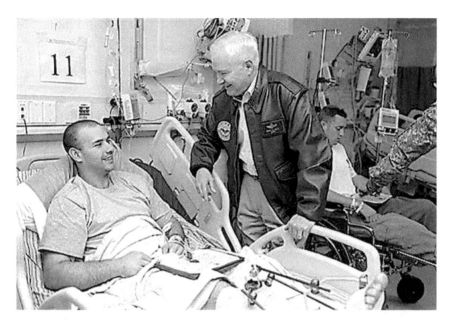

Photograph 40. Secretary Robert Gates in this photograph visits a hospital in Afghanistan in 2011 and awards Purple Hearts to wounded troops. He accepted the post of Secretary of Defense as President of Texas A&M University. Previously the Director of the Central Intelligence Agency, he brought his organizational and intelligence background to focus on the so-called "war on terror" in a manner that protected our military personnel but assured a comprehensive withdrawal strategy in the best interests of the United States. His dedication to the military personnel of the Department of Defense over four years, serving in both Republican and Democratic Administrations, was best summarized in his own retirement remarks: "I've done my best to care for them as though they were my own sons and daughters, and I will miss them deeply."

Gates also recognized that the Defense Department can eliminate much of its duplication and spending on expensive and marginally strategic weapon systems that are largely driven by political needs of certain congressional districts and influential defense contractors.

The Secretary of Defense must reconsider the questionable use of civilian contractor personnel in combat areas, who are often compensated at rates double or triple that of volunteer servicemen. Supposedly these functions were to release the Army, Navy and Marines from mundane tasks like food preparation, housing and construction project involvement, but it has been discovered that many of these no-bid contracts had severe cost overruns, significant corruption and bribery, and minimal oversight by the military itself.

Although food preparation and housing seem safe from changes, use of private contractors for security and indigenous construction need further scrutiny and there must be assignment of enough military officers to provide oversight to prevent fraud or abuse by any contractor operating in a combat zone.

Leon Panetta succeeded Robert Gates as Secretary of Defense and within a short time later after sequestration, resigned and was replaced by former Sen. Chuck Hagel. The Department of Defense under these two Secretaries had been subjected to extensive reviews of its future, particularly with respect to force realignment, sequestration of funds, serious problems of health care facilities, suicide rates, nuclear weapons maintenance, base security after the gun massacres at Fort Hood and Washington Navy Yard, the closing of the facilities at Guantanamo and how military commanders convene court martials and administer non-judicial punishment, alcohol abuse and how the military grants medals and awards.

Photograph 41. Leon Panetta, former Director of the Central Intelligence Agency, was appointed by President Obama to replace the retiring Robert Gates as Secretary of Defense and meets with Senator Richard Durbin of Illinois before his confirmation. Panetta began his governmental career as a campaign aide to Mayor John Lindsay of New York City, but later changed parties as the Republican Party drifted toward the right. President Clinton appointed Panetta as his Chief of Staff. Panetta has always been open-minded and willing to weigh opposing viewpoints to craft reasonable solutions to problems.

Photograph 42. An Air Force veteran, Chuck Hagel was the first enlisted man to serve as Secretary of Defense. Known for his even-handed manner as a Senator, being neither a "hawk" nor "dove", his confirmation was rocky due to his prior commentary on Israeli-Arab relations, his willingness to accept defense cuts in the face of budget deficits, and assent to the gradual withdrawal from conflicts in the Middle East. Hagel advocated increased military pay, improved troop morale, and has worked effectively with the Joint Chiefs. Unfortunately, his siding with the military eventually brought about disagreements with the White House staff over the conflicts in Iraq and Syria, leading to his resignation as head of the largest department of the Federal government.

The Army

The Army is the largest of the armed services and has been placed under great pressure over the past 10 years due to numerous re-deployments to Iraq and Afghanistan. During the tenure of Secretary Donald Rumsfeld, the Army was delegated to a lower status because Rumsfeld deemed it as a service of lesser progressivity. The Chairman of the Joint Chiefs of Staff was an Air Force officer in charge of a ground war that was largely concentrating on counterinsurgency, rather than air warfare. Nevertheless, General Richard Meyers still provide substantial support to ground forces when surveillance and attack drones and aircraft were needed.

The Army has several key weapons at its disposal, including the most advanced battle tank, armored personnel fighting vehicles, good communications, a large helicopter force, and advanced missile defenses against air attack. The recent introduction of more survivable vehicles, such as the Stryker and the MRAP, has helped to provide better protection for soldiers in combat areas.

However, it has been shown of late that better personal armor and protection against explosions which damage the brain are badly needed. This has been a continuation of the same problems that confronted soldiers in World War I, II, Korea and Vietnam, but was largely ignored. Wounds from bullets, shrapnel or other sharp objects that penetrated the body were recognized as worthy of a Purple Heart, but brain trauma was neglected, often leaving veterans in a foggy state, requiring years for partial or full recovery. The Army has finally recognized the importance of brain injury as a true wound.

As these wounded soldiers return to civilian life, their injuries will linger and limit their entry into jobs where their leadership and organizational skills are highly desired. The Army represents the most prominent service to provide a supply of talented people for the future of the United States.

The placement of soldiers in "police" roles where they are ill-equipped has exposed areas where improvements in training are sorely needed. The Army needs to re-examine its role in further conflicts which have been trending toward smaller regional disturbances requiring either peacekeeping efforts or direct counterinsurgency tactics. This means better means of detecting IEDS, clearing mines, and expanded military advisory roles so that the United States is not entirely shouldering the burden of conflict that should be largely taken up by indigenous forces.

It is most evident that the size of the Army must increase to permit a sharp decrease in the number of re-deployments for certain key skill sets, since the Afghan conflict is still on the horizon. This can be accomplished by reducing the size of the Marine Corps, which of late has been assuming many Army functions, rather than concentrating on its mission of amphibious assault.

The Navy

The US Navy is the largest naval force in the world, dwarfing other foreign navies in size, inventory and number of bases. The Navy places high reliance on its carrier forces because they provide the element of force projection from a large battle group that can consist of both strike and air defense aircraft, ship-launched missiles, naval gun bombardment and amphibious assault if necessary.

Along with this carrier-based fleet are strategic and attack submarines. Submarine launched intercontinental ballistic missiles are a substantial deterrent to any foreign adversary willing to attack the United States. Of all the strategic missile forces in the US arsenal, including Minuteman launchers and B-52 aircraft, submarines are the least vulnerable to retaliation.

However, the carrier fleet is vulnerable to foreign submarines and several new land-based anti-ship missiles under development by the Chinese military. Large carrier groups present a very discernable electromagnetic signature due to their radars and heavy emphasis on coordination and communication of their battle elements. The carrier battle group is appropriate for engagement of enemy forces of lesser technology and military weakness but could present problems when carrier groups could be detected by more sophisticated adversaries. Retiring older carriers and their support ships is an area where cost savings can be registered.

The future focus of the Navy needs to be placed on stealth technologies, with greater use of submersibles for sensitive missions, and limiting the number of carrier groups to trouble zones like the Mediterranean, Middle East, the Somalian coast, and the Indian Ocean. The current scourge of piracy indicates the need for fast destroyers and littoral ships in battle groups. The Navy must also render assistance to the Coast Guard in curbing offshore oil well leakage with the development of new deep-sea submarines and robots for use along the US coastline and at other offshore foreign drilling sites.

With the rise of North Korean nuclear militarism and the potential instability by a military takeover after the death of Dictator Kim Jung Il, the positioning of sea-based interceptor ships with missiles to destroy North Korean long-range missiles in their post-boost phase should become a very useful task for American carriers or submarines operating in international waters. This type of interception is far more reliable than space-based destruction by X-rays or explosive air bursts from the anti-ballistic missiles of the Strategic Defense Initiative (SDI).

The F-35 Fighter Aircraft

This new aircraft, jointly developed by the Boeing Company, Lockheed, BAE Systems and Rolls-Royce, is designed to land on short runways and even has the capability of vertical takeoff and landing. It is the most advanced fighter aircraft ever built, and unfortunately, the most expensive. The dual feature of vertical and horizontal takeoff and landing has resulted in less maneuverability and lesser performance. Many experts feel the vertical takeoff feature is unnecessary and limits the capability of this fighter aircraft. Although it has dual roles for the Air Force, Navy and the Marines, the procurement is following in the footsteps of the expensive stealth bombers built for the Air Force. Although each fighter becomes more capable, it also is more expensive, limiting its deployment in conflicts due to the realization that losses of the F-35 could be prohibitively expensive. Moreover, the Chinese have built a similar fighter without the vertical takeoff and landing, outclassing the F-35. Fortunately, the number being built is limited. Unlike the F-14, F-16 and F-22 fighters, which could be upgraded and modified at lesser cost, an expensive advanced fighter like the

F-35 can only be justified if opposing foreign threats are equally lethal or more advanced and are being produced by our adversaries in sufficiently large numbers, requiring an equally large number of F-35s. The export of our own advanced F-14s, F-16s and F-22s appears contrary to our own interests, especially if they fall into the hands of radicals opposed to the United States.

The Marine Corps

This service came to prominence in World War II as the United Sates engaged in many amphibious landings of Pacific islands captured and controlled by the Empire of Japan. It has many adherents in Congress and a very masculine "warrior aura" that is portrayed in its commercials for recruiting. In the recent conflicts of Iraq and Afghanistan, the Marines have become primarily an Army augment, functioning as a land force. Amphibious landings are slow, susceptible to detection, and vulnerable to opposing forces. Many of the landings on the Pacific islands during World War II sustained horrific casualties, which would certainly be repeated if any of our potential adversaries would have weapons of enough lethality supplied to them by any government that exports arms, including China, Russia, North Korea or Iran. Moreover, since the Marines are controlled by the Navy, the need for Marine pilots seems like duplication of effort when Navy pilots would suffice.

There are about 230,000 Marine Corps personnel, a far greater number than will be needed after the cessation of conflict in Iraq and Afghanistan. It seems that the future roles of the Marine Corps need to be reoriented as a focused special expeditionary force, and as an augment to Army Special Forces. Their amphibious role still has validity, as there are many islands and coastal areas such as Sri Lanka and Indonesia where Marines may be needed in the future. Amphibious landings in Somalia to neutralize pirate sanctuaries and other potential trouble spots like Libya are plausible scenarios for future deployments. The number of Marines could be reduced by 100,000, whereas the Army could be increased by 100,000 personnel.

The Air Force

Once an augment of the Army during and for a short time after World War II, it became evident to senior staff that commanding officers of infantry and armored ground forces had limited strategic knowledge of the needs and capabilities of air power. The Air Force became a separate service in 1948 and became a key component of the strategic defense "triad" of bomber aircraft, land-based ICBMs and ballistic missile submarines. As the Cold War with the former Soviet Union gradually faded from an era of direct engagement to détente to peace treaties whereby nuclear warheads and missile launchers were being reduced, the inventory of air force bombers and ICBMs began to dwindle. Similarly, air defense fighter-interceptor needs also decreased as the Soviets phased out many of their long-range bombers. Although there is a very slim threat of attack from Russia compared to the days of Communist rule, other new adversaries remain, including North Korea, Iran and a growing Chinese military capability which could cause problems if the United States continues to provide advanced weapons to Taiwan.

The B-52 strategic bomber will need replacement in about 10 years, but its successor cannot be a billion dollars per aircraft. Most favorably the new bomber would be a launching platform for a variety of cruise missiles, high energy lasers for killing missiles in their post-boost phase launched by our adversaries, but still able to drop conventional pin-point munitions of substantial tonnage. The new bomber must have advanced capabilities, but not have such a prohibitively high in unit cost that there would be a reluctance to commit them to combat. Designs similar to the FB-111, which have subsonic cruise capabilities to conserve fuel but could convert to speeds above Mach 1 by altering wing and fuselage geometry, are suggested concepts to consider which could make the future reality for an advanced bomber to replace the aging B-52s.

The trend of late for aircraft acquisition is to consider contractors and subcontractors of allied states to build or supply components for refueling tankers to replace the aged KC-135 aircraft. Although ultimately awarded to the Boeing Company, this situation will arise again. Contracting with foreign countries may please our allies that have semi-nationalized aircraft industries, but it places the Air Force in a dependent position in case of shortages for parts and spares and the possible loss of classified material or restricted components to foreign nationals. It is no secret that many countries like China have no compunction about obtaining sensitive intellectual property through espionage to further their own interests. Moreover, defense work contracted to foreign companies means losses of highly-paid American jobs in design, production, logistics and assembly.

The Air Force has most recently become responsible for cyber security, which has become a vital tool of disruption used by terrorist organizations and criminal enterprises. This cyber effort, along with satellite security, is a key area where the Air Force should be expanded. China, Russia, Iran and North Korea have engaged in cyber invasion of Federal agencies and more than 100 state, local and private firms to gain information, disruption or feed misinformation.

Although rarely mentioned, the existence of near-earth object, such as meteors, comets or asteroids, truly do threaten the United States in the future. With its inventory of long-range missiles, the Air Force is most suited to determine methods to force these objects out of their earth-bound trajectories. The recent strike of meteorite in Russia that caused severe injuries and damage was a direct warning of a natural threat to our planet, and one that cannot be ignored.

Finally, the Air Force can provide, with its growing arsenal of computer-guided drones, intelligence aids to the Army, interdiction of hostile forces, and border defense to stem the tide of illegal immigration and smuggling of illegal drugs and weapons flowing in and out of the United States.

The Coast Guard

The Coast Guard, along with the US Merchant Marine, has been the most neglected of the armed services. Only recently has the United States recognized its importance, particularly with the events surrounding the vast leakage of crude oil into the Gulf of Mexico from the Macondo Well owned by British Petroleum, along with the problems of drug smuggling and ship container security on both coasts. Although passenger aircraft is heavily screened, container ships have only minor inspections, primarily on a sampling basis, often relying on foreign entities to ensure that those suspicious cargoes are not loaded onto ships of entry into the United States. The role of the Coast Guard must be a joint partner with the US Customs Service to search vessels for contraband, explosives and drugs, and more funding for this purpose should be allocated in the future.

The Coast Guard also needs funding to develop deep undersea submersibles to monitor offshore oil drilling, and develop technical means to seal well heads, deploy acoustic sensors and scan for the presence of hydrocarbons in cooperation with the US Navy.

The US Merchant Marine fleet has dwindled down to a handful of ships. Instead of allocation of defense funds for more naval combat vessels, these subsidies need to be directed to produce American merchant built in American shipyards. This will provide greater security for incoming cargo, better quality ships, and the ships will be inspected and manned by American crews and armed if necessary by Coast Guard or Marine Corps personnel when operating in hostile waters.

Women in Combat

The recent introduction of women in combat roles needs comprehensive study. In the past, standards of fitness and physical capabilities have been adjusted downward to permit the entry of women into military service. The severe drain of wartime on military personnel in the Iraq and Afghanistan campaigns have drawn attention to the hardships endured by disabled veterans, and to the cost of rehabilitating personnel for continued service in military and civilian life. Whether women wish to bear the weight of harsh conditions of combat, both in and out of theater of operations, this decision now rests with them and their families.

There are many combat roles which do not require great physical strength or endurance, such as intelligence, weapons and drone control, supply and maintenance, submarine and ICBM control, and transportation. Many male officers have risen through the ranks to become general officers with these specialties. However, infantry, armor, artillery and special forces have more demanding physical requirements. Such positions must only be granted to individuals who are fit enough to meet all requirements. Given the current technological aspects of modern warfare, physical requirements are only one aspect of the complete profile of military leadership.

The number of sexual assaults, immaterial of command emphasis and discipline, will continue to be problems because the military brings together aggressive people that are supposed to be ideally synergized with other service members to complete designated military missions. Unfortunately, the same aggression needed for military conflict is often accompanied by exhibitions of dominance and control that many servicemen bring with them upon entry into military life. Involvement of commanders and use of separate trials for offenders can help. However, the overturning of convictions must be confined to separate military courts to limit any command influence that could result in lighter sentences or nullified general discharges.

Veterans Affairs

After World War II, veterans received far better treatment and care than did their fathers after World War I when the Great Depression intervened, and bonuses were suspended, resulting in the establishment of makeshift veteran encampments in Washington, DC which had to be dispersed by force (by no less than Gen. Douglas MacArthur). As the Vietnam War gradually ended after much political and civil unrest, veterans care slid back to less than adequate treatment for many servicemen exposed to dioxin, battle stress and transition back to civilian life. Even after the invasion of Kuwait and the Persian Gulf War, the Veterans Administration disallowed many claims for the inhalation of depleted uranium, traces of nerve gas derived from exploding munitions storage, along with the crystalline dust, vapors and particulates from oil well fires which have long residence in the human body. Called the "Gulf War Syndrome", and only after repeated vocal efforts by veterans groups, this problem was finally recognized as a legitimate claim. Similarly, many affected veterans of the Vietnam War were ignored after being exposed to dioxin ("Agent Orange"), a known carcinogen, which was used as a defoliant agent. Although an effective chemical for deforestation, many areas in Vietnam remain contaminated.

The Veterans Administration was headed by former Army Gen. Eric Shinseki, a veteran wounded during the Vietnam War, who finally recognized that head injury trauma incurred after an explosive blast can severely affect soldiers in the hear-and-now but also in many years to come. In World War I, it was called "shell shock"; in World War II, "battle fatigue". The influence of blast waves on the human body, particularly the brain which can handle only a mild 4% compression or displacement, has long been understood, yet the American military and the Veterans Administration have largely dismissed its long-term significance or minimized its consequences. This problem is particularly severe where personnel are exposed to continual explosions in close proximity from shelling, mines or improvised munitions.

This government spends hundreds of billions of dollars on a conflict, including vast amounts of aid and support to our allies and the countries, so that we can establish a stable government to permit continued American involvement, so our interests can flourish. But laxity sets in after the conflict as we try to "conserve" and "tighten our belts" on the very veterans who provided those victories. These actions say volumes regarding the low priority that both political parties have given to our injured and disabled veterans in the past.

In too many circumstances, veterans are referred to in speeches, but mostly forgotten after the conflicts have ended. It is now apparent after more than 100 years of combat involvement that their wounds are more than loss of arms and legs, physical tears, cuts and punctures. Now that our military is all-volunteer, it is particularly important to any family convincing their sons and daughters to enter the military that they know their offspring will be cared for when required after their service is ended.

What is needed is more than the obligatory "thank you for your service" from legislators and officials; it is addressing medications, physical treatment, psychological counseling and subsidizing former veterans to help care for their wounded and injured brothers and sisters in first-class hospitals and clinics similar to the treatment received by legislators and their aides. It also means examining the number of tours served and the intervals in-between on a rational medical basis, not on an administrative time table of convenience established by high-ranking officers and DOD civilians.

Taxes and Financial Reform

The American tax system is the most complex of any industrialized nation. It is also based on 19th Century notions of classical capitalism, whereby those who receive wages, whether by salary or by the hour, are receiving "ordinary income". In contrast, those buying and selling securities, those receiving dividends or capital gains or their distributions, are members of the "investor" class who are in charge of "capital". This type of income is designated as "extraordinary income". Unfortunately, there is nothing truly "extraordinary" about this income, as the "ordinary income paid to wage-earners takes their intellectual, physical and other labor to create the capital gains of the very corporations that benefit from the preferential tax treatment. In 2007, billionaire Warren Buffet commented on this inherent unfairness that he paid 17% of his income in taxes, largely from capital gains, compared to a 30% tax rate on the income of his secretary, who was paid only $60,000 per year.

The modern enterprise of today relies on many skills to produce, create, manufacture, market, and account for transactions and search for even more talented people that are supposedly "ordinary" to provide the "extraordinary" income out of which corporate executives are often paid. Moreover, the pensions, IRAs and 401K portfolios of "ordinary" wage-earner are largely capital investments but are taxed income when extracted from those portfolios.

In essence, the US tax code is inherently unfair to persons earning less than $100,000, particularly when it comes to Social Security taxes and various itemized deductions. Social Security cuts off at about $118,000, allowing upper income taxpayers relief from a program which is not only used for retirement, but has been drawn upon by the Congress for various other expenditures. This capped level of taxation should be raised to at least $1,000,000. This would still provide upper income earners the ability to receive Social Security after retirement, but because they are far fewer in number and many do not actually retire until near death, the Social Security payout would be only nominal.

Many years ago, deductions could be itemized for credit card interest; auto loan interest; medical and dental expenses were fully deductible without meeting a percentage of gross income to qualify; so were job-related expenses and casualty losses that did not have to exceed a percent of gross income. Today, deductions favor the upper incomes, permitting generous deductions for home mortgage interest and contributions to charity (up to $83,400 for singles and $166,800 for married persons in the 2009 Code). In the 2009 Tax Code, medical and dental expenses must exceed 7.5% of gross income before they are eligible for deduction. For casualty losses, they must exceed 10%. For job-related and unreimbursed travel, expenses must exceed 2% of gross income.

In a real-world case, consider when a family suffers a severe loss due to an earthquake, flood or tornado, sustains substantial injuries to several family members, and has minimal insurance coverage or none at all due to an economic downturn. Their losses would have to exceed almost 20% of their gross income before they could claim deductions. This means that 20% of their income is disallowed before deductibility is valid. Yet another family could claim deductions for their multi-million home for mortgage interest and donate to charity to relieve their tax burden. The lesser income family could hardly have any money remaining to contribute to charity, as the tax code has already rendered them as a "charity case".

The total amount mortgage interest as deductible needs to be limited to 20% of the taxpayer's gross income, a reasonable amount paid for housing out of total income and limited to the primary residence. The interest exemption is presently (for 2010 returns) limited to $135,000 for single filers and $260,000 for married persons filing jointly. Medical and dental expenses are vital to health and should be fully deductible. At present, one must choose between general sales taxes or income taxes, as certain states have no income tax. However, there are many states with both general sales taxes and income taxes. Why must these persons be penalized? Taxes, whether they are real estate or personal property, vehicle taxes, income taxes, sales taxes and any other miscellaneous taxes, are taxes, and should be fully deductible.

Charitable contributions need to be limited to 20% of gross income, similar to home interest. In the interest of improving employee productivity, job-related expenses should not be limited by any percentage of income. The present tax code already stipulates what is and what is not a job-related expense.

After the banking debacle and bailout, credit card interest has soared. For some major credit cards, interest rates are as high as

30%. Credit card interest, up to 10% of gross income, should be eligible for deduction. As a means of stimulating the auto industry, auto loan interest on vehicles less than 5 years of age should be fully deductible, gradually reducing to zero after 10 years of age.

Another means of stimulating American manufacturing would be to make each purchase over $50 in value that was bought on credit eligible for interest deduction if the domestic content was more than 50%. Due to tracking of purchases by universal bar codes, the product could be easily identified, and the eligible interest would be based on the credit card or loan interest rate used to purchase the item.

This would be particularly useful for larger purchases, such as automobiles, refrigerators, stoves, electronic equipment, furniture and other "big ticket" items. For example, a refrigerator costing $1,000 purchased either with a credit card or payment plan with a 20% interest rate, $200 would be fully deductible in the first year if it contained 50% domestic content. The remaining deductible interest would decrease as the item was gradually paid down.

Capital Gains and Dividends

Corporate profits are taxed twice, first as a corporate tax, and then later taxed as dividends are distributed to shareholders. The corporate tax should be decreased substantially from 35% to 15%, and dividends treated as "ordinary income" when received by the shareholder. Capital gains have multiple treatments, depending on their classification and longevity in the hands of the investor. The present rate is low at 15% for "investments", although numerous exceptions in the tax code complicate capital gains reporting.

According to the 2010 tax code, collectibles such as gold, art, antiques, coins or stamps, are taxed at 28%. Small business stocks are taxed at 28% but have a 50% deduction.

Upper income earners have a substantial advantage over those primarily receiving "ordinary" income. Higher executive incomes, including salaries, bonus and other compensations, are often 200 times the earning power of an average employee, permitting substantial buying power of securities which are taxed at a lower rate when sold for profit.

When an executive receives stock options or other forms of compensation other than in salary, the taxation rate is decreased; however, these stock options or stock grants are just another salary augmentation. Supposedly the options are an incentive to increase the price of the stock through efficiencies, creativity and personal contributions of the executive. Most of the increases are simply due to market conditions, rather than by some startling innovative contribution of the executive. As such, these stock options need to be taxed as income, not as capital gains. It is more productive to decrease the maximum corporate tax rate to 15-20%, and tax personal income as function of gross income, with a maximum tax rate of 35%, in the same manner that non-executive employees are taxed.

The granting of options is not an investment per se; it is an incentive to keep an employee for a certain period of time. Since the massive decline of stock prices from 2008 to 2009, executive salaries and stock compensations have increased even more than pre-recession levels. The compensation of executives from the Standard & Poor's

Index of 500 companies has averaged about $9,000,000 per year for executives, whereas the pay of an average employee is about $45,000 per year. Based on 2,000 hours in a typical year of work, this means the executive is paid at a rate of about $4,500 per hour, whereas the average employee is at $22.50 per hour. There is no rationale to explain that an executive is creatively or diligently working 200 times harder than an average employee.

The failure of the Dodd-Frank Act to curb executive pay by direct approval from shareholders will further exacerbate increased risk and greater demands for compensation. Because the "advisory" nature of shareholders voting on pay, it is seriously incumbent on institutional investors and mutual fund managers to bear the greatest responsibility to stave off further compensation excess by corporate boards in the future.

Although capital gains taxation is purposely kept at 15% to stimulate investment, it is evident that much of it flows to foreign corporations and not into the establishment of new American enterprises or increasing efficiency or profitability in existing American businesses. There clearly needs to be a better determination of what the higher differential tax rate should be for foreign investment compared to domestic investment. An increase of 8-10% higher taxation on foreign capital gains would provide more incentive for domestic investments.

There are several recent trends which clearly indicate that the preferential tax rate for capital gains is being abused by so-called "day trading", "fast trading" and "short sales". This abuse has been badly exacerbated by the ever-increasing amount of computer activated trading. There are several brokerage firms that hold securities for less than an hour, even minutes, whereby the upswing of the Dow or other indexes are gauged, and then trades are executed involving millions of shares. Although only fractions of a dollar may be gained on each share, the profits gained are largely based on the magnitude of the trade.

Although seemingly clever and taking advantage of the tax code, these computer trades can cause instability in the market, and literally are not "investments" per se. They create no real capital but are merely adaptations of the derivatives of mathematical calculus that take advantage of the fleeting rate trends that appear on a day or less basis on a given stock exchange or index. These transactions, particularly those where securities are held for less than a day, should have a Federal transaction fee of 1% of the value of the trade for those securities held less than a day, and 2% for less than an hour.

"Short sales" have also been problematic, particularly with investment funds engaged in "hedging". The abnormal volume of short sales in the collapse of 2008 indicated a signal that investment bankers clearly had some indication of the impending disaster. Like derivatives, short sales should be subject to a Federal transaction fee a 1% fee, since they partly contributed to the massive downfall of the stock market in 2008.

Derivatives in recent years have been a serious problem for the financial sector, along with credit default swaps. These so-called "creative" financial instruments are largely private transactions, whose general opaqueness has caused many of the holders of these instruments to wonder what collateral they were based on. It has been demonstrated through Congressional testimony that many of the packages of mortgages lacked sufficient backing in terms of mortgage holder qualifications. This involved granting of mortgages to persons without enough assets, income, and job stability. Frequently the housing was priced far beyond its inherent value. Many of the derivatives were based on the erroneous assumption that housing values could never decrease. When gasoline prices rose in 2008, it exposed the tip of a financial iceberg that many mortgage holders were barely above water, causing defaults to rise, along with foreclosures. As in the Great Depression of the 1930s when stocks were overvalued caused by rampant speculation, so too were the highly leveraged derivatives based on real estate properties of specious value.

It should be fairly obvious that these instruments should have been fully disclosed to any purchaser, and that the rating agencies of Moody's, Standard & Poor's and Fitch should have properly rated these instruments, just as municipal and corporate bonds are accurately rated. However, due to the relatively recent introduction of derivatives into financial trading, their ratings should have been checked on a random sampling basis by Federal regulators. It is startling to realize that new financial instruments like derivatives had not been examined carefully, just as a new model vehicle is scrutinized and analyzed for flaws after its market introduction.

To limit the growth of these instruments, a transactions fee of 1% should be imposed to permit their adequate oversight by the Securities and Exchange Commission, or by any subsequent rating agency developed in the future.

The recent financial collapse should be evident that the financial industry cannot, nor seems to be even inclined, to police itself. Purchasing securities should not be a constant "buyer beware" when the industry declares such instruments as "securities", when in reality they are not truly "secure" but are an exercise in serious risk management by investors.

Mortgages and Financial Lending

Although bitterly fought against by the Republican Party, it should be evident to any rational observer that not only must consumers be protected against unwarranted banking policies, but there must a lawful sense of uniformity for mortgages, loans and credit cards. This national uniformity not only helps consumers, but benefits businesses and investors.

There is no question that home ownership brings many benefits to the United States and American families. These benefits include a driving force for consumer acquisition of home improvement materials, appliances, utilities and jobs associated with housing construction. Other benefits are lessening of population crowding and better sanitation, improvements in overall health, lower crime rates, and higher academic progress for young people due to community cohesiveness and increased parental involvement. These advantages were translated into the formation of two large quasi-governmental entities known colloquially as "Fannie Mae" and "Freddie Mac", which guaranteed the defaults on mortgages.

Although these organizations have been helpful in increasing home ownership in the United States, it is evident that such guarantees of default should only be borne if a realistic set of standards is established by Congress and adhered to by these mortgage backers. This includes a decent credit report and a down payment of 20% or more. Calls for a phase-out of these mortgage guarantees would mean increases in interest rates for loans with private backing.

No mortgage should be granted to persons who have an unstable work history, continually missing payments, very poor credit scores, an insufficient assets-to-debt ratio commensurate with the value of the property being acquired, and an inability to provide equity for a down payment, and no bankruptcy in the last 5-7 years. This means that owning a home is not an "American dream" but should be one of the symbols of "American achievement". Dreams are fleeting, whereas achievement is concrete and has a real basis in terms of accomplishment.

Credit cards have been much of the problem with increasing debt and instability in the United States. It should be evident that there needs to be a maximum interest rate in the United States, limited to 35% per annum. Not only would this place restrictions on credit cards, but it would virtually eliminate the car title and payday loan companies that prey upon the poor and low wage earners that are barely able, or sometimes unable, to move beyond a paycheck-to-paycheck existence.

Mergers and Acquisitions

Mergers and bank acquisitions, particularly of investment banking which now permeates commercial banking after the Glass-Steagall Act was repealed during the Clinton Administration, have resulted in the creation and bailout of banks "too big to fail". Although the recent Troubled Asset Relief Program (TARP) bailout has resulted in some or most of the payback of Treasury funds in the long run, with interest to boot, the problem of size and domination remains. The Dodd-Frank financial reform attempts to resolve this by permitting a "smooth" bankruptcy (a true oxymoron). Although large banks have advantages, they do not promote competition. Nor did any of the much smaller banks receive significant assistance due to the massive size of the TARP to address the severe crisis caused by these large banking entities. A plurality of banks limits the spread of "bad paper", because not every bank desires such exposure to risky financial instruments, given the wide range of conservatism to hearty acceptance of financial innovation in the banking world, whereas a limited number of megabanks can be infected at a faster rate.

Several financial analysts have recommended that substantial taxation be levied on banks that have assets above a certain percentage of the US Gross Domestic Product (GDP). The amount of assets exceeding a pre-set level would incur a taxation penalty of those assets by the Federal Government. Values of assets exceeding 1.5 to 2.0% of GDP have been suggested. This would prevent any bank from gaining too much market share, as it would not be in their financial interest to do so when taxes imposed would be on the order of a 35% penalty on those assets above the set percentage level of GDP. The taxation penalty would shunt monies from any of this excess size back to the US Treasury.

Another means to prevent bailouts of banks "too big to fail" is to severely limit any mergers or acquisitions that could potentially result in combined bank assets exceeding that 1.5% to 2% of GDP. Large mergers and acquisitions limit both regional and national banking competition. These measures would probably only occur if the next Treasury Secretary is not an investment or large commercial banker, but an independent financial analyst or a courageous academic. Congress must recognize that competition breeds its own watchfulness.

Government regulators are often co-opted into remaining aloof or tolerant of malfeasance, which is precisely what occurred with the Securities and Exchange Commission (SEC) in the Madoff investment scheme. When financial analyst Harry Markopolos reported several times to the SEC that the Madoff investments were a Ponzi-pyramid scheme, he was rebuffed and ignored. Only when the Madoff-Ponzi falsity unraveled did the SEC become hyper-alert, but it was too late for the majority of Madoff investors. In the sage words of Peter Lynch, the most successful financial analyst of Fidelity Investments, one must always avoid any investment schemes "...that seem too good to be true."

Manufacturing Policy
During and after World War II, the United States was the world's leading manufacturer. Manufacturing, which creates products, also drives innovation, and compensates the best minds of its citizenry through research, development, patent acquisitions and the formation of new industries. For many years, the United States led in the production of advanced aircraft, electronics, and automobiles. American factories and infrastructure, unlike its adversaries, were not destroyed by war.

American corporations sought overseas markets in allied countries, those of its previous adversaries, and in the developing countries. As cost of living and wages in the United States gradually increased, the lower labor costs and the lack of environmental regulations, and the ease by which foreign countries adopted American methods, foreign sources for manufacturing became quite attractive. American manufacturing began a slow decline. According to the Bureau of Labor Statistics, from 1979 to 2010, approximately 16,000,000 American manufacturing jobs were lost, with the sharpest decline in the last ten years. Americans increased their demand for material goods by leveraging their home equity, and dramatically expanded their credit card debt. The rise of "big box" retail stores, who continually sought lower bids on a variety of consumer goods, ushered in a huge influx of foreign merchandise. Many of these large merchandisers often abandoned US suppliers just for a few pennies difference on many products. American manufacturing continued to slide downward.

On the shelves of the big box retailers today, we see products once made in the United States now made in China, Mexico, or Korea, often priced at the level of a similar or even superior product made in the US. When it comes to apparel, we see products from India, Bangladesh, Pakistan, United Arab Emirates and Mexico which have virtually replaced American clothing and shoes.

The marketing of Chinese products is particularly deceptive, whereby cheap and often markedly inferior products are given American-sounding brand names, such as "Chicago Electric" (not made in Chicago) or "Pittsburg Tools" (not made in Pittsburgh). Many of the products are made from scrap plastics and use inferior components and are easily worn out or broken. To compensate for this inferiority of components, some are made in the United States, but the final product is assembled in China or Mexico. The Chinese in particular have exported numerous products and foodstuffs that are either toxic or contaminated, as shown by high lead content in painted toys, or melamine used as a protein substitute.

The United States lacks a comprehensive manufacturing policy. One possible solution is to reduce the corporate tax rate for companies that actually produce something tangible to 15% or slightly less. These may be companies that produce automobiles, computers, energy-based equipment, machinery and machine tools, appliances and so forth.

One of the most successful programs instituted during the recession was the "cash for clunkers" program, which directed cash payments up to $3,000 for purchase of new automobiles, resulting in a virtual restart of the depressed auto industry. Although $1 billion was first set aside, it was easily snapped up in 1 month, and had to be supplemented again with another $1 billion.

The establishment of a realistic Federal banking support program for the purchase of domestic automobile and consumer related items which meet "Energy Star" requirements with incentives and stable interest rate maximums would be an excellent spur to automobile sales and manufacturing. By pegging a maximum rate, with rate fluctuations based on the prime rate, this will prevent rate gouging and stimulating domestic production.

The Chinese have developed a manufacturing policy that benefits that nation. When wind turbines were built, they must be of Chinese origin. When solar panels were required, they must be Chinese. Yet many of the recipients of project funds from the American Reinvestment and Recovery Act involved the use of foreign turbines and solar panels. We see a substantial number of Chinese, Taiwanese and Korean parts flooding the auto industry, particularly in replacement or aftermarket parts. These parts should have entry inspection and quality check fees to counter such dumping.

Both Federal and State governments can contribute to domestic production by insisting on the enforcement of the Buy America Act. This is particularly important for the acquisition of military hardware, aircraft and other weapons systems. The decision to permit European Aeronautic Defense and Space (EADS) to participate in the US Air Force refueling aircraft contract bidding was wrong-headed. Other bidders besides Boeing, such as Lockheed Martin were not encouraged to provide competing bids with subsidization of their submissions, considering the complexity of such bid entries. Although Northrop Grumman was a partner with EADS, the aircraft design was based on a large commercial airliner built by EADS. It was to be assembled in Alabama, but it was not publicly divulged as to how many components would be made in the United States. The strong dependency on foreign parts for assembly of automobiles in the United States was made most transparent after the tsunami struck Japan in 2011, causing shortages of various electronic devices and auto parts for the production of Hondas and Toyotas.

Industrial unions have finally realized that they can no longer demand ever-increasing benefits and wages. Foreign competitors have learned quickly and present an ever-growing threat to American manufacturing. This means re-emphasis on manufacturing skill, training of American workers, and solidarity that comes with union membership. Rather than having companies expending efforts to break down the drive for union membership, they could reduce turnover recognizing that employees inherently need stability and uniformity of treatment. Before and during World War II, the German government, run by the National Socialist Party, broke down many trade unions in exchange for cooperation from large German industrial firms to produce war materiel to prevent any labor unrest and solidify wages. A similar trend in the United States after World War II to break down union power has resulted in only 11% of all workers as represented by a union, down from 35% after the Korean War. Without union wages and benefits, many workers are barely able to obtain a wage to sufficiently clothe, house and educate their family. The unemployment rate has fluctuated between 8-9% for 2009-2010 due to credit contraction, housing foreclosures and layoffs, all despite various stimulus measures.

With the decline of unions, and the current law that employers must provide health insurance for their workers, this places a greater burden on employers to compete with nations that have no health benefits, no unions, nor do they have to comply with adequate safety and environmental regulations. A government option, whereby insurance plans would be drawn up to cover most medical problems and procedures, would have provided relief for many companies. Not only would this option have provided competition with private insurance plans, it would have eventually decreased costs over time as it enlarged itself into a quasi-governmental entity. That private insurance holds down costs has been shown not to be entirely true; costs are held down by insurance companies by restricting claims, and encouraging realistic costs for medical procedures, but also having insured coverage holders pay the difference. All in all, relieving manufacturing of the burden of insurance coverage for its employees certainly would improve the bottom line.

The Federal tax code needs a direct preference for American products based on domestic content. This is particularly important for items costing $50 or more, which are typically purchased on credit. Previously credit card interest was fully deductible. Now the deduction should be granted based on the interest expended on products with 50% domestic content or more. If the product was a domestic refrigerator costing $1,000 or more, and the credit card interest rate was 20%, the tax-deductible interest would be $200 for that year. As the refrigerator is gradually paid down, the amount of deductible interest would gradually decrease. High value items like automobiles, appliances, electronic equipment and furniture are classic deductible products purchased on credit terms. This deduction would make both consumers and retailers more aware of the domestic content of products and help to stimulate American manufacturing.

The Buy America Act is an excellent starting point to help revitalize American manufacturing, particularly because Federal, State and local governments have so much purchasing power. Similarly, many unions also have large memberships who could leverage their size to provide discounts sales of automobiles, tires, equipment and other American-made products. Unfortunately, many government agencies use the "low-bid mentality" and often skirt the Buy America Act in preference for cheaper foreign products.

The US Product Safety Commission needs to be expanded to be the US Product Quality and Safety Commission, whereby foreign products are scrutinized and examined for the presence of toxic substances, poor quality, inferior reliability and potential for user harm. Much of this work could be subcontracted out to organizations such as the Consumers Union, Underwriters Laboratory, Factory Mutual and many other national laboratories. This would provide direct involvement of the government in examining the performance of imported products and restricting those that do not meet reasonable standards or present a direct threat to the health and safety of the buying public.

Industrial accidents in the United States claim many lives. Recent legislation has strengthened some agencies such as the FDA with closure authority and recall, but much remains to be done with Occupation Health and Safety Administration (OSHA) and the Mine Safety Administration (MSA). The fact that only 11% of all workers are union members further limits actions taken on safe working conditions, particularly in underground mines, construction, rubber and chemical plants. The anti-unionism on the part of corporations and many in the Republican Party borders on irrationality, as so few workers are unionized, compared to about 30% in the 1950s. As many employees transitioned to service work, many industrial unions declined as productivity and automation ramped up. The 11% of workers that are unionized are primarily concentrated in government, aerospace and defense, trucking, steelmaking and the construction trades.

The Obama Administration has made so-called "green" projects a priority. If so, these projects and subsequent jobs should be preferentially awarded to American-owned companies. Awards can be made to foreign-owned companies if they use American-made components and assemble the final product in the United States. Much of our military spending can be used to generate such work, because energy efficiency and productivity are mutual goals of both civilian and military organizations. Rather than spending on weapons of questionable value, the development of high energy wind turbines, solar cells, advanced batteries and capacitors, and the production of biofuels can benefit both the military and civilian sectors of the economy.

Energy and the Environment

For most of the 20th Century, the United States was the largest consumer of energy in the world, principally relying on coal, oil, natural gas and hydroelectric power. Only after World War II when the Eisenhower Administration established its "Atoms for Peace" program did nuclear energy result in the construction of numerous reactors (now at 104) built by a variety of engineering firms and their allied contractors. Its consumption of energy is divided into electrical production for homes, businesses and government facilities; gasoline and diesel fuel for automobiles, trucks, and trains; and natural gas for homes and industrial production.

The principal sources of energy used in the United States are derived from the following: oil, 34%; coal, 23%; natural gas, 20%; biomass fuels, 10%; nuclear fission, 7%; hydroelectric, 3%; with wind turbines, solar and geothermal making up the remainder. Because of the heavy reliance on carbon-based fuel, the transition to so-called "green" energy sources will be based on economics, and by government and public support.

The reliance on oil is gradually decreasing due to the depletion of dwindling oil reserves throughout the world, leading to a long-term effect of gradually increasing costs per barrel of oil.

Distribution of Electricity

The electrical grid, connected to various power producers, shares electrical power through contractual and spot rates. The actual distribution network is aging at a continuing pace, primarily through heavy power consumption during hot climatic cycles, and a growing number of electrical devices drawing power each year due to the continual increase in the American population. Most of the distribution network is outdoors and subject to wind and electrical storms, overheating at various connections, subjected to transformer failures and numerous ground faults. There have been instances where the various power producers fed to the electrical grid due to ground faults, transformer explosions or interrupter glitches, causing massive blackouts over large areas. There have been so-called "brown-outs" when electrical demand has been so intense that required voltage levels could not be sustained.

Lighting consumes approximately 20% of the nation's power needs. Many of these lighting fixtures are wasteful, generate too much heat, and are inefficient. The gradual phase-out of incandescent bulbs, augmented by direct energy credits for the use of halogen and light-emitting diode (LED) bulbs can provide a dramatic reduction in the gradual increase for more electrical power. Many of the exterior street lighting fixtures used today are very inefficient, scattering light in many directions rather than concentrating on light distribution over roadways, intersections and sidewalks. Any city desiring "esthetic" lighting needs to closely evaluate light lumen distribution in specific areas carefully before purchasing fixtures with inferior efficiencies.

Recently there have been proposals to upgrade the electrical grid with so-called "smart technology" where electrical consumption can be directly monitored by wireless transmitters, and eventually appliances could be programmed to apply their peak demand at certain hours, but also reducing electrical rates for consumers at hours where demand is minimal. This technology appears promising, but credits to electric utilities to upgrade existing electrical distribution networks make more sense in the immediate future. Because of the computer nature of these "smart grid" systems, they are susceptible to unauthorized hacking and could present national security problems if adequate controls are not mandated.

Much of the secondary electrical distribution network in residential and commercial areas is still above ground and quite antiquated. Although convenient for repair, exterior electrical distribution networks are very susceptible to storm damage, subject to overheating during high ambient temperature extremes, and are vulnerable to collisions with ground vehicles. Underground distribution cables would require armoring in conduit or other protective trenches to prevent disruption or electrical shorting to ground in case of excavation of construction. Investment credits to place these antiquated above-ground electrical distribution networks to underground status would substantially reduce their susceptibility to storm damage or overheating. This would increase their resistance to electromagnetic pulse events sustained during high sunspot activity.

Automobiles and Trucks

The United States has the largest fleet of automobiles and trucks in the world, with at least one automobile for every three persons. Rather than attempting to convert to completely electric vehicles, several approaches need to be taken to reduce fuel consumption of the more than 130,000,000 vehicles in the United States.

Conventional spark-ignition (SI) and compression-ignition (CI or diesel) engines are inefficient power sources at 35% efficiency due to the substantial amount of heat loss required to maintain proper engine temperatures for proper ignition. Their drive train efficiencies are about 80-85%. However, this is not to say that SI and CI engines should be cast aside, since they pack far more energy per pound of fuel than the energy stored in batteries of equivalent weight. In addition, SI engines with multiple valves per cylinder, fuel injection, turbo or super chargers have a high volumetric efficiency of fuel and air. They can be excellent power sources if their size is not too large, where cooling becomes a problem.

The advantage of automobiles with electric motor drives is their high efficiency (85-90%) and torque. A vehicle that uses a small CI engine to drive a motor-generator, with relatively small battery storage, can be a very efficient combination. In this configuration, the electric motors are drive motors, whereas the SI engine is primarily the motive force for a very large efficient generator or alternator, and the batteries are smaller storage devices used for starting if there is no longer any fuel for the small SI engine. The Chevy Volt is a variant of this system, which has also been used in other hybrid drive vehicles.

In contrast, battery storage vehicles are primarily limited to short commuter distances, but their long-range travel is constrained. Because of the size of the United Sates, and the concentration of vehicles in large cities, both spark-ignition-generators-electric drive and all-electric vehicles should be subsidized. In the meantime, improvements in SI and CI engine efficiency needs constant improvement, whereby vehicles can be taxed based on [brake hp + vehicle weight]. This mechanism of taxation discourages purchases of cars and trucks with higher vehicle weight and inordinate horsepower, both of which consume greater amounts of fuel. Along with fuel taxes, this should provide adequate funding for maintenance and repair of existing highways.

Fossil Fuels and Climatic Change

Disagreements persist as to whether the carbon dioxide (CO_2) and methane (CH_4) produced by human activity have raised planetary temperatures even more than cyclical sunspot activity. CO_2 and CH_4 are the principal atmospheric gases which re-reflect infrared radiation from the sun back onto the planet. CO_2 is produced from the oxidation of carbon-based fuels, such as coal, gasoline, diesel fuel, natural gas and other hydrocarbons. Methane is produced by coal mining, the decaying of plant matter, and from the digestive gases of animals. Carbon dioxide is consumed by plants by the process of photosynthesis to provide oxygen and water vapor.

When there is substantial sunspot activity, there is a general heating of the planet and disruption of communications due to increased amounts of radiation from the sun. When there is minimal sunspot activity, as occurred in the United States in the 1880s, the weather is cold. Many scientists in recent years have been more closely monitoring ocean temperatures, the melting of continental and alpine glaciers, and sampling ice cores from both Greenland and Antarctica to note what CO_2 levels were in past history. Changes in tree ring growth have also been studied. With the surge in energy demand in China, which has overtaken the United States as the world's largest energy consumer, there is a significant concern that Chinese reliance on coal for energy production could tip the scales toward even more rapid planetary warming.

When increased Chinese demand for coal consumption is coupled with the continual logging of forests in tropical South America and other logging areas in North America, Africa and Indonesia which absorb CO_2, there would be an increase in CO_2 and other "greenhouse" gases that could cause substantial increases in planetary temperatures. A year-by-year assessment of this matter by neutral environmental scientists on behalf of the US government and industrial interests is needed to discern warming and climatic changes and correlate them with sunspot activity and total CO_2 and methane emissions. Putting the controversy aside over the release of CO_2 from combustion of hydrocarbons causing climatic change, it makes sense that there must be a general reduction of the burning of carbonaceous fuels because they release other potentially harmful gases such as sulfur dioxide and particulates that contain mercury, arsenic and other toxic compounds.

Many governmental officials have advocated the use of "cap and trade" to supposedly reduce our energy dependence on hydrocarbon-based fuels. This mechanism sets "caps" on the amount of CO_2 emissions from various point sources. If the emitter exceeds those "caps", the producer can "trade" credits from another producer who has not exceeded the set limits by paying for those emission credits. The problem with this system, which sounds "economic" in nature, is that emissions limits may not be realistic or are arbitrarily set. It also prevents corporations that are well off to simply pay for the credits but continue to avoid upgrading facilities to reduce emissions as a "business expense". The "cap and trade" system discourages innovation; it also taxes certain forms of energy in a non-economic way. If the burning of hydrocarbons is to be taxed, the fuel should be taxed on the basis of CO_2/BTU/pound of fuel [kg of CO_2/k Joules/kg of fuel]. Coal, with its higher carbon content, lesser BTU value and the more CO_2 it produces per pound upon oxidation, would be taxed more than natural gas, methane or propane.

Another major reason why this rationing system is faulty is that in order to reduce planetary CO_2 and CH_4 emissions, every nation must participate, with emphasis on the rising industrialized nations to reduce their reliance on hydrocarbon combustion for electrical production, heating and for transportation. China and India, the most populous nations on earth, have both indicated that they should not be penalized for improving and expanding their GDP without using hydrocarbon fuels. They cite that leading Western nations gained their higher economic status by using the same fuels that they are now trying to restrict and tax.

Fuels in the United States are already taxed, and under the present economic conditions, cap and trade and the additional tax burdens on fuels need to be deferred until the US economy full recovers from its present recession, and a rational system of carbon taxation is developed.

Coal and Coal Gas

The United States has the greatest coal reserves and is projected to last for the next 400 years. About 70% of the nation's electrical power is produced by coal-fired plants. The burning of coal, which is primarily carbon in solid form, is not as efficient as the burning of natural gas or coal gas. Coal produces more CO_2 as a function of its calorific value, which varies substantially from anthracite coal at the highest value, to lignite at its least. Coal also produces sulfur dioxide, and depending on the source where it is mined, varying levels of mercuric and arsenical oxides.

The conversion of coal to coal gas, a hydrogen-methane derivative, is one of the means to convert "dirty" coal to a cleaner fuel. Coal gas is typically a blend of several gases, including, on average: hydrogen at about 50%; methane 35%; carbon monoxide 10% and ethylene 5%. These percentages depend on the feedstock and the process used. Some CO_2 is produced during the production of coal gas, but it is substantially less than with anthracite or bituminous coal, which are mostly carbon, some hydrocarbons, iron sulfide and other non-combustible constituents. The CO_2 produced from burning coal gas is less than that of coal, and the BTU per pound of coal gas is at least 50% greater than coal. Coal gas combustion only produces about 20% CO_2 compared to coal at nearly 98%.

The use of coal gas was used during World War II. The advantage of methane and natural gas from underground sources is that CH_4 is a molecule with four hydrogen atoms and one carbon atom. When methane is combusted, its products of oxidation are CO_2 and H_2O, with substantially less CO_2 than with coal. This is a promising process to use for the vast coal reserves of the United States.

There are two other technologies which can reduce the amount of CO_2 released into the atmosphere. The first method burns coal in a fluidized bed which is agitated with combustion air, with the coal surrounded by solids which tend to absorb much of the CO_2. This process is advocated by the Foster Wheeler Corp.

Another method is the more controversial CO_2 sequestration process which forces CO_2 into reservoirs containing large calcium or magnesium deposits which can then trap or form calcite or dolomite. Unfortunately, many of these formations are also aquifers, whereby water used for drinking and other purposes can then become acidified with the introduction of CO_2, forming carbonic acid. Other waste products from the coal of coal, such as sulfur dioxide and various nitrogen oxides, could also find their way into the aquifer. This process needs extensive testing and monitoring before it can ever be considered for wide-scale adoption.

Although many environmentalists complain about the combustion of coal, it will be the fuel of economic choice used for many years in the United States and China. The problem of CO_2 emissions will be a long-term issue, but it should be realistically addressed by objective analysis and investigation.

Natural Gas

Natural gas has a high calorific value and lesser CO_2 content, and contains fewer trace contaminants than coal. The United States has abundant sources of natural gas. Reserves of natural gas are located in geologic formations where petroleum is trapped, in various deep underground shale deposits, and in coal deposits. In coal mines, the natural gas is not recovered, but is considered an undesirable explosive hazard that could kill or injure miners or disrupt mining operations. To extract natural gas from shale formations, hydraulic fracturing ("fracking") has been used to open the shale by injecting water mixed with methanol, benzene, ethylene glycol and other proprietary chemicals under high pressure.

Hydraulic fracturing can lead to the introduction of undesirable chemicals into aquifers, contaminating drinking water. Reports of the presence of natural gas emanating from tap water have surfaced in several drilling areas. Although this process may be a potential source of a valuable fuel, it must be approached with great caution before widespread damage is incurred.

Nuclear Power

Nuclear power has been proposed in recent days as the supposed solution to a CO_2-free power source, along with solar and wind power. Nuclear power has shown itself to be most expensive energy on a cost per kilowatt basis, compared to coal or natural gas. The construction of nuclear power plants is a slow process that must consider various safety redundancies in the form of containment, multiple back-up systems, and higher-priced materials of construction, to contain any radioactive leakage.

Unlike reactors in France, which have the same design, American reactors have different designs and are built by different contractors to specifications of the power producer and the Nuclear Regulatory Commission (NRC). The lack of configuration control complicates inspection and multiplies the number of reactors that can fail. In coal-fired pressure vessels, there are fires and explosions, but no radioactivity is released.

Before the recent tsunami-induced failures in Japanese reactors, there were two very serious instances which occurred in the United States where failures in cooling systems lead, or almost lead, to the inability to shut down the reactor. In the Three Mile Island incident, a substantial amount of radioactivity was released and there was incipient melting of reactor materials. In an incident rarely reported by the news media, an American nuclear reactor at Browns Ferry, AL sustained a severe electrical fire in its cable room, which could have prevented the reactor from shutting down. The NRC recommended the use of CO_2 to suppress the fire, the usual practice for electrical fires, but its ineffectiveness prompted the local fire department to use water. Fortunately, the fire was suppressed, and the control cables did not short to ground.

In the former Soviet reactor at Chernobyl, Ukraine, a seemingly harmless exercise in shut down led to the worst dispersal of radioactivity on record. Leakage of radiation from this reactor continues to this day, with recent reports of apparent degradation of the graphite and steel used to envelop the abandoned core.

The problem of storing radioactive waste products persists. In the United States, most radioactive waste is being stored at each plant, with disagreement continuing over the complete activation of a large underground depository in Nevada. Rather than transport this waste to a single site, it makes more sense to store it in regional locations in remote, seismically stable areas. If the Nevada site somehow becomes contaminated, there are no backup sites for waste disposal if individual reactor pools can no longer accommodate more waste.

Nevertheless, nuclear power should be considered as one of several power sources, along with wind, solar and geothermal power generation. Recent events indicate that the present reactors in the United States need to be critically evaluated whether their backup cooling water systems for the main reactor vessel and the spent fuel water pools can function in locations where seismic events frequently occur and at what magnitude. Many of these plants have been operating for 40 years or more, and it makes sense that a state-of-the art reactor design with proper configuration controls should be under consideration for future reactors to replace any decommissioned units.

Wind, Solar and Geothermal Power

For wind, solar and geothermal, each of these power technologies has favorable geographic locations in the United States. For solar power, the Southwest and parts of southern California are ideal locations due to ample sunshine; for wind power, the Midwest and the northern plains are flat areas with vast acreages of farmland and consistent wind; for geothermal power, there are select locations in Washington State, Wyoming, Oregon and Arkansas which have hot springs where wells can be drilled for access. The advantage of all these power technologies is that they are not dependent on the combustion of hydrocarbons. Both private and public investments in the form of "energy bonds" are definitely needed to spur further dispersal and installation of solar panels, wind turbines and geothermal wells for American power needs.

There have been several recent developments in solar and wind technologies which increase their attractiveness year-by- year. There are several firms developing "printable" solar cells which do not rely on silicon wafers, and they have efficiencies comparable to silicon style cells. They have been proposed as "solar cell shingles" for roofing. Conventional solar cell arrays have also been deployed in many locations, although their payback periods are still quite long.

Wind turbines have also increased in terms of power output and efficiency. Numerous wind farms have been constructed, particularly in the Midwest and Southwest. A typical wind turbine produces about one megawatt (MW) of power. Using aerospace methods, turbine blade designs have been optimized and their safety improved. New turbine technology should "piggyback" onto existing designs, and their needs to be accelerated depreciation credits set aside for American firms to build these turbines rather than importing foreign turbines.

Geothermal energy has been the least developed of the technologies due to the salinity and corrosiveness of the geothermal waters used to heat these reactors. However, newer alloys have been developed to minimize this problem, and like any newer technology, it needs technical and fiscal support from both public and private sources. Of all the power technologies mentioned, geothermal is the most natural, has the highest efficiency, produces no CO_2, but has been the least exploited.

National Identification

There is a vital need for a national identity card for several reasons, including national security, determination of immigration status, voting and census taking. Each of these requirements is constitutionally mandated, and they take precedence over the right to privacy. There are many advocates of the so-called fundamental right to privacy, based on the 4th Amendment, which states that "The right of the people to be secure in their persons, houses, papers and effects, against unreasonable searches and seizures shall not be violated..." The key words in this amendment are "unreasonable searches". Asking for a person's identity card to determine their status is not unreasonable. Travelers abroad certainly would not object to providing their passport to authorities upon civil request and asking persons unknown who seem conspicuously out of place in a certain context is not unreasonable. Moreover, private or public corporations, such as banks, routinely ask for identification when cashing a check, or require identification for a job application where citizenship may be mandatory for employment or asking for identification when entering a restricted area.

The current de facto identification in the United States is the driver's license, which upon face value, is not a realistic means of establishing complete status. In fact, many persons do not drive, or their licenses have expired, or they may be minors, or they may be of foreign origin as students or visiting the United States, or they may be illiterate or disabled.

The means of establishing identity varies from state to state. Many states do not have adequate means of preventing duplication or falsification of identity cards and the picture on the licenses are often faded or difficult to distinguish, particularly if the person has dark skin coloration where features cannot be fully distinguished due to the poor quality of the cameras used. Physical descriptions are often limited to height, weight, hair color and eyes, of which weight, hair color and eyes are easily altered if there is intent to defraud identity. What is needed are more accurate means by which identity can be discerned, such as by fingerprints, ear shape, blood classification or iris appearance, in addition to the more obvious parameters previously described.

Clearly identifying more than 300,000,000 persons in the United States is not an easy task. The Federal government, along with each state receiving compensation for this task, would gradually start this process. For those persons already requiring known identity, such as military personnel, police and firefighters, governmental officials, pilots and corporate personnel who travel frequently, would easily have their national identity established. The general population would gradually receive national identity card notifications through license renewal, voting, census and at birth registry.

The Immigration and Naturalization Service (INS) would notify permanent legal residents first, and anyone applying for a visa would receive a foreign visitor ID with a radio frequency identification (RFID) chip embedded in their card. Universities and colleges would require any foreign students to have such cards prior to enrollment. Persons with hardships, such as elderly persons or those in hospitals, would receive special treatment as a courtesy to their situation. It is recognized that this process would take time, but as the general population would gradually recognize its value, it would progress at a faster clip than anticipated. There is no question that a small percentage of the population would refuse any national ID, but would in the long run, find the inconvenience not worth the resistance, especially if they had been arrested for some infraction of various laws or entry into restricted places, or denied the use of certain forms of transportation.

Immigration

This is one of the most controversial issues facing the United States today. In the early days of this Republic, immigration from Europe and Asia provided both labor and capital to expand and industrialize the United States. This immigration continued up to the entry into World War I, with large migrations of Irish, Germans, Italians, Poles, Swedes and Jews along the East Coast and the Midwest. Even after World War II, there were large numbers of displaced persons from war-torn Europe entering the United States.

Certain service industries and the agricultural sector have long welcomed the ebb and flow of non-citizens to work in various jobs supposedly of "no-interest" to American workers, particularly from Mexico and South America. The restaurant and hotel industry have long supported and looked the other way regarding the national origins of its workers. Significant portions of their wages find their way back to Mexico and other foreign countries. Some illegal immigrants have demanded Social Security (SSI) benefits because SSI taxes were paid, even though they lack citizenship.

The 14th Amendment to the Constitution guarantees that "All persons born or naturalized in the United States, and subject to its jurisdiction, are citizens of the United States and of the State wherein they reside." This amendment provides a simple avenue for any illegal alien to give birth to a child and that child is thereby a citizen. These children will attend American schools, and ultimately become "Americanized" as long as the parents remain in the United States.

Two recent propositions do need to be considered. The first is whether the child of illegal immigrants that has attended American schools up to high school, but was not born in the United States, should be permitted to attend college or awarded scholarships, or those who have served in the US military, be granted citizenship. It appears that this concept does have merit, as this would be the same naturalization process that a legal immigrant would go through prior to the grant of American citizenship. Military service, by its very nature of swearing allegiance to the Constitution, is a more rigorous test for citizenship.

The other proposed route, which addresses those families who are primarily here for economic gain or convenience, is to change the Constitution by simply amending the 14th Amendment. That change would automatically grant citizenship to anyone born in the United States if one or both parents are citizens. The amendment process is slow and contentious, but this is only solution in the long run to determine birthrights for Americans.

Those immigrants without proper visas or valid work permits who desire no actual pathway to citizenship often represent a drain on public schools, medical care, and housing. At the extreme end of this immigrant stream are the undesirable elements that come in the form of gangs and illegal activity. No one considers this a simple problem.

There are some solutions, although many immigrants may find them unfriendly. The first solution, as outlined in the section on national identity, requires any alien to obtain an alien registration identity card, which would not necessarily mean deportment. Only those who have committed felonies or are clearly unbalanced should be immediately deported. If an employer recognizes that the alien is providing proper service for his pay, and has committed no crimes, the alien would be permitted to remain for at least one year if authenticated by the employer that the worker is truly or critically needed. However, if there are American citizens that desire that work, the alien would have to make arrangements to depart the United States within 6 months. If after advertisement of the work in the leading newspapers of the area, and no responses from native Americans are received, the lack of applicants would provide the alien a work permit. If this cycle goes on for several years, and the employee speaks fluent English, his application for legal residency should be considered. This mechanism takes the punitive action away from both employer and alien but recognizes the reality that both aliens and citizens are competing alike for jobs.

Clearly the United States needs immigrants with certain critical skills, such as physicians, lawyers, translators, trade specialists, computer scientists, engineers and electronic technicians from various countries. These immigrants should receive higher priority than others. However, there must be critical controls on the entry of immigrants coming from or educated in countries that have shown hostile intent toward the United States, such as North Korea, Iran, Sudan, Somalia, Syria, Libya, Saudi Arabia, Afghanistan and Pakistan. Immigrants from these and other countries need to be limited, and their presence known and closely monitored. The use of alien ID cards with RFID tracking permits finding their location and travels and limits their length of stay. The excuse of "losing the card" and not reporting its loss immediately would be grounds for immediate deportation.

Aliens who have demonstrated good skills in adapting to the United States, and do not attempt to impose their philosophy or doctrines of their native country during their presence in the United States can certainly enhance their consideration for citizenship. The learning of English must be mandatory before any citizenship is even considered.

There have been some disturbing trends where many immigrants have indicated that the mandatory use of English for governmental purposes only is not in their interest. Some have declared that their governmental meetings be conducted in Spanish, not English. In the past, most immigrants tried to integrate themselves into American society by learning English, and have their children speak the language fluently. The requirement that governmental and business services must be in English, Spanish and other languages is antithetical to unison and sharing a common American experience.

We have seen the bitter effects of forced bilingualism in Canada, where French and English are the mandatory official languages taught in schools and for government functions. Many French speakers of Quebec felt they were given short shrift in Canadian affairs. The Province of Quebec attempted at one time to require airline pilots to speak French over their airspace, which created boycotts of flights into Quebec, strong objections and outright refusals from pilots, and a potential aircraft safety hazard. At one point, Quebec threatened secession from Canada over the issues of the French language, its culture and influence in Canadian life.

The requirement for English to be the official governmental language of the United States does not mean that other languages are restricted; clearly foreign languages are very useful in certain business transactions, and foster connectivity with other countries. However, for an American citizen to vote and grasp political and financial issues, this responsibility comes with an understanding of the English language.

Education

In recent years, there has been much hand-wringing over the supposedly poor condition and output of American secondary schools. Much of the problem has been overly exaggerated by both politicians and the media, based on selected comparison tests of students in various developed countries vs. American students, which supposedly inferred the massive failing of US schools. Yet these same countries vie to send their graduates to US colleges and universities for further education, and there are many top high schools in the United States that produce from year-to-year highly talented and gifted graduates that fare very well in college and later life.

Why is there such a disparity in schools in Mississippi, Alabama and New Mexico vs. schools in New York or Massachusetts or

California? Many conservatives advocate "local control" of schools, frowning heavily on certain subjects that may clash with their religious sensibilities, beliefs or ideologies, and the "federalization" of schools. Subjects like biology, ecology, evolution and certain elements of history seem to evoke the greatest uproar over content and interpretation of facts. Many education "reformers" point to the use of vouchers, charter schools and private education as the means to overcome the supposed bureaucracy of unionized public schools. Yet when it comes to measurements proposed by the Bush Administration in its "No Child Left Behind" testing program to weed out "failing" schools, it is the voucher and charter schools that generally score less on standardized tests than do the public schools. "Home" schooling produces the least qualified graduates.

It is not only differences over subject matter and teaching methods that cause substantial variation from one school to another, and from state-to-state. Property taxes have long been the principal source of school revenue, levied on homes and business property. Although this seems logical, but property values in one community vs. another, or the types of businesses in one city compared to another, can make quite a difference. For example, in some rural school districts, the spending per pupil can be 3-4 times less than that of suburban school district where property values are so markedly different that the teachers of the more affluent community receive so much greater pay and better facilities as to be basically, and sometimes utterly unfair to students, no matter where they live.

There are remedies to this problem, both of which require State and Federal aid to school districts that cannot make up the difference by further taxing a property base that is gradually declining in size and value. It should be incumbent on each state to determine the average spending per pupil. With this value, the average spending per pupil can be determined nationwide. The cost of living varies from state-to-state, and a cost-of-commodities adjustment would be made to determine what level of Federal education aid each state would receive. Each state would be required to provide at least 40-50% matching funds to receive the Federal subsidy for each of its schools. Each school would receive an amount based on the number of students enrolled in that school. Private or parochial schools could leverage their tuition if their average per pupil cost is less that of the public schools. These schools could receive state or federal funds if they do not require every student to attend classes that are basically religious indoctrination and attendance at religious services if the parents are opposed to such education for their children. This would be relatively rare, except for certain inner-city schools, where parochial schools may be accepting students of different religious persuasions to keep enrollment at a sufficiency level. Many of these schools would forgo federal and state support just to preserve their independence from secular governmental control.

What would such State and Federal aid require of the schools receiving it? There are five areas of concentration where national standards make sense in terms of receiving an American education. They include proficiency in the English language and its general literature; mathematics, science, economics and constitutional government. First and foremost is the teaching of the English language, reading and writing clear and concise letters, reports and documents, which seems to have been a subject area in decline and neglect due to the influence of television and visual learning. The reading selections should be modern and current; this includes newspapers, magazines, intelligent novels and non-fiction, and minimizing the requirements of antiquated readings of Chaucer and Shakespeare that are historically interesting but are often of minimal value in today's world. The teaching of mathematics, progressing from algebra to geometry to trigonometry, should be mandatory for all students. For those desiring more technical or professional careers, the study of advanced algebra, calculus and statistics should be emphasized. Basic science, including chemistry, physics, plant and human biology would be mandatory. The basics of economics, business law and the functions of all levels of government would also be required. These are not subjects which draw controversy, in contrast to subject areas like history, religion, or social studies, which are best left to each state to determine the appropriate curriculum.

Critics often point out methods to improve our schools, often targeting education unions and associations for protecting "incompetent" teachers. There are methods to determine whether students are receiving an adequate education, but close scrutiny and the use of testing is necessary to screen whether students learned anything of value during each half year. Testing needs to be conducted by independent contractors or state monitors so that school officials cannot tamper with results. Another method is to place less reliance on "multiple choice" tests but require students to give written answers to general questions or problems. This eliminates the problem of erasing wrong answers to obtain "improvement" in school scores.

The Armed Services have frequently employed the use of visual aids, practice sessions, test measurement, classroom participation and actual assessment of teacher skills by evaluating the number of students who are able to progress in a particular area of study. Both the instructor and the student are held accountable. The student must account to his commanding officer why he failed; typically, it means no advancement in grade and pay. The instructor is also held accountable and must state why the failing students under his tutelage failed to progress or grasp the subject area. New York State has long held Board of Regents examinations in various subjects to assure that individual schools are not simply passing students along without sufficient knowledge. Not only does a system that passes those who lack skills breed contempt, it does a marked injustice to the student who realizes later that he or she is bereft of learning and becomes a drag on society and his family.

How do we recruit good teachers? Good teachers do not have to attend a "teachers college". On the contrary, there are many semi-retired persons, former military personnel, those skilled in certain trades and professions who are natural teachers and would receive a welcome reception by students from a teacher who comes from the "real world". Teaching along these lines invites a one-year apprenticeship, and upon its conclusion, the "specialist teacher" may decide to stay or if ineffective, be advised to move on to other pursuits. This type of interplay will be beneficial to both experienced traditional teachers and their specialist counterparts as a mutual learning experience. Other mentoring systems that have shown promise include matching a meritorious teacher with a younger teacher to counsel and suggest improvements or recommend teaching ideas to further the younger teacher's career. Teachers who do not measure up after repeated mentoring should be used either in an administrative capacity or terminated if completely ineffective.

There has been a depressing trend where male students have been lagging behind their female counterparts in recent years. About 30 years ago, schools were scolded for not addressing the needs of female students. As a result, we have seen college enrollment to be about 60% women and 40% men, and the so-called wage gap virtually has disappeared in such field as chemistry, law, mathematics and medicine. In many cases, the starting pay of women has exceeded that of men in various fields, except for business executives, where pay is beyond both reason and actual performance and return-on-investment.

This development should re-awaken many high schools to wonder whether we really need all classes to be "co-ed". It may be better to have some separate classes for boys taught by men to improve their outlook and scores in certain classes, particularly in literature, English language and biology where topics can be discussed in a vein more appropriate to the aptitudes and attitudes of males.

Disruption and discipline in schools has always been problematic, particularly where there is no home guidance, nor any parental respect toward education. There may be illegal drug or violence problems in the home, or just simple rebelliousness on the part of the student. Whatever the cause, if numerous disruptions have been incited by one or more students, states need to organize so-called "boot camp schools" or "amendatory schools" which take the student away from the school environment to a suburban or rural location with dormitories for a more rigidized and structured environment. Such schools would concentrate on basic literacy, elementary mathematical skills, and providing a practical education where employable skills will be learned, such as carpentry, plumbing or welding, and extensive use of physical programs so that excess energy is channeled into sports rather than violence directed against others or property. Graduates would receive graduate equivalency diplomas (GEDs) if they pass state requirements for awards.

Clearly state laws must be passed to define the criteria by what actual disruptions, their number and magnitude, are required for such transference, as many parents would object, but would most likely yield when confronted with actual witnessed reports and the extent of disruption or injury that was caused by the student in question. The dismissal from school of disruptive students serves no real purpose under the age of 16, at which most states no longer require mandatory education. Many parents may desire their children to attend such "amendatory schools" up to the age of 18 years, given their inability to provide for their child's education if the disruptive student is released onto the parent's own recognizance.

There is a growing trend in the United States to have children without benefit of marriage. Not only does this present problems of child support, but it is well established that family support is critical to a child's education. Keeping parents married and properly nurturing their children and their education is not always sustained by the initial romantic love for a long period of time. Just like other incentive programs, there is a need for a bonus program for marriage. Upon being married, the couple would receive $5,000 to begin their lives together to establish a residence and provide basic necessities for their children. This grant would only be awarded if the couple has children. To provide additional encouragement to remain married, the couple would receive $4,000 on their second anniversary, $3,000 for their third, and $1,000 for their fourth anniversary. This program would decrease some of the difficulty in searching for parental support, lessen some of the welfare support, and involve fathers and mothers in their children's lives and education.

Affirmative Action, Genderism and Sports Excess

Since much of the civil rights legislation passed in the 1960s, there has been remarkable progress regarding racism and advancement of minorities in the United States. In the area of sports, virtually all the domestic professional basketball players are "black" or dark-skinned, with most of the lighter-skinned players from foreign countries. The National Football League (NFL) has a high percentage of black players, at about 60%. There are a large number of minority legislators in both Federal and State governments, in addition to the President of the United States being of mixed race, as well as many other high-ranking elected officials and corporate executives, generally reflecting their numbers in the general population. There is no question that there are certain sections of the country where affirmative preferences are apparently needed, but there will always be imbalances in selections for any position. There are similar "set-asides" for "women-owned" businesses, although it is well-documented that women in general control

60% of all expenditures on both every day and out-of-the-ordinary expenses in the United States.

The earning power of certain sections of this country varies sharply from one location to another. If affirmative action is to be offered, it should be based on either family or individual income or assets, and not just based on skin color or national origin. There should be a certain color-blindedness to these programs, because in certain circumstances there may be more deserving poor Caucasians, reddish, yellow or tan-skinned persons based on need and intelligence or motivation in certain circumstances, rather than using a simple population quota for persons whose skin is darker. Use of a population quota based on a selected minority population in the United States has been used in legal cases for college admission for "diversity" and "balancing", but it is not constitutional equality, and is not the best course of action in all cases or circumstances.

Women have achieved remarkable gains in recent years, not only in many fields of professional endeavor, but also those of high school and collegiate sports programs, which are often established at the expense of men's programs. This area of gender-based "set-asides" needs to come to an end.

There also is a stream of excessive money that is flowing into collegiate sports for coaches and players into football, basketball, baseball and other lesser sports. Many of the salaries of these coaches exceeds that of top faculty members, and the attention lavished on these sports programs drains away funds from educational programs, whereby scholarships to play football, basketball, baseball and hockey sometimes outnumber scholastic scholarships.

Many of these collegiate players are not college students per se; many leave before graduation or take courses that are of no use after their sports careers are over. There is no question that sports recognition brings attention to a college, and provides student camaraderie, but having star athletes who can barely articulate, are rude to spectators, receive money under the table, and are more concerned about after-game activities than grade points should be in a professional developmental minor league sponsored by the NFL, the National Basketball Association (NBA) or Major League Baseball (MLB).

Genderism has also extended itself to the distribution of various government contracts in the form of set-asides for "women or minority-owned" enterprises. Granting points to bidders for public government contracts just based on gender or color violates the concepts of merit and equality under the constitution. Many women have entered the work force after changes in divorce laws of many states, where grounds were no longer mandatory and the concept of "no-fault" divorce prevailed. The mother was usually awarded custody of the children, forcing her to strive for a much higher wage or salary than previously acceptable, along with the fact that many more women have college degrees than in prior times. In 47 out of 50 of the largest metro areas of the United States, women in their 20s without children make more money than their male counterparts. The typical pay difference is about 18% more for women.

Awarding a construction contract to a woman-owned enterprise based on her degree in English literature vs. a contractor with substantial experience in civil engineering and construction is inherently wrong-headed practice. This is not to say that companies headed by women with construction experience should be penalized; the correct policy dictates that government contract work should be awarded based on prior experience and good work.

The Second Amendment of the Constitution

There is probably no greater area of controversy over the wording of the Constitution than the wording of the Second Amendment. That amendment states that "A well-regulated Militia, being necessary to the security of a Free State, the right of the people to keep and bear Arms, shall not be infringed." At the time of the founding of the Republic, many states had concerns that a strong central government with a Federal Army could usurp their right to bear arms, lessening the power of the States and inviting Federal intervention each time there were riots, disorder or any uprising within the State. The militia today consists of the National Guard of each State, which can be nationalized if necessary to intervene in certain conflicts. Although not present at the founding of this Republic, each state and municipality, both large and small, now have police forces which are armed and serve the public. The police and the guard members of each State are now the modern "Militia" described in the Constitution.

Except for war zones, the United States leads all other industrialized nations in the possession and production of hand guns and rifles and the greatest number of mass shootings. The sheer proliferation of guns makes them a very difficult product to regulate and prevent their use in crimes, suicides, and accidental deaths. At the present time, based on the estimated number of guns produced, it is estimated there is one handgun available for every two persons in the United States.

A recent ruling of the Supreme Court, *Heller vs. Washington, DC,* awarded the right of individuals to have handguns in the home for protection. Five justices interpreted the amendment to indicate that the "right of the people" was to be taken in the ordinary sense, meaning that the bearer of arms was not just in the military or former military, a policeman, or a security guard, but any citizen. The four opposing justices felt that the amendment applied to only military personnel and the police, as has been the case for many years. Another similar ruling struck down the handgun ordinances of the City of Chicago.

In response, the City of Chicago revised its ordinance stating that handgun possession is legal, as long as it is confined to storage in the home per se, and could not be taken outdoors. Further, purchases of guns were limited to transactions outside of Chicago and the number of handguns purchased and held was restricted. In some western states, attempts to permit handguns to be carried openly were passed. Logical restrictions should indicate that those persons openly carrying handguns clearly present a general threat to most persons, because handguns or other similar weapons are only openly displayed by police officers, guards and special agents in most ordinary circumstances. In areas where home invasions and burglaries are common, it makes sense for persons to receive handgun permits for protection. This can be easily verified by crime reports for certain sections of a city or town. Other exceptions would apply to persons carrying special equipment, high value items like diamonds or expensive jewelry, hazardous chemicals, or persons working in areas where animals could present harm or transfer disease.

A license to have handguns or rifles should only be granted to persons with no criminal record, no history of mental illness or domestic violence, and documentation to prove that they live in an area which has presented threats to their personal security. Health professionals, courts and the services should be reporting those patients with mental or psychological disorders to the National Instant Criminal Background Check System Denied Transaction File to prevent these persons from acquiring weapons. These are sane gun controls, limiting guns to persons who truly must have them for legitimate reasons. Clearly automatic rifles, such as the AR-15, and military ammunition belong in the hands of the military, tactical police units and special government agents. The sale and registration of auto/semi-automatic rifles and handguns, amount of ammunition sold, and the number guns held per person, must be closely monitored. Proposals to register these military weapons should be made mandatory because they are not simple weapons of self-defense. Voluntary buybacks of $500 per AR-15, a legitimate number based on the typical price for used rifles on the internet, would reduce the number of rifles available. For those who decide to retain them, registration, annual licensing fees and background checks would be required. This would help to curb illicit gun trafficking, which serves no purpose other than the arming of criminals, gangs and drug cartels.

The Courts

The ability of a judge to be appointed to the Supreme Court of the United States for life is not in line with the other branches of government. All other high offices in the Executive and Legislative branches of the US Government have specific terms where they are limited by (a) two terms of the Presidency or (b) two years for each Representative and (c) six years for each Senator. All legislators must seek re-election after each term, whereas judges of the Supreme Court are neither elected, nor are they limited by any term.

Most judges that are selected for the Supreme Court are in their 50s, where they have compiled sufficient record of achievement before they can be considered for selection. By the time a judge reaches his 80th birthday, aging has taken place and his clerks assume much of his writings and reflection on legal issues. A maximum term of 18 years for Supreme Court judges makes more sense, which is equivalent to three senatorial terms, after which each justice could become a special master for the Court as a Justice Emeritus, whereby he could advise the Court on very difficult cases where his experience and wisdom could be beneficial. Emeritus Justices with a temperament to encourage comity among the younger justices would result in more unified decisions. Once the Chief Justice had assigned the case, the Emeritus Justices would be advisors to clerks and justices formulating the majority opinion.

Another troubling area in the Federal Courts is prosecutorial misconduct. In many cases, innocent persons have been incarcerated due to prosecutors withholding evidence to the defense, fabricating charges, or coaching witnesses to commit perjury, but the prosecutors did not sustain any reprimands or punishments by disbarments, dismissal or severe fines. Unlike defense attorneys or judges who are often held accountable, federal prosecutors are appointed, generally untouched and unpunished. To stop this injustice, special panels of judges with investigatory staffs should be formed to sanction these rogue prosecutors with civil and criminal penalties and disbarment, based on the extent of misconduct committed. To help protect the innocent against these injustices, the preservation of physical and DNA evidence is the key to exoneration. At present, only 16 states have no laws requiring preservation of DNA evidence.

A similar problem is when these prosecutors pursue a case as revenge or a vendetta, whereby the prosecution of the case costs more and far exceeds the so-called "damages against the people of the United States". This behavior occurred during the era of special prosecutors but continues to this day. An example is the prosecution of former Sen. John Edwards regarding the use of private funds to shield his wife from knowledge of his extramarital affair during the campaign of 2008. The amount spent on prosecuting the supposed campaign offense was three times the actual amount expensed. Given the magnitude of private contributions to campaign funds that sloshed around in various election cycles, prosecution of public figures in such a morass is hardly a worthwhile endeavor, particularly when the *Citizens United* decision permitted Republicans to exploit the ruling, and the prosecutor in the Edwards case was a Republican. This prosecution had political fingerprints all over it, and the prosecution was meaningless because Sen. Edwards was ultimately acquitted.

About 30 years ago, it was thought that the illegal drug trade and crime would supposedly halt if individuals with a "lifetime of criminality" would be imprisoned. A "lifetime of criminality" was defined by at least three felonies and numerous misdemeanors and became known as the so-called "three strikes law". Persons committing three or more felonies were to be sentenced to long terms of imprisonment. Unfortunately, so many State and Federal criminal laws had been upgraded to felony status that many persons were sentenced to long terms that were not commensurate with the actual offenses committed. This was especially the case for the possession of illegal drugs.

The "war on drugs" is a losing battle, often sentencing persons to prison for relatively minor offenses, serving longer prison terms than those of murderers, bank robbers, arsonists, embezzlers and terrorists. The billions of law enforcement dollars spent on this "faux war" are literally staggering. The establishment of drug courts by some states solely dealing with those offenses is a major step to forcing rehabilitation through simple confinement in "halfway houses" and mandatory drug treatment and counseling. This approach is far less expensive than imprisonment at $25,000-$30,000 per prisoner per year in a penitentiary.

This is not to say that illicit drugs such as methamphetamine, cocaine or heroin, should be "legalized". What should be emphasized is that possession of these substances clearly present health and safety threats to the public, just as alcohol consumption before and while driving is dangerous. Penalties and forced rehabilitation rather than imprisonment are better avenues for treatment of the illicit drug problem.

One good example to curb the spread of methamphetamine has been the sequestering of pseudoephedrine by pharmacies and requiring signatures and identification prior to purchase if the buyer has no prescription. Purchasing a large quantity is certainly a tip-off, and manufacturers, particularly foreign sources, must account for their sales to legitimate buyers. Regarding heroin, if the United States had purchased the poppy crop in Afghanistan and converted it to morphine for American and worldwide distribution for medical purposes, much of the morphine and heroin would not have made its way onto urban streets. The close monitoring and heavy taxation of "medical marijuana" distributors would also help to curb excessive demand and would provide a direct revenue source for drug treatment and law enforcement. Because the United States is such a diverse and open country, it is doubtful that the use of illicit drugs will ever be tightly controlled. A successful prevention effort would involve medical professionals aiding middle and high school educators about the harmful effects of excessive usage that these drugs have on human health. In this way, drugs are described as toxic, habitual chemicals by intelligent, informed professionals to young people at their most impressionable ages.

In its sweeping decision entitled *Citizens United vs. Federal Election Commission*, the Supreme Court claimed that restricting the establishment of political action committees (PACs) by corporations, unions and the media was "...chilling political speech, speech that is central to the First Amendment's meaning and purpose. The Court ruled that restrictions on speakers to check with Federal Election Commission (FEC) before issuing their message to avoid criminal liability and the cost of defense counsel was the equivalent of "prior restraint", which the five justices of the majority claimed that "...the First Amendment was drawn to prohibit." Further, they naively stated "...a PAC created by a corporation can still speak, because a PAC is a separate association from a corporation."

The Court felt that the First Amendment was "Premised on mistrust of governmental power" and it stands against restricting certain viewpoints or discussions, or only letting "preferred speakers" discuss certain topics. The Court's statement is only partially true, because corporations during the time the framers forged the Constitution were not as powerful as they are today.

Most startling is the statement of the Court in its decision that "It is irrelevant that corporate funds may have little or no correlation to the public's support for corporate ideas. All speakers, including wealthy individuals and the media, use money amassed from the marketplace to fund their speech, and that the First Amendment protects the resulting speech." The Court even topped this statement by concluding "...that independent expenditures, including those made by corporations, do not give rise to corruption or the appearance of corruption." Nor that speakers "...influence over or access to elected officials does not mean the officials are corrupt", nor "will it cause the electorate to lose faith in democracy." It was as if ethical statutes and bribery implications were whisked away by the Court in the majesty of their own words.

The Court further went on to describe prior restrictions on corporate and union contributions as antiquated but did not feel that disclosure requirements of who made the contributions or political advertisements were restrictive.

The isolation, naiveté and ideological divisions of the Roberts Court revealed that they concluded there was an absolutist reading of the First Amendment, not considering that elected officials are routinely influenced to make laws that favor corporate interests that often restrict or markedly minimize the speech of individuals who cannot afford to influence, or even have access to elected officials. Because PACs serve to fund campaigns of public officials selected by corporations, these same officials became virtual representatives of the corporations, making laws of the corporation, by the corporation, and for the corporation.

This decision unleashed a barrage of corporate and wealthy individuals to contribute to various PACs, often overshadowing the contributions gathered from those of lower and moderate incomes on internet web sites. A fierce opposition and criticism of this decisions ensued, and the signers of the decision were derided for their faulty logic and clearly sophomoric interpretation of what is free speech intended for individuals, not corporate, union or other political organizations. The Constitution itself begins with "We the people...", not "We the corporations, unions and the PACs that represent us..."

Justice Roberts initially shrugged off the criticism of *Citizens United*, but eventually seemed to grasp that the decision did not serve the common good, because it leads to elections bought and sold by big money, not big ideas. As such, he sided with the moderates on the Court in their ruling regarding the Affordable Care Act (ACA). The decision, titled *National Federation of Independent Business vs. Sebelius, Secretary of Health and Human Services*, concluded that the penalty described in the law was a tax, although the Court stated clearly that the act compelled commerce, but did not regulate it. This provision of the law was ruled unconstitutional as unable to compel a mandate to have insurance.

What the Court did affirm was the fact that "Neither the ACA nor any other law attaches negative legal consequences to not buying health insurance beyond requiring a payment to the IRS", and it does not regard not having insurance as "unlawful conduct". The Court felt that a tax levied on individuals and business was within the Congress's power to tax and was constitutional.

However, the Court felt that compelling the States to comply with the ACA by threatening them with the loss of Medicaid funds was "economic dragooning", and that the shift to cover the population with incomes more than 133% of the poverty level was too dramatic a transformation and declared the provision unconstitutional. That provision of the law was to be withdrawn, but any offer of Federal help to expand Medicaid of any state "willing to participate" was permissible.

A statement of Court humility emerged in the ruling, apparently stung by its maladroit *Citizens United* decision which tore down years of precedent, the Court intoned: "When a Court confronts an unconstitutional statute, its endeavor must be to conserve, not destroy, the legislation." Let us pray that the Court finds wisdom in its own words in its future decisions.

The Role Police Forces

During the Trump Administration a series of shootings and manslaughter by municipal police led to months-long outbreaks of protests in many big and medium size cities decrying the use of lethal force on persons of color. The first seminal instance was a man selling "loose" cigarettes in New York City, a misdemeanor that by passes the collection of taxes, which is the actual majority their retail cost. The seller was placed on sidewalk pavement whereby officers held him down. Even though he told the officers of his health problems, they ignored his calls that he "could not breathe", resulting in his death. Another incident in Minneapolis where a man used a counterfeit $20 for purchase which was reported to local police. The reluctance of the purchaser to enter a police squad car led to some scuffling and the man was placed downward, where weight was applied to his back and neck for about 8 minutes, resulting in asphyxiation and death. The third highly significant incident occurred in Atlanta where a no-knock warrant was issued, supposedly for possession or sale of illegal drugs. The ensuing break-in of the motel room resulted in a young woman hit by multiple bullets and her death.

The political response has primarily been for better training of officers and decreasing the influence of their unions in protecting offending officers. The controversial concept of "defunding" the police is not as divisive as it sounds; it actually is a diversion of some funds to other agencies that can do a better job of remedying problems rather than police officers with guns and their authority to arrest persons for minor crimes or ordinances. Although the protests focused primarily on one race of people, this sort of police brutality extends and occurs to all persons, whether they are black, brown, red and even white.

Examples of funding diversion include using social service employees to resolve domestic disputes; using psychologists and social workers to resolve problems or intervene with police to better handle persons with mental difficulties, such as schizophrenia, bipolar disorder or dementia. With respect to homelessness, many cities and towns can refurbish properties obtained at low cost for temporary shelter for homeless persons, along with providing temporary positions for employment in work not requiring skilled labor. Even traffic control could be handled by private companies instead of police officers. Police work would be confined to robberies, shootings, murder, bombings and other violent crimes, rather expending police time and resources on what is referred to as "soft crime". Many officers complain that they are given tasks outside their expertise; diversion permits them to concentrate on what they do best. Misdemeanors should be treated like traffic tickets; not grounds for arrest and the potential for brutality if compliance is not forthcoming.

Violence in our Culture

When one scans a video store surveying the movies and the electronic games, they are riddled with excessive violence, the use of weapons, blood and bizarre behavior which seems to glorify the lesser elements and baser instincts of our society. Both youth and adults spend many hours a day watching and interacting with this drivel instead of playing sports, having constructive hobbies, volunteering or maintaining their homes or the environment in general.

Presently we tax liquor and playing cards and gambling, yet these violent games and films are supposedly lumped under the rubric of "free speech" and have no excise taxes assessed on them. We spend and an extra \$2-\$3 for an X-rated sexual video which contains no overt killings, brutal savagery or torture, yet these violent R and X-rated films which have no sexual content have no additional excise taxes assigned to them. These video games and films deserve the same treatment as liquor and playing cards or lotteries, whereby at least a 5% excise tax should be assigned to an R or X-rated film or video of a particularly violent nature. The Motion Picture Industry already has a rating system whereby these excise taxes can be directly related. These "V-fees" make sense in limiting the output of this fare where the frequent use of guns and weapons and extreme violence to remedy "problems" has no real social merit and deserves no special treatment better than whiskey, wine, playing cards or lottery tickets.

SHUTDOWN INTERVENTION

During the early months of 2019, President Trump, in conflict with the Congress over the funding of a barrier wall on the US-Mexican border, withheld the pay of employees of governmental employees. This border wall had been one of his many promises offered during his campaign for the Presidency. The wall would extend from the shores of the Gulf of Mexico to the shores of the Pacific Ocean in California. Its estimated cost was \$5.3 billion, ostensibly based on a 2,500-mile-long barrier.

Since the author of this book was a former Federal employee, he decided to offer a compromise solution, but only based on 500 miles, which was purported in various studies of the actual requirements to upgrade or build new barriers in locations where trafficking was very prevalent. An email was sent to the White House outlining a barrier system consisting of driven steel sheet piles, steel angles and plates. Here is that letter email:

This email concerns the construction and design of barriers for the US-Mexican border presently under contention. The so-called "slat" design consists of equal-leg angles sharpened to a point at the top of the barrier. These angles are transversely fastened near the top and at the bottom of the barrier, presumably by welding, to provide rigidity and continuity for the angle barrier. It is suggested that whoever your contractors are that they consider the use of two steel alloys that have both excellent atmospheric corrosion resistance, very high impact toughness and weldability. These alloys are easily painted and have better durability than A588 when scratched and cut. They are ASTM A710 Grade B, which has a minimum yield strength of 70 ksi, or ASTM A606 Type 5, with a minimum yield of 50 ksi. Both these steels are easily welded with off-the-shelf electrodes. For the foundation of the barrier, instead of using reinforced concrete, the use of sheet piling is recommended. Sheet piling can be driven into soils up to 20 ft depth, making by-pass tunneling more difficult. The angle "slats" of ASTM A710 Grade B or ASTM A606 Type 5 steels can then be welded to the sheet pilings, increasing the efficiency of installation. This eliminates relying on the need for trenching and formwork associated with a reinforced concrete foundation needed for a massive masonry wall.

President Trump actually responded in a reply by email:

THE WHITE HOUSE
WASHINGTON

January 3, 2019

Instead of setting politics aside and putting the safety of our country first, Democrats in Congress have continued to obstruct. In doing so, they have refused to come together with Republicans to pass commonsense legislation that provides adequate funding to secure America's borders and prevent a partial government shut down.

As I have said throughout this process, I remain committed to finding an agreemnet that reopens our Government and ensures that our Nation's borders are safe and secure.

I urge Congress to rejoin me in Washington to immediatly pass appropriations legislation that properly addresses the critical issues affecting our Nation's security and prosperity.

Thank you for your email.

Sincerely,

Since Senators Durbin and Schumer were the principal negotiators on the matter of reconciliation with the President, a more detailed cost analysis was sent to them. This analysis is very thorough and is provided to show the reader that these leaders were given an accurate accounting of the true costs of barrier construction. Email and the cost analysis were sent to both Senators Durbin and Schumer, and is as follows:

Dear Senator Durbin,
I am writing to you regarding the current dispute over the issue of border security. This email describes a compromise barrier system for border security which is cost-effective and would apply only to locations where new barriers are needed or replace those which have deteriorated or are known to be ineffective. The unit cost for this system is $2.83 million per mile, which is only 25% of what the President has proposed on a cost per mile basis. This barrier system is limited to only 500 miles. Hopefully this proposal can be used for compromise in negotiations so that Federal employees can go back to work. I have attached a very detailed cost analysis of this sheet pile-angle barrier system for border security for your consideration.

SHEET PILE-ANGLE BARRIER SYSTEM FOR BORDER SECURITY

Design Concept
The design of this barrier system consists of flat sheet piles of 25 ft length driven to a depth of 20 to 23 ft, depending on soil conditions. Modules of 118" width and 20 ft height are then welded to the pilings. Each module has a total of twelve 5 x 5 x ½ equal leg angles that are welded together with three ½" x 12" wide steel plates at the bottom, midpoint and apex of the barrier. Each vertical angle has a 5" space between them. The module has a "shoe saddle" which is bolted and welded to the pilings to provide complete integrity to the barrier.

Each module has been kept within transportable dimensions so that any competent fabrication shop can produce them within days for shipment to construction sites.

Component Cost Breakdown
The cost computations for this system are on a per mile basis so they can be adapted for any length of steel barrier to be emplaced on an as-needed basis.

1. Sheet piles. Each flat interlocking sheet pile is 19.69" [50 cm] wide and is about 25 ft long. Since 1 mile of sheet piling is required, the total number of piles is 5280 ft ÷ (19.69 / 12) = 3,218 piles.

2. Pile and driving costs. According to the 2009 *NASSPA Retaining Wall Comparison Technical Report*, the cost per lineal ft is $143 or $7.53 per square ft. Since a 25 ft pile of 19.69" width and has a surface area of 1.64 ft x 25 ft = 41 ft^2, the cost of installation per pile is 41 ft^2 x $7.53 / ft^2 = $309. Since 3,218 piles must be driven per mile, the pile installation cost estimate is $994,362 / mile.

3. Cost escalation. According to Corps of Engineers data, the cost escalation factor for general construction from 2009 to 2019 is approximately 1.29. The cost of pile installation therefore increases from $994,362 to $1,282,727 per mile.

4. Vertical elements. The vertical elements of the barrier consist of 5 x 5 x ½ thick equal leg angles that are 20 ft in height, with points at the apex of the barrier. They are then welded to ½ x 12" wide plates, resulting in a 118" wide module. Modules have a "shoe" which fits like a saddle onto sheet piling whereby the modules are then bolted and welded to the sheet pilings. Since the modules are 118" wide (9.83 ft), then 537 modules are needed for one mile of barrier.

5. Angles required. For 118" wide modules stretching over 6 flat piles, 12 angles are needed. The total number of angles is therefore 537 x 12 = 6,444 angles per mile.

6. Set up and welding of the modules. A set-up time of 30 minutes is estimated to prepare each module for fabrication. Since set up time is 30 minutes at $75/hr (includes overhead), the total cost for 537 modules is 537 x 0.5 x $75/hr = $20,138. Welding processes used would have a minimum deposition rate of 12 inches/min. A total of 72 inches of welding is required per angle, of which there are 12 angles. Total welding time is 72 x 12 = 864 inches, which would be welded in 72 minutes.

7. Fabrication costs. Since there are 537 modules, total welding time is 72 x 537 = 36,664 minutes = 644 hours. At a rate of $75/hr, the cost of welding is 644 hrs x $75/hr = $48,330. The cost of AWS E7018 electrodes is about $4.25 / lb. Total volume of weld metal for a ½" fillet weld for a module is ½ x ½ x 72 x 6,444 angles = 115,992 in³. The weight of the weld metal is (volume) x (density) = 115,992 in³ x 0.28 lbs/in³ = 32,477 lbs. At $4.25 per lb, the cost of electrodes for all 537 modules is 32,478 lbs x $4.25 = $138,032 per mile.

8. Cost of angles. The total tonnage for the angle portion of the barrier is determined in this paragraph. There are 6,444 angles of dimension 5 x 5 x ½" of 20 ft length at 16.2 lbs / ft, whereby each angle weighs 324 lbs. Total weight of these angles is 324 lbs x 6,444 angles = 2,087,856 lbs. The current average North American steel price for structural sections is about $928 / tonne, which is equivalent to $0.422 / lb. Cost for the angles is $0.422 x 2,087,856 lbs = $881,075 per mile.

9. Cost of plates. The total cost of the ½ x 12" plates of the barrier is determined in this paragraph. There are 4 plates for each 118" wide module, which comes to 472" for each module. The plate volume for each module is 0.5 x 12 x 472 = 2,832 in³. Since steel has a density of 0.283 lbs/in³,

the weight of this volume is 801 lbs. Since there are 537 modules, the total weight of the plates is 801 lbs x 537 = 430,137 lbs. The current price in North America for hot rolled plate is about $1032 / tonne, which is $0.469 / lb. The cost of plates for 537 modules is 430,137 lbs x $0.469/lb = $201,773.

10. Summary of fabrication costs per mile. For 537 modules, the total cost includes set up, welding time and cost of electrodes. Cost of bolts and drilling holes to attach the modules to sheet piling was considered as incidental. The labor costs per mile are $20,138 for set up and $48,330 for welding time. Materials costs are $138,032 for electrodes; $881,075 for angles and $201,773 for plates.

Summary of Costs per Mile

The costs for pile material and driving costs are $1,282,727 per mile. The fabrication costs include welding assembly and material costs for angles, plates and electrodes. Here is an itemized list of costs per mile:

A. Piles and driving costs	$1,282,727
B. Module fabrication	
(1) Set-up	20,138
(2) Welding	48,330
(3) Electrodes.............	138,032
C. Vertical element materials	
(1) 5 x 5 x ½" x 20 ft angles	
....	881,075
(2) 1 x 12 hot rolled plates	
....	201,773
D. Total cost per mile	$2,572,075

Unit Cost Per Mile + Contingencies

The calculated unit cost per mile is $2,572,075. Because there are always unexpected issues that arise during construction, a contingency of 10% was applied to the unit cost per mile. With a 10% contingency, the unit cost is adjusted to $2,829,283 per mile.

According to news reports, only about 500 miles of new barrier need to be emplaced or replace existing barriers or fenced sections that have deteriorated. To fabricate and install 500 miles of sheet pile-angle barriers, the total cost was estimated at $2,829,283 per mile x 500 miles = $1,414,641,250. This estimate of $1.4 billion, which includes a 10% contingency, could be re-adjusted by a 20% contingency which would consider other unanticipated conditions.

The final figures in this detailed cost analysis were used directly by the negotiators with President Trump at $1.375 billion for 486 miles of barrier. Ultimately the offer was rejected by the President, who desired the entire 2,500-mile length of the barrier. Although no agreement was reached on wall funding, at least the shutdown was terminated, and Federal employees went back to work. Subsequently the President sought funding by taking appropriated funds from other agencies, much to the dismay of the Congress.

GROUNDS FOR IMPEACHMENT

Since his election in 2016, the Trump Administration has been a chaotic organization, both in policy and in radical dismissals of cabinet officers confirmed by the Senate.

Immigration policy has been discriminatory, in frequent violation with court orders confirmed under previous administrations, rife with a clear animus toward persons from certain countries of origin. This included persons with Islamic backgrounds, Hispanic origins, and other persons of color. Although this country needs persons with substantial skills, this is not always present when large contingents of refugees arrive seeking asylum. However, the clear need for persons willing to do manual labor in agricultural and service work of generally lesser pay than skilled labor can be satisfied by training such refugees and assisting them and their children in learning the English language.

Trump intervention in trade policy has been disastrous both for importers and the stock market in general. Looking for domestic sources on such short notice has been problematic for many manufacturers when tariffs were imposed on goods from China and other countries.

The lack of diplomacy with European allied leaders and deprecation of NATO led to the resignation of Generals Mattis (Secretary of Defense) and McMaster (National Security Advisor). Due to disagreements with Secretary of State Rex Tillerson over foreign policy, he was replaced by Mike Pompeo, a hawkish Congressman from Kansas. Trump has gone through three National Security advisors, Generals Flynn and McMaster and John Bolton. He has named a fourth advisor, who was an aide to Bolton.

Although such chaos would be grounds for separation in any decent corporation or organization, none of these policies or events are actual grounds for impeachment. The Constitution lays out specific grounds in Section 4 of Article II: "The President, Vice President and all civil Officers of the United States, shall be removed from Office on Impeachment for, and Conviction of, Treason, Bribery or other high Crimes and Misdemeanors." Moreover, in Article III, Section 3, Treason is also defined: "Treason against the United States, shall consist only in levying War against them, or in adhering to their Enemies, giving them Aid and Comfort."

The actual articles of impeachment submitted by the House Judiciary Committee to the Senate are shown in an appendix to this section at the end of this book. They are sparse and make few references to violations of statutory law, a fatal flaw that was exploited by counsels for the defense of President Trump. In this book, references are cited where the President directly violated specific statutes of the US Code.

This section of the book is divided into two parts. The first part concerns the actions regarding the intervention of Russia in the 2016 election, cyberattacks and false postings of negative information on the internet. The second part is based on the actions of the President with respect to his attempts to obtain information on a potential rival whereby he withholds military and financial assistance to Ukraine of $390,000,000 until the President of Ukraine holds a press conference stating that Joe and Hunter Biden are under investigation.

After the firing of FBI James Comey, a special investigation was undertaken by former director of the FBI Robert Mueller III. The final report of Director Mueller and his staff provided details in great depth regarding the interactions between officials of the Trump campaign and other appointed officials after the election with the Russian government. Wikileaks, an internet ally of the Russian government with a history of distributing damaging political information, was also involved. The Mueller report also describes efforts by Trump himself and his subordinates to obstruct investigations into his conduct, not only including his interactions with the government of Russia, but also financial transactions relating to his businesses and political activities.

Trump has long been interested in establishing hotels in various parts of the world, including Russia and particularly in Moscow. He had indicated his desire to build lavish penthouses for President Putin and his close associates. During testimony before the Congress, Trump's personal attorney Michael Cohen had indicated that Trump had only pursued the Presidency to further publicize the Trump "brand" and did not seriously consider that he would win the election.

The so-called "Steele Dossier" was actually a notification to the FBI by British intelligence that there was a long-standing interest by Trump in Russia to obtain real estate locations for his hotels and casinos. Russian officials had a preference for Trump over Hillary Clinton, who they considered as essentially hostile to their government and her disapproval of the manner how officials were elected and maintained their positions and power in Russia.

When Trump was notified of Russian interactions with respect to election interference, he elected not only to ignore such warnings, but went out of his way to treat the information as if it was derived from "partisan Democrats", even though most intelligence operatives are politically neutral, often lean Republican or are donors to the Republican Party; some are Democrats.

The following are specific grounds for impeachment based on violation of existing laws enumerated and described as criminal acts in the United States Code of Laws (US Code). They include aiding and abetting criminal acts, abrogation of the oath of office, obstruction of justice, and recently, extortion and bribery to obtain adverse information on an upcoming political opponent from the Ukrainian government.

Aiding and Abetting Criminal Acts

In the midst of the campaign, Trump called on the Russian government in a most public manner: "Russia, if you're listening, find the 30,000 missing emails of Hillary Clinton." Immediately after this announcement, the Russian internet hacking organization GRU began searching emails of the Democratic National Committee and distributed the emails they had obtained through downloads to Wikileaks.

This supposedly "flippant" request for hacking of emails started only because prior knowledge and communication between the Russian government and the Trump campaign had already been established.

Wikileaks distributed thousands of emails from the computer files of the Democratic National Committee intent on damaging the Clinton campaign.

Roger Stone, a close associate of President Trump, acknowledged their receipt. Other meetings to obtain adverse political information were conducted in Trump Tower in New York by Trump's son Donald Jr. and Paul Manafort, their campaign manager, who had extensive political ties with members of the Ukrainian government that had strong ties with Russia. Subsequently Manafort shared polling data such that better social media advertisements could be targeted to specific voting districts to improve Trump's chances of election.

Prior to the election, several election boards of the various States were hacked in attempts to determine status of voting rolls, as to who is registered and their identities. Presumably the intent of hacking was to possibly disrupt the registration status of voters where party affiliation is known based on what primary the voter casts a ballot. Since many of the States would not disclose the extent of hacking, it remains indeterminate whether this directly affected election results.

The elements for the aiding and abetting of a criminal act and its conviction are described in 18 US Code Section 2, sub section 2474, as follows: (1) the accused had specific intent to facilitate the commission of a crime by another; (2) had the requisite intent of the underlying substantive offense; (3) assisted or participated in the commission of the underlying substantive offense; and (4) that someone committed the underlying offense.

Trump and his associates clearly intended to have emails hacked and facilitated it by invitation to the Russian government, and brazenly stated so. They assisted in the dissemination of the hacked emails in cooperation with Wikileaks, and it is obvious from intelligence and FBI reports that the GRU, an agency of the Russian government, committed the offense.

The crime committed was a violation of the Computer Fraud and Trespassing Act. This law is described in 18 US Code Section 1030 Subsection (3). It is unlawful to trespass on non-public or government computers, especially intending to access and obtain something of value. The elements of this crime are: (1) knowingly access a protected computer; (2) intend to defraud the owner of the computer; (3) access furthered the defraud, and (4) obtained anything of value exceeding $5,000.

In the case of the GRU, the Trump campaign associates, most logically with the assent of Trump himself who requested it, the hacking was not "harmless or incidental" but purposeful and was intended to obtain political information considered as secret or confidential. The political information, if obtained by other means, would certainly have cost more than $5,000. At this moment in time, its value is probably immeasurable, considering that Mr. Trump was elected President.

Bribery and the Foreign Corrupt Practices Act

In the newest set of revelations, it appears President Trump did not take heed regarding the solicitation of negative information about his political opponents from foreign sources. His actions through his representatives Gordon Sondland, Ambassador to the European Union, his personal attorney Rudy Guiliani and Chief of Staff Mick Mulvaney, withheld $391,000,000 of military security funds before Ukrainian officials announced that investigations of Hunter Biden, a board member of Ukrainian energy company Burisma, were publicly announced. According to a whistle blower complaint filed in 2019 regarding his conversations with the President of Ukraine, Trump repeatedly requested negative information regarding the activities of Hunter Biden, son of former Vice President Biden, when he was a board member of the Ukrainian natural gas company Burisma. If such information was not received, the military aid to Ukraine to fend off Russian separatists previously passed by the Congress would be withheld. This is a simple case of requesting something in turn for a price. It is bribery and extortion based on the promised release of millions of dollars intended for the defense of Ukraine in exchange for negative information on the Vice President Biden and his son Hunter. This offense is grounds for impeachment as specified in Article III, Section 4 of the Constitution, and was a violation of the International Anti-Bribery and Fair Competition Act of 1998 and the Foreign Corrupt Practices Act.

Bribery is well defined in18 US Code Section 201 entitled "Bribery of Public Officials and Witnesses. This act covers all public officials. Most pertinent is subsection (b) which states that "whoever directly or indirectly gives, offers or promises anything of value (in this case $391,000,000) to any public official...with intent to (A) influence any official act and also in (c) (B) directly or indirectly gives, offers or promises anything of value to any public official, for or because of any official act performed or to be performed by such public official..."

It is surmised that the House Judiciary Committee did not invoke this statute is because the actual acceptance of the bribe was not completed because of the invention of the whistleblower who reported the bribe to the Inspector General of the National Security Council.

According to the Department of Justice, since 1977, the anti-bribery of the Foreign Corrupt Practices Act of 15 US Code Section 78 dd-1 has applied to all US citizens and foreign issuers of securities. The act specifically states "by any means of instrumentality (in this case transfer of military assistance funds) a promise to pay, or authorization of the payment of money to any person...to a foreign official in his official capacity, induce the foreign official to do..an act in violation of his lawful duty or secure an improper advantage..." is "unlawful". Because this is primarily a securities act, this may be the reason why the articles of impeachment only refer to abuse of power, rather than bribery per se because one might consider that the President was not issuing any "security", although the $391,000,000 was for "military security" purposes.

Impoundment Control Act
The withholding of these funds to aid Ukraine in its defense from Russian incursion, which had been approved by Congress and even signed into law by Trump himself, was a violation of the Impoundment Control Act (2 US Code Sections 681-688). In its decision regarding the withholding of this military security assistance, the General Accounting Office (GAO), notified the ranking members of the House and Senate Committees on Appropriations that Trump was required to notify the Congress if those funds were placed in abeyance and the reason why they were placed on hold. Contrary to this requirement, Trump thought he could secretly withhold the funds transfer, but was identified by a whistleblower, thought to be a CIA employee.

The GAO decision summarily states that the statute, Supreme Court case law, and the Constitution itself indicates that there is "... no basis to interpret the Impoundment Control Act as a mechanism by which the President may unilaterally abridge the enacted period of availability of fixed-period appropriation. The Constitution vests in Congress the power of the purse and did not cede this important power..."

According to the GAO letter to the Congress, the "Constitution does not authorize the President 'to enact, to amend or to repeal statutes.'" He must faithfully the laws, and take care that funds are obligated within the period of their availability. If extensions are required, the Congress must be notified. Trump ignored all these requirements by withholding funds without any notice to Congress, which has the sole authority over obligation of funds.

The Director of National Intelligence, a Trump appointee, withheld the whistleblower complaint from the House Intelligence Committee, also a statutory requirement. The unclassified portion of the complaint was released and indicated an attempt to obtain negative information from a foreign source for a domestic campaign. Suppression of witnesses to testify who heard the conversation between Trump and the President Zelensky of Ukraine and hiding the transcribed unclassified conversation into secret files can be construed as obstruction of justice.

Subsequently in an appearance before his supporters, Trump characterized the whistleblower and any of the witnesses to his conversation with Zelensky as "spies" and further stated that spies in the past were treated as traitors. Spies were often executed, particularly during wartime. Having a President conveying such a veiled threat is unseemly for someone occupying such high office. Trump bristles with the concept and intentions of whistleblowers who negatively report on his activities but would probably praise them if they disclosed information beneficial to his own interests.

The entire concept of a whistleblower started when accountant Ernest Fitzgerald reported on the cost overruns on the C5-A aircraft and received death threats. Similarly, death threats were made against whistleblower Dr. Jeffrey Wigand who reported on how the Brown & Williamson tobacco company withheld data on the carcinogenic and addictive nature of chemicals added to cigarettes. Whistleblowers are persons who realize that criminality and fraud must be reported to stop the activity, lest it result in public harm. By withholding military aid to Ukraine, more casualties of Ukrainians and further incursion of Russian forces could occur if the request for damaging political information was not obtained. Because the Defense Department opposed the withholding of funds that were appropriated by the Congress, they were subsequently reinstated to defuse the issue.

Obstruction of Justice

Obstruction of justice was the basis by which President Nixon resigned from office. He did so because he was a lawyer who firmly believed in the force of law, and the Republicans in Congress felt the evidence against Mr. Nixon was too compelling to support his continuance in office. That situation is not applicable today with the Republican Party no longer operating as the "loyal opposition" and literally railing against the intelligence and investigatory agencies they previously considered as always above board. In general, they are treating disclosure of adverse information as disloyalty and any officeholder of their party in agreement with the intelligence findings as eligible for targeting in a primary election.

In stark contrast with Nixon, Mr. Trump considers lawyers to be useful for his own purposes and a means to counter any moves by governmental or law enforcement officials that could impede his objectives. In his many business ventures, he used his lawyers to intimidate smaller firms who performed construction work to either reduce their payments due, or to stymie their efforts after they imposed liens on his various properties.

The start of the Mueller investigation began when Trump invited then FBI Director James Comey to dinner at the White House. Trump inquired whether he was under investigation by the FBI. Although informed that he was not, Trump was not convinced and fired Comey. This resulted in the appointment of former FBI director Mueller as Special Counsel, resulting in very serious disclosures of the many interactions between Trump campaign officials and the Russian government.

Other obstructions occurred prior to the dismissal of Comey. Trump was careful to require other subordinates to stop investigations or have others dismiss investigating agents. He asked his former campaign manager Corey Lewandowski and White House lawyer Don McGahn to arrange the dismissal of Attorney Jeff Sessions, who had recused himself from any investigations involving Trump campaign contacts and the Russian government.

Sessions also had contacts with Russian officials but denied such contacts in Congressional testimony. Concerned with perjury and possible penalties, he dismissed Deputy Director McCabe who was investigating whether there was enough evidence to charge Sessions with perjury. In a subsequent meeting, Trump requested that Sessions "unrecuse" himself from the Russia investigation.

Sessions was replaced by William Barr, an attorney who previously had served in the Bush Administration. Since his appointment to Attorney General, Barr has acted as a loyal defender of the President and is an avowed protector of the executive branch of the US Government. Barr, like the recent appointee Brett Kavanaugh to the Supreme Court, is an advocate of the "unitary theory of government".

The "unitary theory of government" purports that the President controls all agencies of executive authority, effectively limiting power of Congress to control or limit the powers of executive officers who are only subordinate to the President. According to this theory, independent agencies, such as the Federal Reserve or Special Counsels like Robert Mueller, are supposedly "unconstitutional" because they have discretion to act beyond the control of the President.

However, Congress does have such constitutional authority in Article I, Section 8, last paragraph: "To make all Laws which shall be necessary and proper for carrying into Execution the foregoing Powers, and all other Powers vested by this Constitution in the Government of the United States, or in any Department or Officer thereof." This section clearly enumerates that the Congress has power over the Executive and can require any Department, create any governmental instrumentality, or require any executive to comport in accordance with the laws they pass. Considering at the time of the writing and ratification of the Constitution, the founders were very aware of the powers of their former king. They wanted the source of governmental power to be lodged with representatives of the people, not in a powerful executive who could be completely independent and rule without consent of the electorate. The unitary theory of government is an overreach advocated by those who desire executive conduct to be above, or out of the reach, of certain laws passed by Congress.

There were additional efforts by the President to claim "executive privilege" for his subordinates and ordered their refusal to testify before Congressional committees. During many of their hearings under oath, they claimed such privilege or lack of recall of events. In the case of his personal attorney Michael Cohen, when his office records were seized by a search warrant, he urged his attorney to "stay strong" and not "flip". After Cohen realized that his sentencing would occur, he cooperated with legal authorities, whereby Trump termed him a "rat".

The statute governing of obstruction of justice is located in 18 US Code Chapter 73. Sections pertinent obstruction of justice to President Trump and his associates are as follows:

(1) 1505, Obstruction of Proceedings before Departments and Committees, as shown by Trump not permitting staff officers to appear before committees, claiming "privilege", or providing very limited testimony, or even defiance to comply with committee requests.

(2) 1510, Obstruction of Criminal Investigations, as shown by the dismissal of Attorney General Sessions, FBI Director Comey and Deputy Director McCabe.

(3) 1511, Obstruction of State and Local Law Enforcement, as shown by refusal to cooperate with the Attorney General of New York regarding income tax filings and bank records.

(4) 1512 and 1513, Tampering with, or Retaliating against, a Witness, Victim or Informant, as committed by Paul Manafort, his campaign manager prior to his trial and encouragement by Trump to remain loyal.

(5) 1516, Obstruction of Federal Audit, a long-standing problem where Trump has resisted any disclosure of his Federal income tax returns.

(6) 1517, Obstructing of Examination of a Financial Institution, which relates to his opposition and filing of countersuit to prevent disclosure of his dealings with Deutsche Bank.

(7) 1521, Retaliating against a Federal Judge of Federal Law Enforcement Officer by False Claim or Slander of Title, which relates to his conduct with respect to immigration judges and terming FBI and other intelligence personnel as "traitors" and causing their dismissal.

Violation of Federal Election Law

Prior to his election, Trump was concerned about public knowledge of his prior exploits of womanizing and involvement in sexual activities considered as unappealing for someone seeking the office of President. Trump had sexual interactions with many women; he bragged about his inability to contract sexually transmitted diseases during the period of his military deferral from the Vietnam Conflict.

A published photograph of a smiling Trump standing next to adult film star "Stormy Daniels" (actual name Stephanie Clifford) at Wicked Pictures indicates his pleasure over the encounter. Similarly, he had sexual interactions with model Karen McDougal (Playboy Playmate of the Year, 1998). Although these are salacious events, non-disclosure payments were made to these women to conceal Trump's sexual activities with them, as testified to by his attorney Michael Cohen before Congress. The payments were intended to silence the women so as not to sully Trump's reputation as a candidate. Because of their magnitude, they can be considered as campaign finance contributions because they were related to a presidential election. Some would argue that these were merely non-disclosure payments, but they are too coincidental and were made specifically to cover up undesirable background information that could have diminished his standing as a presidential candidate.

According to the Bipartisan Campaign Reform Act of 2002, which is codified in 2 US Code 431, the limit that an individual can contribute to his candidacy from his own personal funds is $150,000 + $0.04 x voting population, when there are opposition funds to the candidacy. This limit was not overturned by the *Citizens United* decision of the Supreme Court. However, when the non-disclosure payments were made to Ms. Clifford and Ms. McDougal, Trump's candidacy had not yet been announced, so there was no opposition funding. The non-disclosure payments were more than $150,000, which exceeded the Federal election "threshold limit".

This offense should probably be considered as a "misdemeanor", since it is more of a technical violation of 2 US Code 431, considering the vast sums of money that are involved in political campaigns.

Abrogation of the Oath of Office

When a President is sworn into office, he takes the following oath as required by the Constitution in the last paragraph of Article I, Section One, "I do solemnly swear (or affirm) that I will faithfully execute the Office of President of the United States, and will to the best of my ability, preserve, protect and defend the Constitution of the United States".

The Constitution consists of articles and several amendments, some of which are more important than others. The first 11 amendments were ratified by 1797, of which the first guarantees the "freedom of the press", which today constitutes of both print and electronic media that disperses news to the public at large.

Trump has gone out of his way to describe newspapers and electronic news outlets as distributing "fake news" and disallowed several members of the media to ask questions of him or his spokespersons. He has termed the media as "enemies of the people", which is clearly at odds with his oath to defend their freedom. He could simply not respond to their questions by the phrase "no comment", but instead terms them as a threat to his office.

The founders clearly understood that their revolution against Britain could not have begun without newspapers describing the need for defiance against the crown.

Emoluments

According to Article 2, "The President shall receive, at stated times, receive for his services, a Compensation, which shall neither be increased or diminished during the Period for which he shall been elected, and shall not receive within that Period any other Emolument from the United States, or any of them."

The antiquated word "emolument" is defined by the American Heritage Dictionary as "payment for an office or employment; compensation." The word is derived from old Middle English for the fee paid to grind grain.

The founders were concerned about one state influencing the President over the others, or that he could derive income from his office over and above his compensation determined by the Congress. In the present circumstances, it has been revealed that one of Trump's properties in Scotland received fueling and landing fees from the US Air Force, rather than land or refuel at other more convenient locations. Similarly, he has sent several staff, including the Vice President, to stay at his resorts.

He requested that a G7 meeting of foreign representatives be held at one of his hotels. This offense would probably be considered as a "misdemeanor", although the offenses of aiding and abetting criminal acts and obstruction would be "high crimes" in constitutional parlance. When resistance from the Republican Party surfaced to the proposed G7 stay at his Doral resort, Trump described the emoluments clause of Article I Section 9, which prohibits acceptance of compensations from kings, princes or foreign states, as "phony". To describe constitutional requirements as false or counterfeit is in direct violation of his sworn oath to uphold them.

Treason

The Constitution defines treason in Article III Section 3 as "Treason against the United States, shall consist only in levying War against them, or Adhering to their Enemies, giving them Aid and Comfort."

This offense can only be applied if the United States considers Russia as its enemy. During the "Cold War" following World War II, the United States considered the Soviet Union as an "political enemy" but was its ally during World War II for convenience, since Russia was attacked when Germany was under National Socialist (Nazi) control. The founders could have never conceived of a "cyber war", much less even understood the electronic state of the physical world.

However, during the election of 2016, the United States was under cyber-attack by Russia, but Trump and his associates denied any such actions, sided with Russian President Putin, and Trump literally degraded his own intelligence agencies. One could describe such actions as giving "aid and comfort" to our enemies.

Because the United States is not officially at war with Russia, although its relations and policies are often at odds with the United States, this offense is tenuous at best, but could be considered serious if the United States was in actual conflict where American military forces were engaged against Russian forces.

At present our only conflicts with Russia have largely been confined to "electronic warfare", although electronic hacking and disruption of our electrical grid, sanitary systems and water supply could adversely affect the entire population of the United States.

Electronic warfare may be a portent of the future, rather than an exchange of nuclear weapons, which could put the planet into a semi-permanent condition of "nuclear winter".

Impeachment Acquittal

In the end, all the citations of abuse power presented by House managers before the US Senate, controlled by the Republicans by a 53-49 majority, basically concluded that all of Trump's actions were "insufficient to be impeachable". Only Republican Sen. Mitt Romney of Utah cast a guilty vote; the remainder voted along party lines.

The potential future import of this acquittal of very serious constitutional breaches of established law is that when the Senate is controlled by the same party of the President, impeachment and conviction becomes virtually unlikely. Articles of impeachment submitted by the House will be considered as "insufficient to rise to a level" needed for conviction by the Senate.

It is now understandable why an Independent Party must be established, because one of the major parties during the recent impeachment literally suspended their Constitutional oaths of allegiance to enforce that established laws be faithfully executed by the President. Independent Senators would not be bound to either party but could continue to exercise proper judgment without political pressure applied to them by one of the two major parties. An independent party provides some objectivity which is often missing during these rancorous times.

The Corona Virus

The inability of the Trump Administration to prevent the spread of the corona virus has compounded even more problems for the United States. This is in addition to the lack of cooperation between the House controlled by the Democrats and the Senate controlled by the Republicans.

The novel corona virus was first known by scores of infections which occurred in Wuhan, China. It is known from previous corona virus epidemic, such as SARS-1, that the virus originated from animal species sold in open markets in China. The virus is spherical-shaped, with protein spikes that are spread through aerosols, personal contact, and remain live for several hours on various surfaces, such as paper, metals or ceramics. The virus primarily enters the respiratory system through nasal passages, and then enters the lungs, whereby it reproduces. Depending on the immune response of the person inflected, the Covid-19 disease can result in fever, fatigue, brain fog and breathing difficulty. If the person overcomes the disease and develops immunity, often times there may be residual effects of Covid-19 on the lungs, heart and circulatory system. In some cases, death may result, particularly in the elderly or those with compromised or diminished immune systems. Although multiple vaccines are in developed, none have been approved yet for wide scale use.

Initially a task force created by the Obama Administration to limit the spread of infectious diseases was abandoned by John Bolton, head of the National Security Council, as unnecessary. During Trump's discussions with President Xi of China over trade disputes with that country, Xi indicated that the corona virus originating from the city of Wuhan was "under control". However, it is now apparent that Chinese travelers were actually transmitting this virus throughout the world because it is now known that carriers may be asymptomatic, not showing elevated temperatures, fever or cough.

Although Alex Azar, head of Health & Human Services, warned the Trump cabinet of the danger of the spread of this virus based on his past experiences, his warnings were largely minimized. Trump for months basically stated that the virus was "under control", that it was really a simple influenza that would dissipate in warm weather, and hyped an anti-malaria drug called hydrochloroquinone (HCQ) as a "cure", although the initial French study was based on a limited number of patients and augmented by azithromycin, an antibiotic. Eventually it was determined that the HCQ drug was inefficient and of limited benefit.

Concerned about his record of economic expansion and employment gains, Trump encouraged reopening of businesses to offset the massive unemployment needed to limit the spread of the virus by "stay at home orders" issued by state governors. A large virus relief package was brokered between the House and Senate and the White House to provide for the unemployed and business loans to keep many companies afloat. As this package was put together, it became evident that were critical shortages of protective clothing for health care workers and equipment needed for patient recovery and survival. Trump refused to invoke the Defense Production Act, even though he declared the virus pandemic a national emergency, for fear of antagonizing his corporate supporters. Although he relented by floating massive contracts for medical supplies and ventilators, it became apparent that there were insufficient stockpiles and that much production capacity for supplies was located offshore, increasing our vulnerability.

As the number of corona virus deaths steadily increased above 100,000, blame was placed on state governments rather than an inadequate Federal response. States struggled with reduced revenues and overburdened hospitals; some states reduced cases by use of distancing, closing non-critical businesses and mandatory use of masks and face coverings to limit transmission of the virus. However, the Trump Administration left this up to state and local officials, and for many months, required those around him to practice safer health practices, but did not want to look "weak" by wearing a mask in public.

Subsequently as the number of cases and deaths began to resurge, Republicans opposed greater deficit spending and could not agree with the Democratic House over funding for unemployment, state fiscal relief and vaccine development and distribution. The House had proposed a $3 trillion package whereas the Senate Republicans were at $1 trillion. A compromise is needed, but recalcitrance on both sides seems to be the order of the day. As the parties dither over what is the proper course of action and resolution, thousands of Americans die each week due to a virus that clearly is not a simple influenza, but is advanced in biological survivability and leaves lasting effects even after the patient is supposedly cured. Many experts do not expect this virus to disappear without strict adherence to methods to contain and find an effective vaccine. Whether such a vaccine will provide antibodies that lasts for years to contain or limit virus reproduction is yet fully tested and delivered in large quantities.

After months of Trump indicating that the virus was "under control" or would be extinguished by warm weather and "miraculously disappear", the number of cases continually increased but then started to abate after "stay at home" orders issued by states went into effect, along with the closure of restaurants, bars and physical fitness centers. Trump continually downplayed the importance of masks, often mocking Democrats for their emphasis on them. He held rallies where masks were "optional", only to lead to spread of the virus. Eventually his recalcitrance to face coverings caught up with him and he and his close advisor Hope Hicks caught the virus and required hospitalization.

It is not known when Trump was infected, because although he is tested "regularly", that interval of testing was not disclosed. At his rushed introduction of a conservative judge to the Supreme Court where no face masks or distancing was required, numerous officials caught the virus, in addition to members of the Joint Chiefs of Staff who may have contracted the virus at a Gold Star Mothers event.

After Trump's fever and condition worsened, he was sent to Walter Reed Hospital in Washington where he received the finest treatments available, including the anti-viral drug remdesiver, monoclonal antibodies, an experimental drug not available to the general public, and dexamethasone, an anti-inflammatory steroid. This level of excellent treatment would not have been generally available to the millions of cases who sustained the effects of the virus, nor to the more than 500,00 persons who died from Covid-19 (as of March 2021).

Apparently putting pressure on his military personal physician to have him released from Walter Reed Hospital, Trump returned to the White House and later "tweeted" that "Don't be afraid of the Covid-19"... and "Don't let it dominate your life". This was of little comfort to those who lost relatives to the disease, nor did they have the world-class care available to them like the President. The entire episode smacked of bravado and self-importance rather than treating a pandemic with the seriousness it deserved since the corona virus had taken almost 4 times the number of dead than the Vietnam Conflict in a span of 9 months compared to 5 years in Vietnam.

It is now understandable why an Independent Party must be established, because the two major parties have failed to adequately promote the general welfare and provide domestic tranquility to meet their Constitutional oaths of allegiance. A president must be elected to ensure that established laws are "faithfully executed". Independent legislators would not be obligated to either party and could use logical judgment about major issues and legislation to address them without political pressure from the two major parties.

THE DISTORTION OF THE ELECTORAL COLLEGE

The authors of the Constitution were troubled that the choice for President and Vice President could be selected by mass popularity. They were concerned that candidates of inexperience and potentially lesser moral character could be elected as President. To counteract this possibility, they determined that only knowledgeable "electors" should act as representatives of the general population to select the best choice for president. It was a time when the clear majority of the population voting for president had a limited and compressed sense of what government should accomplish. Similarly, since

Senators would have a term of six years, Senators were chosen by legislatures to represent the state. This was overturned by the 17th Amendment (ratified in 1914) whereby senators are directly elected by the people.

Presently each state legislates how the sum total of popular votes will determine how the electors will vote for President. Only a few states determine this by allocation of the popular vote, whereas the remainder choose a single slate of electors, based on which candidate receives the plurality or majority of votes. Unfortunately, this means that when final voting is tallied, the popular votes for the losing electors are completely negated. This is a distortion of the intent of the voters.

The Elections of 2016 and 2000

There have been two recent elections, in 2016 and 2000, where the selected president failed to capture the majority or plurality of the votes cast. In this chapter, a method to select electors that reflects the intentions of qualified voters is described and proposed for amendment. The proposed changes would bring the Electoral College in line with election procedures used to elect all other public officials, which is by receipt of the majority or plurality of votes cast for the candidates of President and Vice President. This can be either by distribution of votes cast among electors, or by direct popular vote.

Because each state is assigned a certain number of electoral votes, which is based on the number of Representatives and Senators assigned to it, large states like California, New York and Texas have the largest number of electors. However, smaller or lesser populated states like Rhode Island or North Dakota have a greater number of electoral votes that is not in proportion to its voting population.

To receive an electoral vote in California, with 55 electoral votes, an elector representing a specific candidate must receive 1/55 = 1.8% of the votes cast. For a state with only 3 electoral votes, an elector must receive 1/3 = 33% of the vote. In the following table for the presidential election of 2016, if an elector received less than required percentage, those electoral votes were distributed in the following table that best approximates the proportion of votes cast. If the percentages of two candidates are virtually equal, the votes are equally divided if possible. This distribution can be problematic if the number of electoral votes for the particular state is not an even number, and the other candidates received less than the required percentage for that state. The distribution of electoral votes, but only based solely on the popular vote percentages, could also be chosen by the state legislature, or by a state election commission. Since there cannot be fractional electors, the distribution of electoral votes must be fair and equitable, particularly when the number of electoral votes is limited.

Electoral Vote Distribution by State for the Election of 2016

State	Electoral Votes	% Required	% for Trump	Electoral Votes	% for Clinton	Electoral Votes	Others[A]
Alabama	9	11.1	62.9	6	34.6	3	
Alaska	3	33.3	52.9	2	37.7	1	
Arizona	11	9.0	49.5	6	45.4	5	
Arkansas	6	16.7	60.4	4	33.8	2	
California	55	1.8	32.8	18	61.6	34	3
Colorado	9	11.1	44.4	4	47.2	5	
Connecticut	7	14.3	41.2	3	54.5	4	
Delaware	3	33.3	41.9	1	53.4	2	
Dist. Columbia	3	33.3	4.1	0	92.8	3	
Florida	29	3.4	49.1	15	47.8	14	
Georgia	16	6.3	51.3	9	45.6	7	
Hawaii	4	25.0	30.1	1	62.3	3	
Idaho	4	25.0	59.2	3	27.6	1	
Illinois	20	5.0	39.4	8	55.4	11	1
Indiana	11	9.1	57.2	6	37.9	5	
Iowa	6	16.7	51.8	3	42.2	3	
Kansas	6	16.7	57.2	4	36.2	2	
Kentucky	8	12.5	62.5	5	32.7	3	
Louisiana	8	12.5	58.1	5	38.4	3	
Maine	4	25.0	47.9	2	45.2	2	
Maryland	10	10.0	35.3	4	60.5	6	
Massachusetts	11	9.1	33.5	4	60.8	7	
Michigan	16	6.3	47.6	8	47.3	8	
Minnesota	10	10.0	45.4	5	46.9	5	
Mississippi	6	16.7	58.3	4	39.7	2	
Missouri	10	10.0	57.1	6	38.0	4	
Montana	3	33.3	56.5	2	36.0	1	
Nevada	6	16.7	45.5	3	47.9	3	
New Hampshire	4	25.0	47.2	2	47.6	2	
New Jersey	14	7.1	41.8	6	55.0	8	
New Mexico	5	20.0	40.0	2	48.3	3	

State	Electoral Votes	% Required	% for Trump	Electoral Votes	% for Clinton	Electoral Votes	Others[A]
New York	29	3.4	37.5	11	58.8	17	1
North Carolina	15	6.7	50.5	8	46.7	7	
North Dakota	3	33.3	64.1	2	27.8	1	
Ohio	18	5.6	52.1	10	43.5	8	
Oklahoma	7	14.3	65.3	5	28.9	2	
Oregon	7	14.3	41.1	3	51.7	4	
Pennsylvania	20	5.0	48.8	10	47.6	10	
Rhode Island	4	25.0	39.8	2	55.4	2	
South Carolina	9	11.1	54.9	5	40.8	4	
South Dakota	3	33.3	61.5	2	31.7	1	
Tennessee	11	9.1	61.1	7	34.9	4	
Texas	38	2.6	52.6	20	43.4	17	1
Utah	6	16.7	45.9	3	27.8	2	1
Vermont	3	33.3	32.6	1	61.1	2	
Virginia	13	7.7	45.0	6	49.9	7	
Washington	12	8.3	38.2	5	54.4	7	
West Virginia	5	20.0	68.7	3	26.5	2	
Wisconsin	10	10.0	47.9	5	46.9	5	
Wyoming	3	33.3	70.1	3	22.5	0	
Totals	**538**	...	**49.5[B]**	**266**	**50.5[B]**	**265**	**7**

[A]Others primarily included Gary Johnson as an Independent and Jill Stein of the Green Party; Evan McMullin received 21% of the Utah vote.

[B]Percentage was based on total popular votes cast only for Clinton and Trump.

The results of the 2016 election indicate that neither Trump nor Clinton received the required 270 votes for a majority. Because there are 7 electors who had received votes, they could and most likely would have cast their votes for Clinton rather than Trump, since she had received more votes. In addition, there are so-called "faithless electors", who vote their own individual preference, often for someone who is not even a candidate desiring the office of President. If the Electoral College acted in the manner of true representation of the popular vote, the 7 electors not pledged to either Clinton or Trump could have decided the election.

Even more instructive is the election of 2000 between Governor George Bush and Vice President Al Gore. Using the same mode of assignment of electors based on the popular vote in each state, the electoral vote tallies for the presidential election of 2000 are summarized in the following table for the election of 2000.

If the popular vote was properly divided among the electors they actually voted for and their votes for the electors were not eliminated by the meddlesome interference of the legislative "winner take-all" process, Vice President Gore would have been elected, since Bush other independents, most specifically Ralph Nader, would have probably cast their electoral votes for Gore rather than Bush. would not have received the required 270 votes, even including the votes for the independent candidates also running.

Electoral Vote Distribution by State for the Election of 2000

State	Electoral Votes	% Required	% for Bush	Electoral Votes	% for Gore	Electoral Votes	Others[A]
Alabama	9	11.1	56.5	5	41.6	4	
Alaska	3	33.3	58.6	2	27.7	1	
Arizona	8	12.5	51.0	4	44.7	4	
Arkansas	6	16.7	51.3	3	45.9	3	
California	54	1.9	41.65	23	53.5	29	2
Colorado	8	12.5	50.75	4	42.4	4	
Connecticut	8	12.5	38.4	3	55.9	5	
Delaware	3	33.3	41.9	1	55.0	2	
Dist. Columbia	3	33.3	9.0	0	85.2	3	
Florida	25	4.0	48.9	13	48.8	12	
Georgia	13	7.7	54.7	7	43.0	6	
Hawaii	4	25.0	37.5	1	55.8	3	
Idaho	4	25.0	67.17	3	27.6	1	
Illinois	22	4.5	42.6	9	54.6	13	
Indiana	12	8.3	56.7	7	41.0	5	
Iowa	7	14.3	48.2	3	48.5	4	
Kansas	6	16.7	58.0	4	37.2	2	
Kentucky	8	12.5	56.5	5	41.4	3	
Louisiana	9	11.1	52.6	5	44.9	4	
Maine	4	25.0	44.0	2	49.1	2	
Maryland	10	10.0	40.2	4	56.6	6	
Massachusetts	12	8.3	32.5	4	59.8	7	1
Michigan	18	5.6	46.2	8	51.3	10	
Minnesota	10	10.0	45.5	5	47.9	5	
Mississippi	7	14.3	57.6	4	40.7	3	
Missouri	11	9.1	50.4	6	47.1	5	
Montana	3	33.3	58.4	2	33.4	1	
Nebraska	5	20.0	62.3	3	33.3	2	
Nevada	4	25.0	49.5	2	46.0	2	
New Hampshire	4	25.0	48.1	2	46.8	2	
New Jersey	15	6.7	40.3	6	56.1	9	

State	Electoral Votes	% Required	% for Bush	Electoral Votes	% for Gore	Electoral Votes	Others[A]
New Mexico	5	20.0	47.85	2	47.91	3	
New York	33	3.0	35.2	12	60.2	20	1
North Carolina	14	7.1	56.0	8	43.2	6	
North Dakota	3	33.3	66.7	2	33.1	1	
Ohio	21	4.8	50.0	11	46.5	10	
Oklahoma	8	14.3	60.3	5	38.4	3	
Oregon	7	14.3	46.5	3	47.0	4	
Pennsylvania	23	4.3	46.4	11	50.6	12	
Rhode Island	4	25.0	31.9	1	61.0	3	
South Carolina	8	12.5	56.8	5	40.9	3	
South Dakota	3	33.3	60.3	2	37.6	1	
Tennessee	11	9.1	51.2	6	47.3	5	
Texas	32	3.1	59.3	19	38.0	13	
Utah	5	20	66.8	3	26.3	2	
Vermont	3	33.3	40.7	1	50.6	2	
Virginia	13	7.7	52.5	7	44.4	6	
Washington	11	9.1	44.6	5	50.2	6	
West Virginia	5	20.0	51.9	3	45.6	2	
Wisconsin	11	9.1	47.6	5	47.8	6	
Wyoming	3	33.3	67.7	2	27.7	1	
Totals	**537**	...		**262**		**271**	**4**

[A]Others primarily included votes Ralph Nader as an Independent; Pat Buchanan of the Reform Party and Harry Browne of the Libertarian Party. In the Alaska voting, Nader received 10.1% of the vote, which was transferred to Gore to bring him above 33%. Similarly, lesser percentages attributed to Nader that were not sufficient to receive an electoral vote were assigned to Gore.

It is entirely clear that either (a) the popular vote should be used to elect the president, which is the method used in every other elected office not subject to appointment, or (b) allocation of votes to electors in direct proportion to the popular vote for them in each state. The second method preserves the slight electoral advantage given to the smaller states, which was the original constitutional intent of the founders. Since Gore received the majority of the popular votes, the electoral votes for the independents could have cast their votes for Gore. Bush would not have received the required 270 votes, even including the votes for the independent candidates also running.

To prevent further recurrence of the election of a president who has insufficient support of the voting population, a constitutional amendment must be proposed that determines who shall be elected as President of the United States in a manner that represents the actual intentions of voters in all states.

The election of 2020 is still disputed due to recalcitrance of President Trump to accept certifications of the states, especially those states where he prevailed in 2016. His principal claim is that mail-in ballots do not provide "equal representation", although balloting by mail has been accepted practice going back to the Civil War. He filed a motion to have the Supreme Court intervene, along the attorney general of Texas and 17 other states, that certain states were not following directions from their "legislatures" and that absentee ballots did not have direct checks against voter registrations, an allegation disputed by the states of PA, GA, MI and WI. Many states chose mail ballots due to crowded conditions in voting sites where the corona virus could easily spread. Although Trump referred to mail ballots as subject to "fraud", they are equivalent to in-person ballots since signatures and addresses are verified. The courts also dismissed many of the frivolous lawsuits submitted, ostensibly filed to delay the transition from the Trump to Biden Administration. The election of 2020, when represented by state electoral votes distributed in proportion to popular vote, is actually quite close, due to over-weighting of southern and western states votes for Trump. Here is a summary of the election of 2020:

Electoral Vote Distribution by State for the Election of 2020

State	Electoral Votes	% Required	% for Biden	Electoral Votes	% for Trump	Electoral Votes	Others[A]
Alabama	9	11.1	36.6	3	62.3	6	
Alaska	3	33.3	43.0	1	53.2	2	
Arizona	11	9.1	49.4	6	49.1	5	
Arkansas	6	16.7	34.6	2	62.6	4	
California	55	1.8	63.8	35	34.1	19	1
Colorado	9	11.1	55.4	5	41.9	4	
Connecticut	7	14.3	59.3	4	39.2	3	
Delaware	3	33.3	58.8	2	39.8	1	
Dist. of Columbia	3	33.3	92.9	3	5.5	0	
Florida	29	3.4	47.9	14	51.2	14	
Georgia	16	6.3	49.5	8	49.2	8	
Hawaii	4	25.0	63.7	3	34.3	1	
Idaho	4	25.0	33.1	1	63.9	3	
Illinois	20	5.0	57.6	12	40.6	8	
Indiana	11	9.1	41.0	5	57.1	6	
Iowa	6	16.6	45.0	2	53.2	4	
Kansas	6	16.7	41.3	2	56.5	4	
Kentucky	8	12.5	36.2	3	62.1	5	
Louisiana	8	12.5	39.9	3	58.5	5	
Maine	2	50.0	52.9	1	44.2	0	
Maine 1	1	50.0	59.9	1	37.2	0	
Maine 2	1	50.0	40.9	0	56.9	1	
Maryland	10	10.0	65.3	7	32.9	3	

State	Electoral Votes	% Required	% for Biden	Electoral Votes	% for Trump	Electoral Votes	Others[A]
Massachusetts	11	9.1	65.6	7	32.6	4	
Michigan	16	6.3	50.6	8	47.9	8	
Minnesota	10	10.0	52.6	5	45.4	5	
Mississippi	6	16.6	40.4	2	58.2	4	
Missouri	10	10.0	41.3	4	56.9	6	
Montana	3	33.3	22.4	1	56.9	2	
Nebraska	2	50.0	39.4	0	58.5	2	
	1	50.0	40.9	0	56.9	1	
	1	50.0	54.7	1	43.4	0	
	1	50.0	22.4	0	75.6	1	
Nevada	6	16.7	50.1	3	47.7	3	
New Hampshire	4	25.0	52.8	2	45.6	2	
New Jersey	14	7.1	57.2	8	41.6	6	
New Mexico	5	20.0	54.3	3	43.5	2	
New York	29	3.4	56.7	16	41.9	12	1
North Carolina	15	6.7	48.7	7	50.0	8	
North Dakota	3	33.3	31.9	1	65.5	2	
Ohio	18	5.5	45.2	8	53.4	10	
Oklahoma	7	14.3	32.3	2	65.4	5	
Oregon	7	14.3	56.9	4	40.6	3	
Pennsylvania	20	5.0	49.9	10	48.9	10	
Rhode Island	4	25.0	59.6	3	38.9	1	
South Carolina	9	11.1	43.4	4	55.1	5	
South Dakota	3	33.3	35.6	1	61.8	2	
Tennessee	11	9.1	37.4	4	60.7	7	
Texas	38	2.6	46.5	18	52.1	20	
Utah	6	16.7	37.8	2	58.0	4	
Vermont	3	33.3	66.4	2	30.8	1	
Virginia	13	7.7	54.3	7	44.3	6	
Washington	12	8.3	58.4	7	39.0	5	
West Virginia	5	20.0	29.6	1	68.7	4	
Wisconsin	10	10.0	49.6	5	48.9	5	
Wyoming	3	33.3	26.7	0	70.4	3	
Totals	**538**	...		**269**		**267**	**2**

Since there are 2 electoral votes for independents, they could have cast their votes for Biden (assuming no party requirements), making his total electoral votes 271, since Biden had more than 7 million votes than Trump.

Trump Administration Challenge to the Electoral College

Even before Donald Trump entered the Presidential Primary in 2016, he declared that the Electoral College process for selection of the President was "rigged". After his election, he ceased in that depiction of a "rigged election". Not until his loss in 2020, did he again declare the current electoral process as "rigged" and "fraudulent". His complaints were amplified by his numerous political allies, including the support of the Attorney General of Texas, who filed a lawsuit to intervene on his behalf to the Supreme Court. Numerous other lawsuits were filed in state and local courts alleging fraud, illegal balloting, discarding of ballots and other voting irregularities. All these lawsuits were dismissed on the basis of lack of evidence and were termed as either frivolous or "without merit".

The basis for filing this motion from the State of Texas was an assertion that it had "original jurisdiction" against the states of Pennsylvania, Georgia, Michigan and Wisconsin, all of which where the popular vote was relative evenly split between candidates

Biden and Trump. Because the differences are about 1-3%, they are colloquially termed as political "battlegrounds". Although these states changed their voting procedures to account for the corona virus pandemic, many other states also revised their voting requirements. The Texas motion argued that only legislatures can make such changes for presidential elections and alleged that Article II of the Constitution was violated. Further objections included public ballot boxes, waivers of signatures and corrections, and that opportunity for fraud greatly increased due to counting of absentee ballots.

Although Texas cited no instances of fraud, a claim was made that "it is not necessary to prove that fraud occurred..." but that these States had supposedly deviated from the way that their legislatures would choose electors. The claim by Texas that it had "original jurisdiction" was as if their intervention was equivalent to a water rights claim between states or a boundary dispute. Texas further stated that "non-legislative actors lack authority to amend or nullify election statutes", alleging that state and county election agencies and officials were supposedly acting without authority. Claims for intervention were needed because Texas alleged that "executive branch election officials, or by judicial officials, in Defendant States of Pennsylvania, Georgia, Michigan and Wisconsin, are in violation of the Electors Clause", and that electoral votes cast by those states were "not constitutionally valid".

Texas objected because its votes would be "unlawfully diluted by illegal votes", and further claimed their motion was "timely", even though it was filed after the election. Texas justified its direct filing to the Supreme Court because there was a "case or controversy" raised and that President Trump had "suffered an injury in fact" by those particular states who had caused him such injuries, so Texas "requested relief [which] would redress injuries." In particular, Texas insisted that absentee balloting, intended to protect voters from exposure in close quarters from the corona virus with in-person voting, was supposedly causing fraud, whereby Republican poll watchers were not able to closely observe ballot processing.

The State of Pennsylvania, acting on behalf of the other defendant states, vigorously responded to the Texas motion. Pennsylvania stated that its legislature had authorized mail-in voting in its Election Code, as did many other states that voted for Trump. Further, State and Federal courts had invalidated claims of voting irregularities, and because of "distance and unfamiliarity" of Texas with Pennsylvania law. Flat out, Pennsylvania dismissed allegations that poll watchers were not allowed to closely observe processing because of the social distancing virus requirements of 6 feet. Pennsylvania stated that minor ballot defects could be corrected, such as a missing address on the declaration, did not void a ballot, and was permissible by law. It was also declared that the allegation that late ballots were not segregated as "utterly false", because three-day extensions were granted due to the large deluge of absentee ballots.

Texas had inserted in its complaint that supposedly a statistical analysis showed that Trump was ahead by in-person voting, but that absentee voting reversed that lead was improbable. This allegation was declared as "nonsense", because the analysis relied on the 2016 results, which were two separate and distinct events.

Pennsylvania dismissed the Texas claim of original jurisdiction because Texas has no jurisdiction "...over the election procedures of four sister states." The most critical statement made by Pennsylvania as defendant is that "Far from trying to vindicate its sovereign or quasi-sovereign interests, Texas is ultimately seeking redress for the political preferences of its citizens who voted for President Trump." Significantly stated by Pennsylvania is that if Texas is granted intervention, "...this frivolous process will proceed to the Supreme Court every four years, and such lawsuits could be filed against any state, not just the four states at hand."

Pennsylvania objected the claim of standing because that required a "triad of injury in fact, causation and redressability", where there were no injuries in fact, nor traceable to a violation of the Electors Clause because they were rejected by the courts, and that no sovereign interests of Texas were not at stake. The Texas motion was described as "untimely" and "moot" because changes to election laws were made these states (and many other states) before the election, which is when Texas should have filed, and that the delay should not be rewarded, because mail-in ballot had already been approved by the Pennsylvania Supreme Court prior to the general election. Pennsylvania defends itself that there was no violation of the Electors Clause and that the argument is without merit because it is turning "state law into Federal law." Precise distancing of poll watchers is not granted in any Pennsylvania state law, other than permitting "their presence in the room."

In rather blunt terms, Pennsylvania states "Indeed, Texas' argument is so untethered from the actual state of the law that it makes the remarkable claim that a state legislature's power to direct the manner by which presidential electors are appointed is 'plenary'." However, such plenary power is not in effect because the Pennsylvania state constitution directs otherwise. Moreover, the Texas claim that the equal protection amendment was violated, which applies to persons within a particular state, not one state versus another, and that variations in county election procedures are permissible.

In summary, Pennsylvania states that "Texas seeks to invoke this Court's original jurisdiction to achieve the extraordinary relief of disenfranchising all Pennsylvanians who voted and 1/10 of the voters of the entire Nation." Further, "Texas asks this Court to bring 'only discredited allegations and conspiracy theories that have no basis in fact and ... contort its original jurisprudence in an election where millions of people cast ballots...sometime risking their very health and safety to do so."

Fortunately, the Supreme Court would not take up the motion, basically stating that Texas lacked standing to take any action by the Court against the other states. Its decision is succinctly stated in a single sentence: "Texas has not demonstrated a judicially recognizable interest in the manner in which another state conducts its elections."

After the dismissal of the Texas lawsuit, Trump continued to remark about the supposedly fraudulent nature of his defeat at the polls. He importuned Vice President Pence to see if an intervention at the counting process of electoral votes cast by the states could be either suspended or overturned. Pence consulted with constitutional scholars and was advised that his role was largely as a witness and that he lacked any ability to suspend or block counting.

Numerous supporters, including Trump's personal lawyer Rudy Guiliani, urged Trump followers to engage in "mortal combat" against the counting of votes and demonstrate against the electoral counting process on January 6, 2021 as per the Constitution. Trump encouraged their march on the Capitol, extolling in his tweet to "be there, will be wild" and to "fight like hell" and other clear urgings to "stop the steal" of the election which Trump frequently claimed that he won the election by a "landslide" (actually he lost by a landslide of the popular vote by 7 million). The word "fight" was used multiple times, whereas the word "peaceful" was only cited once, clearly an attempt of plausible deniability. Several crowd participants waved Trump banners and Confederate flags, indicative of presence of white supremacists, "MAGA" hats, many wearing combat fatigues and body armor, gas masks and deploying "bear spray" and surged forward toward the Capitol. The more militant members of the riot stormed the Capitol, breaking down windows and doors, injuring numerous Capitol police officers and killing one officer by striking his head with a fire extinguisher. Some members of the crowd called for the murder of the Speaker of the House and the hanging of the Vice President. They even constructed a mock gallows outside the Capitol entrance to supposedly indicate intentions of further action.

The members of the House and Senate were escorted to safer locations in the Capitol by the police as the riotous members entered the House and Senate floor and member offices, some gathering souvenirs and others ransacking offices or preening to take "selfies" of the occasion with their cameras. A total of five persons were killed and numerous police officers and people were injured in the insurrection.

After calls were made by Capitol Police and the Mayor of the District to the Secretary of the Army and Acting Secretary of Defense for assistance, the District of Columbia and Maryland National Guards were activated and a curfew was imposed. During this time, Trump simply observed the calamity on television and made no attempt to either calm the rioters or made any effort to call the National Guard. After calm was restored, numerous arrests were made and the rioters were dispersed. The counting of electoral votes then commenced the next day and Joseph Biden was elected President. Many of the legislators who previously disputed the election still clung to their positions, as if to burnish their credentials for Trump voters in future elections rather than decry the seditious nature of Trump's actions and those of his militant supporters.

After the rioters had breached the Capitol and the political fallout began to register, Trump unequivocally stated that his words to his supporters were "totally appropriate".

The Second Impeachment Trial of Donald Trump

Incensed at his behavior and lack of contrition and inaction during the crisis, Speaker Pelosi and Democrats in the House drafted Articles of Impeachment, which are included afterwards in a separate section of this book. This approach was taken because Pence would not, nor was able, to muster sufficient majority of cabinet members to remove Trump by invoking the 25th Amendment.

The possibility of Trump resigning prior to the inauguration was deemed unlikely. The Senate Majority Leader McConnell deferred action on impeachment after Trump left office, even though the offenses were committed during his time in office. There are several precedents where public officials have been impeached after leaving office or after resignation. The deferment of the trial until after the inauguration proved to be a prescient gambit on the part of Senator McConnell.

The impeachment has caused a split between moderate and radical Republicans, many of whom voted to stop the impeachment because Trump had left office. Sen. Rand Paul called the impeachment after a President had left office "unconstitutional", although the sedition was committed during his time in office. The second set of Articles of Impeachment of former President Trump are included with the first set in this book.

The trial managers from the House of Representatives were experienced lawyers, most of whom previously had been prosecutors before becoming legislators. Their presentation of facts regarding the storming of the Capitol relied not only on eyewitness statements, but placed emphasis on tying Trump's prolific and often caustic and critical tweet commentary to the timeline of events. They tied together his obvious tolerance of violence and pandering to extremist elements that literally absorbed his words that the election was "stolen" from him. His supporters had gathered a crowd filled clearly with persons who believed his long-term calls to "stop the steal" by disrupting the counting of the electoral balloting at the Capitol.

Videos of the violent clashes between Capitol and DC Metropolitan Police and the rioter were difficult for the Senators to watch as it brought back traumatic memories. These videos were thought that they make impressions on wavering Republican Senators how serious the incitement of insurrection was on the part of Trump. The House managers did a thorough job in presenting how prior complaints about election "fraud" and "rigging", in addition to dismissal of lawsuits by the courts over an extended period of time prior to and after the 2020 election led to frustration on the part of Trump and his supporters, which was set to culminate on January 6, 2021 when the electoral ballots would be counted, led to a potentially lethal riot. Given Trump's personality which would not permit him to be cast as a "loser", he continued to maintain that he won the election "by a landslide" and heartily agreed with his supporters that they should "stop the steal". He instructed them to march down Pennsylvania Ave. to the Capitol and that he "would be with them", although this statement was entirely rhetorical since he actually retreated to the White to watch the spectacle on television.

The rioters breached the barricades and police lines with poles, pikes, bear sprays and protective gear and they entered both the House and Senate. The Secret Service and the Capitol Police led the legislators off to safer locations. Some carried Trump and Confederate flags and ransacked offices and posed for "selfies" with their telephones, which would later be used against them. Videos presented indicated that the rioters claimed that they were "invited" there by the former President Trump. During this time, Trump made no effort for several hours to contact National Guard units in the District of Columbia or Maryland to quell the riot and occupation of the Capitol.

House Minority Leader Kevin McCarthy called Trump to implore the rioters to cease and desist, since it was evident their penchant for blood was growing after their success in penetrating the Capitol. According to Congresswoman Beutler, who was present during the conversation, Trump told McCarthy, "Well Kevin, I guess these people are more upset about the election than you are" to which McCarthy replied "Who the fuck do you think you are talking to?" in reference to his position and prior support of Trump.

As the rioters progressed through the Capitol, Senators and the Vice President, who was there with family members to witness the counting of ballot totals, were escorted to safety. In his frustration that his Vice President would no longer be useful in obstructing the counting, he called newly-elected Senator Tuberville to see whether he would carry out ballot obstruction. Since Tuberville was also in danger, as was the Vice President, he deferred any action and told Trump he had "to go". As a furtherance of incitement, Trump sent his supporters a tweet that his Vice President didn't have the "courage" to uphold his belief of election fraud, causing his most rabid supporters to chant "hang Pence" and refer to him as a "traitor". This deprecation of Pence is most ironic because he was following the requirements of the Constitution. That Trump would sacrifice his loyal Vice President to rioters and turn to another freshman Senator who he supported and defeated his former Attorney General Jeff Sessions in a primary, indicated that any disloyalty to Trump would be subject to deprecation, dismissal or severe penalties.

After many of his White House staff urged him to calm his riotous supporters, in his farewell, Trump told his supporters that he "loved them" and that they were "very special", even after the loss of life, numerous injuries, trespass and destruction of Federal property.

The Trump defense lawyers were overwhelmed by the evidence shown, and defended their client claiming insufficient due process, that Trump's address to the riotous crowd was not incitement of insurrection, and that the trial was unconstitutional because the former President was now a "private citizen".

Their claim that due process was absent carried little weight because he had access to legal counsel, and that the discovery process was cut short because the trial was deferred by the Senate which was under Republican control until after the inauguration of President Biden.

Trump's legal team frequently referenced the Supreme Court case of *Brandenburg vs. Ohio* regarding the limits of "free speech", claiming that elected officials have the highest protection of their speech to provide "robust discussion" of ideas and policy. That decision contained three requirements to determine incitement, including intent to speak, imminence of lawlessness and the likelihood of lawlessness. Trump certainly had the intention of speaking to the crowd when he importuned them to "fight" or "fight like hell", and because he knew many of the supporters included the "Proud Boys", "QAnon" and the "Oath Keepers", all groups who have posted threatening commentary and have a penchant for violence. He directed them to the Capitol, and even when the violence did commence, he further incited them by stating that his Vice President didn't have the "courage" to "stop the steal". Since impeachment is not a criminal trial, and does not result in criminal penalties, but just removal from office and the possibility of not securing any future public office, the citation of the Brandenburg decision was not completely analogous. However, all three requirements were actually met, especially after the conversation with Leader McCarthy and the lack of "courage" tweet while Pence was receiving death threats.

The Trump legal team exploited the ambiguity of the Constitution whether a former President can be impeached after he leaves office, even though the offense occurred while he was in office. Although the Senate voted with the support of only a few Republican Senators that the trial was constitutional, the Trump lawyers still asserted that the trail was not constitutional.

The final vote came to acquit the President by 57 for removal and 43 for acquittal, where 67 votes (2/3 of the Senate) are needed for conviction. When House manager Rep. Eric Swalwell was asked why he didn't have enough votes to convict, he stated he needed "more spines", a reference to Republican Senators more concerned about remaining in office where they could be deprecated or "primaried-out" by Trump supporters in their States, rather than acting as true jurors to vote guilty when presented with an obvious set of facts.

After the acquittal vote was recorded, Senate Minority Leader Mitch McConnell sharply denounced former President Trump in a Senate speech shortly after McConnell voted to acquit him. Ironically, much of the speech reiterated the legal arguments of the House managers, where McConnell said that Trump was "practically and morally responsible" for the riot that penetrated the Capitol on January 6. Moreover, McConnell stated that the riot was a result of "... an intensifying crescendo of conspiracy theories orchestrated by an outgoing president who seemed determined to either overturn the voters' decision or else torch our institutions on the way out...There is no question, none, that President Trump is practically and morally responsible for provoking the events of the day, and continued to watch the events unfold on television...A mob was assaulting the Capitol in his name...These criminals were carrying his banners, hanging his flags and screaming their loyalty to him." McConnell agreed that the rioters were acting on Trump's behalf and they overtly stated so when confronted by police...."Having that belief was a foreseeable consequence of the growing crescendo of false statements, conspiracy theories and reckless hyperbole which the defeated president kept shouting into the largest megaphone on planet earth."

Then McConnell stated, however, it was unconstitutional to convict a president who was no longer in office, which justified his vote not to convict. This statement was largely predetermined, since his deferral of a Senate trial after inauguration was a precursor for his vote, even though he cited Trump for high crimes and misdemeanors. His gambit of deferring the trial after Biden was elected gave cover to himself and the remaining Republican

Senators who voted to acquit Trump. However, seven Republican Senators did vote to convict, including Burr of North Carolina, Collins of Maine, Murkowski of Alaska, Romney of Utah, Sasse of Nebraska and Toomey of Pennsylvania.

The seeming contradiction by Sen. McConnell is based on the constitutional statement in Article I Section 3, last sentence "... but the Party convicted shall nevertheless be liable and subject to Indictment, Trial and Punishment, according to Law." If Trump is subject and accused by other jurisdictions of insurrection, he could be punished according to either Federal or State laws, and barred from holding any future office in accord with the Fourteenth Amendment Section 3 which permits disqualification from holding office if the person was "...engaged in insurrection...or given aid and comfort to the enemies thereof."

This duality of position on the part of McConnell indicates separation within the Republican Party between traditional moderates and its more radical elements, who believe in immigration restrictions, unfettered sales of rifles and guns, anti-abortion laws and discrimination on the basis of religious beliefs, and limited reliance on foreign allies.

The two recent impeachment trials have shown that one party must have at least 60 Senate seats to override a filibuster and the ability to sway at least seven Senators of the opposition party. Without this, impeachment becomes a "show trial", albeit even when considerable evidence is provided for guilt of the accused, because party loyalty and the search for a technicality to acquit becomes imperative to maintain political power and position.

THE BIDEN ADMINISTRATION

The Biden Administration got off to a rocky start with the events of January 6, 2021, when the Capitol was stormed by armed protestors that attempted to delay or stop the counting of the resulting of ballot totals and electoral votes from each state to assure that former Trump was elected instead. These events are described in detail in the second impeachment proceedings in the last part of this book. A panel of legislators also examined the actions of President Trump and his advisors and supporters in televised hearings regarding the origin and the events of January 6, 2021. Republican legislators Liz Chaney of Wyoming and Adam Kinzinger of Illinois were specifically targeted by their party for their leadership in the hearings, whereby Cheney was eventually defeated in her re-election bid, and Kinzinger declined to run again in his district.

Biden considered himself as a compromiser and a friend to both sides of the aisle. He was able to muster support with enough Republican support to pass an infrastructure rebuilding and repair bill, which Trump was never able to put together. To counter the growing conservative tilt of the Supreme Court, his moderate nominee Judge Brown was confirmed by the Senate. He re-affirmed support for the Affordable Care Act, which prohibits refusal to provide insurance coverage for people with pre-existing conditions.

During his tenure, the Russian army under command of their President Vladimir Putin, decided that increasingly independent Ukraine must be "re-united" with Mother Russia. This sent oil and natural gas prices soaring throughout Europe and the United States. Initially there was immediate bi-partisan support of Ukraine, but

Biden and some of the DOD generals showed hesitance in providing advanced American offensive and defensive weapons to Ukraine, such as F-16 fighter jets and Patriot missile batteries, for fear of their capture by the Russians. Inevitably, Republicans started to complain about the $70 billion price tag for this support, which became a standard Republican talking point that the money should be "spent at home". The irony of the remark is potent because tax cuts during Trump Administration predominantly were aimed for the wealthy, not the general population.

The Biden Administration was also confronted by the conflict between the militants of Hamas in Gaza vs. the Likud government of Israel headed by Benjamin Netanyahu. An initial strike by Hamas on kibbutzes, killing slightly more than one thousand Israelis, which led to Israelis bombing Gaza with American munitions. More than 40,000 Palestinian men, women and children were killed. These acts were condemned by the International Criminal Court, citing Netanyahu specifically as a war criminal since he had targeted innocent civilians and infrastructure in his effort to eliminate Hamas. Biden was a long friend of the Jewish community at home and abroad but could not ignore the outcry of the Arab-American community in the United States, particularly in Michigan, a key battleground state.

Biden ran for re-election because he felt he was ironically "best fit" to oppose the re-election of Trump. He indicated before his 2nd candidacy that he would be a single-term president in the 2020 election. However, faced with the prospect of a second term of Trump, he decided he should run again. After his disappointing debate with Trump, the Democratic Party and its leaders and major donors proposed that he step aside. Biden's explanation was that he had a "cold" and was tired from travel. Most ironic is that former Speaker of the House Nancy Pelosi, who had received the Presidential Medal of Freedom from Biden, was one of the leaders behind the Biden ouster. It was reported that Biden was furious over this betrayal from Pelosi and several other of his "friends". Money donations were drying up from major donors, and Democrats were panicking about losing the closely divided House and Senate.

There was justification for concern because Biden exhibited signs of pre-Covid, described as a "cold" after the debate, but was confirmed Covid exposure several weeks later. He was administered Paxlovid, a Pfizer anti-Covid supplement. Also, the White House log showed there were multiple visits by a physician who specialized in Parkinson's disease. When questioned by the press, the White House communications officer said disclosure would violate "national security". Biden's gait and occasional loss of memory were possible indicators, but Parkinson's disease was never confirmed by any official medical diagnosis.

Although Democrats preached about "democracy", Biden chose to run again, but his incumbency had blocked other candidates during the earlier primaries. More experienced governors and legislators could have sought the office. During his weakened state after sustaining Covid, Biden relented and proposed that Vice President Kamala Harris replace him. Party officials opposed candidates being considered and voted on at the Convention, which had been the nomination method used for more than 100 years. Instead, the Convention was used as an ideological sales pitch.

Trump at his convention gave a rambling speech, aimed at revenge over his fate being cited for violation of fraud statutes by emphasizing non-existent widespread fraud in only the battleground states. His theft of highly classified documents was actually the most serious offense. He was convicted of covering up campaign expenses and falsification of records in the State of New York.

The Democrats vilified independent Rep. Robert Kennedy, Jr when he declared his candidacy and accused him of being an "anti-vaxxer", although he testified under oath before Congress that all his children were vaccinated. He stated that if elected, he would invite Democrats, Republicans, Independents, and Libertarians to be members of his cabinet, based on ideas and knowledge. Whether he will draw votes away from Trump or Biden remains to be seen.

Biden subsequently gave an address stating that he was stepping aside for the "good of the country". In reality, he was abandoned by his own party of many years. It was pure political spin of the party and Biden, indicative of how adverse political events affecting each major party are brushed off. The entire anti-democratic process demonstrated the need for competitive primaries and that an Independent Party to have the same ballot access and equal media coverage. During Trump's campaign, two assassination attempts were made, and both persons were originally Trump supporters. One was a depressed person seeking fame, the other quite irrational. The harsh rhetoric emanating from both parties apparently provided justification of actions for both shooters. Words actually do matter....

THE FUTURE OF THIS REPUBLIC

This book is intended to provide recommendations and insights to re-orient the major parties towards a modern and realistic understanding of the Constitution. If compromise between the opposing Republican and Democratic Parties does not appear soon, an Independent Party of the Republic will be needed to bridge the present impasse. The inability of the Republican Party to oppose clearly unconstitutional conduct by conviction and removal from office by impeachment is an indication that the "checks and balances" inherent to the Constitution are not fully engaged and that oaths of office are not taken with the seriousness and gravity originally intended by the founders.

Although the Tenure of Office Act was ruled as "unconstitutional" by the Supreme Court long ago, the recent turnover of appointed officials during the Trump Administration, a new law must be passed which overturns the concept that appointed officials serve "at the pleasure of the President." This criterion for dismissal has been frequently cited by proponents of the unitary theory of government. A revised version of the Tenure of Office Act, which has a basis because the Senate confirms the appointee, would require that the President can only dismiss the appointee if he or she commits serious offenses, such as bribery, malfeasance, direct obstruction to carry out the requirements of established statutes or confirmed perjury either in sworn testimony before Congress or in a United States or State Court of Law. Offering contrary opinion or speaking on public matters that may not conform to the President's policies shall not be grounds for dismissal.

Unfortunately, the Supreme Court in 2024 decided that the actions taken by the President if within "executive core functions" are immune from prosecution. This decision has been widely condemned as giving virtual carte blanche to a President who abuses power. Although the decision claims that the "founders" wanted a strong executive, they would not have added impeachment to the Constitution, along with the checks and balances of the legislatures of federal and state governments. This exception is laid out in the Tenth Amendment, where powers not enumerated by the Federal government, "...are reserved to the States respectively, or to the people." The assertion that because the Supreme Court is a separate branch of government, they also claim immunity, but the Constitution says otherwise in Section 8, subsections (9) and (18). It was envisioned by the founders that representatives of the people determine what powers and funding the other two branches of government shall have.

Secondly, the United States is at a crossroads remarkably similar to the times of Theodore Roosevelt and William Jennings Bryan where commercial and corporate interests dominated American life, and literally bought influence through their wealth to change laws in their favor. Large corporations and trusts at that time sought to suppress wages and living standards of the general working population. In this era of outsourcing, job losses and demands for tax breaks for the upper 2%, many legislators and governors are asking for further sacrifices from the general population. Over the last 20 years, there has been a general redistribution of income toward upper incomes, whereas the poor and the middle-class incomes have largely remained stagnant in terms of wealth distribution. When legislators and governors do the bidding of corporate interests and ask for sacrifice from their constituents alone, the nature of our democratic republic has changed, whereby the power of government is no longer based on the will and consent of the people but is the will of the special corporate and wealthy interests.

Even in time of a pandemic, we see legislators, particularly Republicans, who are willing to grant tax relief to the upper classes and yet grumble about deficits when needed stimulus programs offer support to the middle and lower classes. With deaths to the Covid virus exceeding 1,000,000 at the time of this writing this 5th Edition, where previous unemployment was at severe levels and record economic losses were sustained, these events cannot be ignored. Serious events, such as the widespread Covid virus, may require deficits to bring about recovery for the general population, just as the founders intended during their writing of the post-revolution Constitution to provide for the "general welfare" of the people. The wealthy must share a commensurate burden to control deficits, just as the upper and middles classes have done for years in the past.

By adopting realistic and timely "constitutional blueprints" and embracing the spirit of the Constitution and its intent "...to form a more perfect Union, establish justice, insure domestic tranquility, provide for the common defense, promote the general welfare, and secure the blessings of liberty to ourselves and our posterity...", any truly American political party that proposes and believes in common-sense solutions for the common good can sustain itself, and continue to truly represent the greatest cross-section of the people of the United States as intended by the Founders in its Constitution.

PHOTOGRAPHIC CREDITS

Photo	*Subject*	*Source*
1	Theodore Roosevelt	Library of Congress
2	William J. Bryan	Library of Congress
3	Woodrow Wilson	Library of Congress
4	Calvin Coolidge	Library of Congress
5	Herbert Hoover	Library of Congress
6	Franklin Roosevelt	Library of Congress
7	Wendell Willkie	Library of Congress
8	Franklin Roosevelt, Joseph Stalin, Winston Churchill	Library of Congress
9	Thomas Dewey	Library of Congress
10	Harry Truman	Library of Congress
11	Gen. Dwight Eisenhower	Library of Congress
12	Pres. Eisenhower	Library of Congress
13	Kennedy Bros.	Library of Congress
14	Lyndon Johnson, Robert McNamara	Library of Congress
15	Richard Nixon	Library of Congress
16	Gerald Ford	Library of Congress
17	Jimmy Carter, Fritz Mondale	Library of Congress
18	Camp David	Library of Congress
19	Ronald & Nancy Reagan	Library of Congress
20	Ronald Reagan	Official White House Photo
21	George H. W. Bush	Official White House Photo
22	Clintons, Al Gore	Library of Congress
23	George W. Bush	Library of Congress
24	George & Mitt Romney	Library of Congress
25	John McCain	Official Senate Photo
26	John & Elizabeth Edwards	AP Photo; Getty Images
27	Barack Obama	Wiki Public Domain
28	John Boehner	Official House Photo
29	Trump, Kislyak & Lavrov	Tass News Agency
30	Evan Bayh	Official Senate Photo
31a	Adam Kinzinger	Official House Photo
31b	Ben Sasse	Official Senate Photo
32	Kent Conrad	Official Senate Photo
33	David Petraeus	Official Army Photo
34	Ralph Nader	Library of Congress
35	Wesley Clark	Official Army Photo
36	Angus King	Official Senate Photo
37	Bernie Sanders	Senate Photo
38	John Huntsman	State Dept. Photo
39	Robert McNamara	Library of Congress
40	Robert Gates	Official DOD Photo
41	Leon Panetta	Official CIA Photo
42	Chuck Hagel	Official DOD Photo
Covers	Eagle, Flag, Washington DC	iStock I

ARTICLES OF IMPEACHMENT

The *first set of articles* against then President Trump are presented here:

CONGRESS OF THE UNITED STATES OF AMERICA,
IN THE HOUSE OF REPRESENTATIVES,
December 18, 2019.

RESOLUTION

Resolved, That Donald John Trump, President of the United States, is impeached for high crimes and misdemeanors and that the following articles of impeachment be exhibited to the United States Senate:

Articles of impeachment exhibited by the House of Representatives of the United States of America in the name of itself and of the people of the United States of America, against Donald John Trump, President of the United States of America, in maintenance and support of its impeachment against him for high crimes and misdemeanors.

ARTICLE I: ABUSE OF POWER

The Constitution provides that the House of Representatives "shall have the sole Power of Impeachment" and that the President "shall be removed from Office on Impeachment for, and Conviction of, Treason, Bribery, or other high Crimes and Misdemeanors". In his conduct of the office of President of the United States--and in violation of his constitutional oath faithfully to execute the office of President of the United States and, to the best of his ability, preserve, protect, and defend the Constitution of the United States, and in violation of his constitutional duty to take care that the laws be faithfully executed--Donald J. Trump has abused the powers of the Presidency, in that:

Using the powers of his high office, President Trump solicited the interference of a foreign government, Ukraine, in the 2020 United States Presidential election. He did so through a scheme or course of conduct that included soliciting the Government of Ukraine to publicly announce investigations that would benefit his reelection, harm the election prospects of a political opponent, and influence the 2020 United States Presidential election to his advantage. President Trump also sought to pressure the Government of Ukraine to take these steps by conditioning official United States Government acts of significant value to Ukraine on its public announcement of the investigations. President Trump engaged in this scheme or course of conduct for corrupt purposes in pursuit of personal political benefit. In so doing, President Trump used the powers of the Presidency in a manner that compromised the national security of the United States and undermined the integrity of the United States democratic process. He thus ignored and injured the interests of the Nation.

President Trump engaged in this scheme or course of conduct through the following means:

(1) President Trump--acting both directly and through his agents within and outside the United States Government--corruptly solicited the Government of Ukraine to publicly announce investigations into--

(A) a political opponent, former Vice President Joseph R. Biden, Jr.; and

(B) a discredited theory promoted by Russia alleginthat Ukraine--rather than Russia--interfered in the 2016 United States Presidential election.

(2) With the same corrupt motives, President Trump--acting both directly and through his agents within and outside the United States Government--conditioned two official acts on the public announcements that he had requested--

(A) the release of $391 million of United States taxpayer funds that Congress had appropriated on a bipartisan basis for the purpose of providing vital military and security assistance to Ukraine to oppose Russian aggression and which President Trump had ordered suspended; and

(B) a head of state meeting at the White House, which the President of Ukraine sought to demonstrate continued United States support for the Government of Ukraine in the face of Russian aggression.

(3) Faced with the public revelation of his actions, President Trump ultimately released the military and security assistance to the Government of Ukraine, but has persisted in openly and corruptly urging and soliciting Ukraine to undertake investigations for his personal

political benefit. These actions were consistent with President Trump's previous invitations of foreign interference in United States elections.

In all of this, President Trump abused the powers of the Presidency by ignoring and injuring national security and other vital national interests to obtain an improper personal political benefit. He has also betrayed the Nation by abusing his high office to enlist a foreign power in corrupting democratic elections.

Wherefore President Trump, by such conduct, has demonstrated that he will remain a threat to national security and the Constitution if allowed to remain in office, and has acted in a manner grossly incompatible with self-governance and the rule of law. President Trump thus warrants impeachment and trial, removal from office, and disqualification to hold and enjoy any office of honor, trust, or profit under the United States.

ARTICLE II: OBSTRUCTION OF CONGRESS

The Constitution provides that the House of Representatives "shall have the sole Power of Impeachment" and that the President "shall be removed from Office on Impeachment for, and Conviction of, Treason, Bribery, or other high Crimes and Misdemeanors". In his conduct of the office of President of the United States--and in violation of his constitutional oath faithfully to execute the office of President of the United States and, to the best of his ability, preserve, protect, and defend the Constitution of the United States, and in violation of his constitutional duty to take care that the laws be faithfully executed--Donald J. Trump has directed the unprecedented, categorical, and indiscriminate defiance of subpoenas issued by the House of Representatives pursuant to its "sole Power of Impeachment". President Trump has abused the powers of the Presidency in a manner offensive to, and subversive of, the Constitution, in that:

The House of Representatives has engaged in an impeachment inquiry focused on President Trump's corrupt solicitation of the Government of Ukraine to interfere in the 2020 United States Presidential election. As part of this impeachment inquiry, the Committees undertaking the investigation served subpoenas seeking documents and testimony deemed vital to the inquiry from various Executive Branch agencies and offices, and current and former officials.

In response, without lawful cause or excuse, President Trump directed Executive Branch agencies, offices, and officials not to comply with those subpoenas. President Trump thus interposed the powers of the Presidency against the lawful subpoenas of the House of Representatives, and assumed to himself functions and judgments necessary to the exercise of the "sole Power of Impeachment" vested by the Constitution in the House of Representatives.

President Trump abused the powers of his high office through the following means:

(1) Directing the White House to defy a lawful subpoena by withholding the production of documents sought therein by the Committees.

(2) Directing other Executive Branch agencies and offices to defy lawful subpoenas and withhold the production of documents and records from the Committees--in response to which the Department of State, Office of Management and Budget, Department of Energy, and Department of Defense refused to produce a single document or record.

(3) Directing current and former Executive Branch officials not to cooperate with the Committees--in response to which nine Administration officials defied subpoenas for testimony, namely John Michael "Mick" Mulvaney, Robert B. Blair, John A. Eisenberg, Michael Ellis, Preston Wells Griffith, Russell T. Vought, Michael Duffey, Brian McCormack, and T. Ulrich Brechbuhl.

These actions were consistent with President Trump's previous efforts to undermine United States Government investigations into foreign interference in United States elections.

Through these actions, President Trump sought to arrogate to himself the right to determine the propriety, scope, and nature of an impeachment inquiry into his own conduct, as well as the unilateral prerogative to deny any and all information to the House of Representatives in the exercise of its "sole Power of Impeachment". In the history of the Republic, no President has ever ordered the complete defiance of an impeachment inquiry or sought to obstruct and impede so comprehensively the ability of the House of Representatives to investigate "high Crimes and Misdemeanors". This abuse of office served to cover up the President's own repeated misconduct and to seize and control the power of impeachment--and thus to nullify a vital constitutional safeguard vested solely in the House of Representatives.

In all of this, President Trump has acted in a manner contrary to his trust as President and subversive of constitutional government, to the great prejudice of the cause of law and justice, and to the manifest injury of the people of the United States.

Wherefore, President Trump, by such conduct, has demonstrated that he will remain a threat to the Constitution if allowed to remain in office, and has acted in a manner grossly incompatible with self-governance and the rule of law. President Trump thus warrants impeachment and trial, removal from office, and disqualification to hold and enjoy any office of honor, trust, or profit under the United States.

Speaker of the House of Representatives.

Attest

Clerk.

The *second set* of Articles of Impeachment pertain to the actions of former President Trump on the 6th of January of 2021 when electoral votes were constitutionally intended to be counted and but were disrupted by an insurrection.

Congressional Bills 117th Congress]
[From the U.S. Government Publishing Office]
[H. Res. 24 Engrossed in House (EH)]

<DOC>
H. Res. 24

In the House of Representatives, U. S.,

January 13, 2021.

Impeaching Donald John Trump, President of the United States, for high crimes and misdemeanors.

Resolved, That Donald John Trump, President of the United States, is impeached for high crimes and misdemeanors and that the following article of impeachment be exhibited to the United States Senate:

Article of impeachment exhibited by the House of Representatives of the United States of America in the name of itself and of the people of the United States of America, against Donald John Trump, President of the United States of America, in maintenance and support of its impeachment against him for high crimes and misdemeanors.

article i: incitement of insurrection

The Constitution provides that the House of Representatives "shall have the sole Power of Impeachment" and that the President "shall be removed from Office on Impeachment for, and Conviction of, Treason, Bribery, or other high Crimes and Misdemeanors". Further, section 3 of the 14th Amendment to the Constitution prohibits any person who has "engaged in insurrection or rebellion against" the United States from "hold[ing] any office . . . under the United States". In his conduct while President of the United States--and in violation of his constitutional oath faithfully to execute the office of President of the United States and, to the best of his ability, preserve, protect, and defend the Constitution of the United States, and in violation of his constitutional duty to take care that the laws be faithfully executed--Donald John Trump engaged in high Crimes and Misdemeanors by inciting violence against the Government of the United States, in that:

On January 6, 2021, pursuant to the 12th Amendment to the Constitution of the United States, the Vice President of the United States, the House of Representatives, and the Senate met at the United States Capitol for a Joint Session of Congress to count the votes of the Electoral College. In the months preceding the Joint Session, President Trump repeatedly issued false statements asserting that the Presidential election results were the product of widespread fraud and should not be accepted by the American people or certified by State or Federal officials. Shortly before the Joint Session commenced, President Trump, addressed a crowd at the Ellipse in Washington, DC. There, he reiterated false claims that "we won this election, and we won it by a landslide". He also willfully made statements that, in context, encouraged--and foreseeably resulted in--lawless action at the Capitol, such as: "if you don't fight like hell you're not going to have a country anymore". Thus incited by President Trump, members of the crowd he had addressed, in an attempt to, among other objectives, interfere with the Joint Session's solemn constitutional duty to certify the results of the 2020 Presidential election, unlawfully breached and vandalized the Capitol, injured and killed law enforcement personnel, menaced Members of Congress, the Vice President, and Congressional personnel, and engaged in other violent, deadly, destructive, and seditious acts.

President Trump's conduct on January 6, 2021, followed his prior efforts to subvert and obstruct the certification of the results of the 2020 Presidential election. Those prior efforts included a phone call on January 2, 2021, during which President Trump urged the secretary of state of Georgia, Brad Raffensperger, to "find" enough votes to overturn the Georgia Presidential election results and threatened Secretary Raffensperger if he failed to do so.

In all this, President Trump gravely endangered the security of the United States and its institutions of Government. He threatened the integrity of the democratic system, interfered with the peaceful transition of power, and imperiled a coequal branch of Government. He thereby betrayed his trust as President, to the manifest injury of the people of the United States.

Wherefore, Donald John Trump, by such conduct, has demonstrated that he will remain a threat to national security, democracy, and the Constitution if allowed to remain in office, and has acted in a manner grosslyincompatible with self-governance and the rule of law. Donald John Trump thus warrants impeachment and trial, removal from office, and disqualification to hold and enjoy any office of honor, trust, or profit under the United States.

Speaker of the House of Representatives.

Attest:

Clerk.

TERMINATION OF THE AFGHANISTAN CONFLICT

On September 11, 2001, four American civilian airliners were hijacked by terrorist cells recruited by Osama Bin Laden, a wealthy Saudi who had previously participated in purging the Soviet armed forces from Afghanistan. Bin Laden resented the presence of American forces in Saudi Arabia subsequent left after the Gulf War where the Iraqi Army had invaded Kuwait but was repelled by coalition forces.

Initiation of the Conflict

In this attack against the United States, two airliners struck the World Trade Center in New York City twice, with another striking the Pentagon in Washington, and a fourth aircraft intended to strike the Capitol in Washington. However, passengers aboard the plane destined to strike the Capitol attempted to overwhelm the hijackers by ramming into them and the cockpit, but the plane ultimately crashed in rural Pennsylvania, killing all aboard. Not only did this multi-aircraft attack kill more than 2,753 civilians in New York City, but led to the loss of many businesses, long term injuries to firefighters and police due to inhalation of toxic dust. The attack disrupted New York City, the financial capital of the United States, along with 184 persons losing their lives at the Pentagon, and 40 more killed in the plane crash in Pennsylvania.

After this attack, the George W. Bush Administration sought to destroy the training grounds for the Al-Queda terrorist cells located in remote parts of Afghanistan. The hunt to kill or capture Osama Bin Laden and his Al-Queda network was the beginning of a conflict that would span over four different administrations and consume an estimated expenditure of 4 trillion dollars and the massive loss of American, Iraqi and Afghan lives over a 20 year period of conflict.

Within this 20 year conflict, the peak level of US and allied military forces confronting its adversaries in Afghanistan reached a peak of approximately 100,000 troops, resulting in 2,400 deaths and far more numerous casualties of US and allied military personnel, including the Afghan military and civilian population. It is estimated that about 177,000 national military and police from Afghanistan, Pakistan, Iraqi, and Syria were killed. Approximately 50% of American and Allied deaths and injuries in Iraq and Afghanistan were caused by rocket-propelled grenade fire and improvised explosive devices, with the remaining 50% due to vehicle crashes, electrocutions, heatstroke, friendly fire, and suicides in both theaters. The number of post-traumatic stress syndrome cases and suicides of US military due to these conflicts has not been entirely accounted for as of this writing.

The initial phases of the drive to destroy Al-Queda in Afghanistan were not entirely successful due to ability of Al-Queda to sequester in hidden caves and escape to the neighboring sanctuary of Pakistan. As military personnel flowed into Afghanistan, they were dispersed to various provinces and established a large airbase at Bagram. The existing government was friendly to the United States since its President Hamid Karzai had previous oil business dealings with Bush.

Although the initial purpose was to destroy all terrorist training sites and neutralize Al-Queda, the doctrine of counterinsurgency was employed to build up, train and pay salaries to an Afghan Army to provide a general sense of security for the Afghan population. The building of roads, clinics and schools was intended to engender relationships with the United States and its allies. These efforts would encourage a degree of awareness that democracy could be established in a relatively poor and fragmented country.

Unfortunately, this reconstruction effort was to be accomplished in the midst of intimidation by the Taliban, a large armed fundamentalist force intending to ultimately control Afghanistan. They were not going to impose an Islamic theocracy on Afghanistan, similar to other Islamic nations. This seemingly positive counterinsurgency agenda was unfortunately continually confronted by intimidation by the Taliban in the form of attacks using conventional weapons, raids, and roadside explosives. This new theocracy, as designated by the Taliban, would become the Islamic Emirate of Afghanistan.

The purpose of military forces was to counteract the Taliban and training Afghans in the use of tactical and defensive weapons. Military personnel from the United States and its NATO allies were not specifically trained for building activities, which complicated this rebuilding effort. Building efforts were supposed to be filled by the US State Dept. and other non-governmental organizations whose efforts are typically funded by charitable contributions and other grants from foundations. This was the mission of the State Dept. and non-governmental organizations, and their support was nominal at best.

The threat of insecurity from the Taliban plagued rebuilding efforts and that military forces of the United States and its NATO allies were not trained to be builders. Such Building projects and military support in many cases were not integrally connected and many military personnel complained that their primary mission of military security, training the Afghans in tactics, weapon operation and engaging Taliban threat forces, was being subordinated to construction efforts.

The number of military personnel in Afghanistan would diminish because the second Bush Administration diverted its attention from Afghanistan by engaging in Iraq for a second time after it was alleged that the Saddam Hussein regime had "weapons of mass destruction". This diversion of resources from Afghanistan to the Iraqi theater of operations lessened the support of the original mission in Afghanistan, which was to establish an Afghan army capable of defending the country and build its infrastructure, and to securing those facilities built for the Afghans, or those in current construction by military or civilian contract personnel.

The Afghan government and its various civilian and military officials, according to US Inspector General reports, had engaged in corruption by diverting funds intended for military personnel for their own purposes. Examples were withholding of pay, lack or shortages of uniforms and purchase of inferior boots and equipment for the Afghan Army. The senior officer corps of the Afghan Army often lacked respect for their troops and the troops under their command would not provide adequate loyalty under such conditions. However, there were reports of specific instances where Afghan troops did give aggressive support to US and NATO forces against the Taliban which apparently indicated that providing training and weapons was doing some good.

However, many of the roads and facilities built for the Afghans were not sufficiently sustained and needed repair or were abandoned. The US Inspector General concluded that many projects may not have been particularly useful in the first place, were hampered by the insecurity of the Taliban, or were due to frequent rotations of senior military and civilian officials of the United States and its NATO allies.

The Obama Administration provided a continuation of force presence through a "surge" force to counteract both the Taliban and destroy Al-Queda. This surge was not universally supported within the Obama Administration, including Vice President Biden, who had disagreements with assessments of key generals serving in Afghanistan. Particularly notable was the disrespect that General Stanley McChrystal had for the Vice President when he referred to him as "Vice President Bite-Me", ultimately leading to his resignation. Several key officials later indicated that after Osama Bin Laden had been killed in Pakistan that the Afghan conflict should then have been concluded.

During his campaign for President, Donald Trump complained about "endless wars" and sought to conclude them if elected. After his election, he withdrew forces from Syria which had been engaging ISIS, a radical branch of Al-Queda, which also had been trying to establish their own Islamic emirate. This withdrawal put our Kurdish allies at risk, whereby many Kurdish civilians were subsequently killed by ISIS.

After serving in office for almost four years, in order to garnish his credentials for re-election, Trump and his Secretary of State entered into an agreement with the Taliban to withdraw American and Allied forces from Afghanistan, now called the Doha Agreement, where it was negotiated and signed by the United States and the Taliban in February 2020. Here is the published official agreement as signed by the United States and Taliban representatives.

The Doha Agreement

Agreement for Bringing Peace to Afghanistan between the Islamic Emirate of Afghanistan which is not recognized by the United States as a state and is known as the Taliban and the United States of America February 29, 2020 which corresponds to Rajab 5, 1441 on the Hijri Lunar calendar and Hoot 10, 1398 on the Hijri Solar calendar A comprehensive peace agreement is made of four parts:

PART ONE

1. Guarantees and enforcement mechanisms that will prevent the use of the soil of Afghanistan by any group or individual against the security of the United States and its allies.

2. Guarantees, enforcement mechanisms, and announcement of a timeline for the withdrawal of all foreign forces from Afghanistan.

3. After the announcement of guarantees for a complete withdrawal of foreign forces and timeline in the presence of international witnesses, and guarantees and the announcement in the presence of international witnesses that Afghan soil will not be used against the security of the United States and its allies, the Islamic Emirate of Afghanistan which is not recognized by the United States as a state and is known as the Taliban will start intra-Afghan negotiations with Afghan sides on March 10, 2020, which corresponds to Rajab 15, 1441 on the Hijri Lunar calendar and Hoot 20, 1398 on the Hijri Solar calendar.

4. A permanent and comprehensive ceasefire will be an item on the agenda of the intra-Afghan dialogue and negotiations. The

participants of intra-Afghan negotiations will discuss the date and modalities of a permanent and comprehensive ceasefire, including joint implementation mechanisms, which will be announced along with the completion and agreement over the future political roadmap of Afghanistan. The four parts above are interrelated and each will be implemented in accordance with its own agreed timeline and agreed terms. Agreement on the first two parts paves the way for the last two parts. Following is the text of the agreement for the implementation of parts one and two of the above. Both sides agree that these two parts are interconnected. The obligations of the Islamic Emirate of Afghanistan which is not recognized by the United States as a state and is known as the Taliban in this agreement apply in areas under their control until the formation of the new post-settlement Afghan Islamic government as determined by the intra-Afghan dialogue and negotiations.

Author's Note: For the sake of brevity, the phrase "the Islamic Emirate of Afghanistan which is not recognized by the United States as a state and is known as the Taliban" will be abbreviated as "the ... Taliban"; in addition, as of this writing, the "Islamic Emirate of Afghanistan" has not yet been recognized as a nation-state by the United Nations.

PART TWO

The United States is committed to withdraw from Afghanistan all military forces of the United States, its allies, and Coalition partners, including all non-diplomatic civilian personnel, private security contractors, trainers, advisors, and supporting services personnel within fourteen (14) months following announcement of this agreement, and will take the following measures in this regard:

A. The United States, its allies, and the Coalition will take the following measures in the first one hundred thirty-five (135) days: 1) They will reduce the number of U.S. forces in Afghanistan to eight thousand six hundred (8,600) and proportionally bring reduction in the number of its allies and Coalition forces. 2) The United States, its allies, and the Coalition will withdraw all their forces from five (5) military bases.

B. With the commitment and action on the obligations of the ... Taliban in Part Two of this agreement, the United States, its allies, and the Coalition will execute the following: 1) The United States, its allies, and the Coalition will complete withdrawal of all remaining forces from Afghanistan within the remaining nine and a half (9.5) months. 2) The United States, its allies, and the Coalition will withdraw all their forces from remaining bases.

C. The United States is committed to start immediately to work with all relevant sides on a plan to expeditiously release combat and political prisoners as a confidence building measure with the coordination and approval of all relevant sides. Up to five thousand (5,000) prisoners of the ... Taliban and up to one thousand (1,000) prisoners of the other side will be released by March 10, 2020, the first day of intra-Afghan negotiations, which corresponds to Rajab 15, 1441 on the Hijri Lunar calendar and Hoot 20, 1398 on the Hijri Solar calendar. The relevant sides have the goal of releasing all the remaining prisoners over the course of the subsequent three months. The United States commits to completing this goal. The ... Taliban commits that its released prisoners will be committed to the responsibilities mentioned in this agreement so that they will not pose a threat to the security of the United States and its allies.

D. With the start of intra-Afghan negotiations, the United States will initiate an administrative review of current U.S. sanctions and the rewards list against members of the ... Taliban with the goal of removing these sanctions by August 27, 2020, which corresponds to Muharram 8, 1442 on the Hijri Lunar calendar and Saunbola 6, 1399 on the Hijri Solar calendar.

E. With the start of intra-Afghan negotiations, the United States will start diplomatic engagement with other members of the United Nations Security Council and Afghanistan to remove members of the ... Taliban from the sanctions list with the aim of achieving this objective by May 29, 2020, which corresponds to Shawwal 6, 1441 on the Hijri Lunar calendar and Jawza 9, 1399 on the Hijri Solar calendar. .

F. The United States and its allies will refrain from the threat or the use of force against the territorial integrity or political independence of Afghanistan or intervening in its domestic affairs.

PART THREE

In conjunction with the announcement of this agreement, the ... Taliban will take the following steps to prevent any group or individual, including al-Qa'ida, from using the soil of Afghanistan to threaten the security of the United States and its allies:

1. The ...Taliban will not allow any of its members, other individuals or groups, including al-Qa'ida, to use the soil of Afghanistan to threaten the security of the United States and its allies.

2. The ... Taliban will send a clear message that those who pose a threat to the security of the United States and its allies have no place in Afghanistan, and will instruct members of the ... Taliban not to cooperate with groups or individuals threatening the security of the United States and its allies.

3. The ...Taliban will prevent any group or individual in Afghanistan from threatening the security of the United States and its allies, and will prevent them from recruiting, training, and fundraising and will not host them in accordance with the commitments in this agreement.

4. The ...Taliban is committed to deal with those seeking asylum or residence in Afghanistan according to international migration law and the commitments of this agreement, so that such persons do not pose a threat to the security of the United States and its allies. The ...Taliban will not provide visas, passports, travel permits, or other legal documents to those who pose a threat to the security of the United States and its allies to enter Afghanistan.

PART FOUR

1. The United States will request the recognition and endorsement of the United Nations Security Council for this agreement.

2. The ... Taliban seek positive relations with each other and expect that the relations between the United States and the new post-settlement Afghan Islamic government as determined by the intra-Afghan dialogue and negotiations will be positive.

3. The United States will seek economic cooperation for reconstruction with the new post- settlement Afghan Islamic government as determined by the intra-Afghan dialogue and negotiations and will not intervene in its internal affairs. Signed in Doha, Qatar on February 29, 2020, which corresponds to Rajab 5, 1441 on the Hijri Lunar calendar and Hoot 10, 1398 on the Hijri Solar calendar, in duplicate, in Pashto, Dari, and English.

Withdrawal of Forces

The Doha Agreement signaled to the Afghan Army that American and Allied military personnel would no longer be available, leading to their demoralization. They had become highly dependent on foreign support which would be terminated by a specific timetable. Deadline for the beginning of withdrawal of forces was to begin on May 1, 2021 during the new Biden Administration and completed at the end of August 2021. This also included civilian support personnel, US citizens and those Afghans granted Special Immigration Visas. The Trump Administration had slowed down this process earlier to limit the number of Afghans entering the US; fortunately, other countries were willing to accept them as immigrants seeking asylum.

The general staff at the Pentagon and Afghan field officers recommended a small reserve force to protect the environs of Kabul, the capitol of Afghanistan and the US Embassy to process visas for Afghans desiring to leave due to their prior alliances with US and NATO forces. President Biden and some general officers conceded that a remaining force might trigger Taliban resistance and result in resumption of conflict. Although Biden and Trump both agreed that US forces should be withdrawn to end the conflict, Trump did not cooperate at all with the Biden Administration because he bitterly disputed the election results and the loss of the Presidency.

Biden had expected that the 130,000 Afghan Army would resist the Taliban and was given assurances of resistance by President Ghani when he met earlier with Biden, even though the Taliban was gradually taking control of many provinces, and eventually surrounded Kabul. It was reported by the Afghan Ambassador to the United States that the "palace" (meaning the staff of Ghani or Ghani himself) had given orders to the Afghan Army "to lay down their arms", although some sporadic opposition was given to Taliban forces in some provinces. Subsequently President Ghani and some advisors fled the country, taking their corrupted monetary gains with them, much to the dismay of the Army and their family members who felt they might be subject to serious Taliban reprisals.

The withdrawal bordered on "organizational chaos", due to the abbreviated time for withdrawal. Nevertheless, 142,000 persons exited the country, although there were still several US citizens unaccounted for or did not want to leave Afghanistan. The Taliban largely stuck to the Doha agreement and did not directly kill anyone attempting to leave but did verbally threaten or beat many Afghans that crowded at the gates of the Karzai airport in Kabul. This unseemly picture, as well as 13 military personnel and 160 Afghans who were killed by an ISIS suicide bomber slipping through the crowd, resulted in heavy criticism of President Biden and his general staff at the Pentagon.

What the future brings to the Afghan population under Taliban rules and governance remains to be seen. The Taliban seeks international recognition from the United Nations for rebuilding and cooperation from its former adversaries to provide capital, foreign exchange and relaxation of sanctions. The Taliban left the US Embassy intact, which is at least a positive sign. Whether the Taliban remains true to the conditions of the Doha Agreement with the US and its allies carries a significant level of uncertainty as of this writing.

INDEX